ALIENS AND ENGLISHNESS
IN ELIZABETHAN DRAMA

Covering a wide variety of dramatic texts and performances from 1550 to 1600, including Shakespeare's second tetralogy, this book explores moral, historical, and comic plays as contributions to Elizabethan debates on Anglo-foreign relations in England. The economic, social, religious, and political issues that arose from inter-British contact and Continental immigration into England are reinvented and rehearsed on the public stage. Kermode uncovers two broad 'alien stages' in the drama: distinctive but overlapping processes by which the alien was used to posit ideas and ideals of Englishness. Many studies of English national identity pit Englishness *against* the alien 'other' so that the native self and the alien settle into antithetical positions. In contrast, *Aliens and Englishness* reads a body of plays that represents Englishness as a state of ideological, invented superiority – paradoxically stable in its constant changeability, and brought into being by incorporating and eventually even celebrating, rather than rejecting, the alien.

LLOYD EDWARD KERMODE is Associate Professor in the Department of English, California State University, Long Beach. He is the editor of *Three Renaissance Usury Plays,* and co-editor, with Jason Scott-Warren and Martine van Elk, of *Tudor Drama before Shakespeare, 1485–1590: New Directions for Research, Criticism, and Pedagogy.*

ALIENS AND ENGLISHNESS
IN ELIZABETHAN DRAMA

LLOYD EDWARD KERMODE

California State University,
Long Beach

CAMBRIDGE
UNIVERSITY PRESS

CAMBRIDGE UNIVERSITY PRESS
Cambridge, New York, Melbourne, Madrid, Cape Town, Singapore, São Paulo, Delhi

Cambridge University Press
The Edinburgh Building, Cambridge CB2 8RU, UK

Published in the United States of America by Cambridge University Press, New York

www.cambridge.org
Information on this title: www.cambridge.org/9780521899536

First published 2009

Printed in the United Kingdom at the University Press, Cambridge

A catalogue record for this publication is available from the British Library

Library of Congress Cataloguing in Publication data
Kermode, Lloyd Edward.
Aliens and Englishness in Elizabethan drama / Lloyd Edward Kermode.
p.   cm.
Includes bibliographical references and index.
ISBN 978-0-521-89953-6 hardback
1. English drama–Early modern and Elizabethan, 1500-1600–History and criticism.
2. Aliens in literature.   3. National characteristics, English, in literature.   I. Title.
PR658.A45K47 2009
822'.309352691–dc22   2008049679

ISBN 978-0-521-89953-6 hardback

For aliaunts and butterboxes

Contents

Preface

NOTE ON THE FRONTISPIECE

The frontispiece and cover illustration is from Jost Amman's *Gynaeceum, sive, Theatrum mulierum* [*The Theatre of Women*] (1586). The book is a collection of prints from fine wood engravings, each image accompanied by eight lines of Latin text by François Modius (1556–97). The title-page notes that the book is designed to present 'The female costumes of all the principal nations, tribes, and peoples of Europe . . . in commendation of the female sex, and for the especial gratification of such as by their manner of ordinary life, or from other causes, are hindered from distant travel, but at the same time take pleasure at home in the costume of various people, which is a silent index of their character.'[1] Costumed appearance of figures is of primary importance throughout this study as various dramatic 'types' and disguises question early modern notions of social, political, gendered, and religious 'character'. Amman's 'married lady of London' is what Pisaro's daughters are aspiring to in their attempt to shed their Portuguese nationality in William Haughton's *Englishmen for My Money*. This matron also, according to the dedicatory letter by the printer Sigmund Feyerabend of Frankfurt (1528–90), represents a moral goodness that we see being strived for in Robert Wilson's *The Three Ladies of London*. The text accompanying the image tells us that Amman's London matron has rosy cheeks deserving of a wealthy husband. She is thus a poignantly optimistic version of *Three Ladies'* Lady Conscience, who is by contrast offered the stability of marriage only by the laughable Simplicity and whose 'reddy and white' 'cheeks' attract the wealth of corrupted Lady Lucre. Amman's presentation of women, and Feyerabend's covert *instruction* of women, as on one hand a locus of national glory and praise and on the other hand the obvious site for corruption and failure to maintain moral uprightness, are further touchstones for the interplay of gender, national security, cross-border traffic of bodies and habits, wealth, and religious conscience in the comedies and histories discussed in *Aliens and Englishness in Elizabethan Drama*.

NOTE ON QUOTATIONS

Quotations from early modern texts have retained original spelling with the exceptions of silent i/j and u/v correction and modern title capitalization.

Quotations from Shakespeare are taken from *The Norton Shakespeare*, 2nd edition (2008).

Acknowledgements

This book has taken a long time to write. And rewrite. And rewrite again. Meredith Skura and Edward Snow gave me helpful guidance throughout its initial phase. The book was rewritten during a Barbara Thom Fellowship at the Huntington Library; it was rewritten again a few years later in response to the bulk of new published material on British studies and 'London plays'; and it was substantially revised over the past couple of years thanks to the incisive and extensive readings of several anonymous readers. My gratitude is due to Sarah Stanton, Rebecca Jones, and everyone else involved in producing this book at Cambridge University Press. To Martine I owe almost everything else.

Rewritten sections of two previously published essays appear in Chapters 3 and 5: 'The Playwright's Prophecy: Robert Wilson's *The Three Ladies of London* and the "Alienation" of the English', *Medieval and Renaissance Drama in England* 11 (1999): 60–87; and 'After Shylock: the "Judaiser" in England', *Renaissance and Reformation* 20 (1996): 5–25.

The frontispiece is reproduced by permission of the Huntington Library, San Marino, California.

CHAPTER I

Introduction – aliens and the English in London

ALIENS, FOREIGNERS, CITIZENS

Tens of thousands of Continental migrants passed in and out of London and other major English towns during the reign of Elizabeth (1558–1603). The merchants of London were used to seeing aliens in their midst, Germans and Italians in particular being a significant presence since the twelfth century. But wars and military occupation in sixteenth-century northern Europe changed the complexion of the immigrant body in England. Protestants migrated in waves after the 1567 news of Alva's troop deployment to the Netherlands and after the fall of Antwerp in 1585, and a number of French Protestants made their way to England after the Paris Massacre of 1572.[1] Edward VI had established French and Dutch churches in London in 1550, when the resident alien population of England was at its peak, and these institutions continued to act as religious, social, and organizational community centres for the immigrant population throughout the century.[2] Among the religious refugees, however, were economic migrants, and this mixed group caused significant tension in the capital. On the one hand, the new residents brought new skills and stature to English production and trade. On the other hand, they were seen to be economically and ideologically dangerous: they clustered and traded among themselves, sent money abroad instead of reinvesting it in England, and practised religion that was influenced by extremists and attracted good members away from the Church of England.

Resentment against the aliens caused friction between English classes. Landlords benefited from the new immigrants as renters of cheap accommodation, while apprentices and journeymen saw aliens as stealers of jobs from the English. Reformed Christian immigrants were transnational 'brothers' against the Catholic beast, but the problem of extreme Protestantism from the Continent continued to trouble the queen.

I

Moreover, the question of rights to work in the city of London was a constant point of debate between the mayor, the guilds, and the Privy Council.[3] All these groups were similarly concerned about the size and impact of the alien population, and the Crown maintained a policy of dispersal, planting immigrants in provincial towns to spread both the wealth and the worry of the new communities. With perhaps 50,000 Continental aliens coming into England during Elizabeth's reign and living in clustered – and therefore visible – communities, it was not surprising if a perception of an 'alien invasion' was in the air.[4] But placed in the context of the general rise of English and 'British' residents in London, the contemporary censuses (the Returns of Strangers) show a proportional *decrease* in the Continental alien presence in the latter half of the century: from 12.5 per cent in 1553, to 10 per cent in 1571, falling to between 5 and 6 per cent in 1593.[5] Indeed, Elizabethan London's population was growing at an extraordinary rate, a phenomenon underpinned by migration from within the 'British Isles'. In the year 1600, London was over sixteen times larger than Norwich, the next most populous English town; fifty years later, it would be second only to Paris in European city population.[6] Frustrations about overcrowding and economic strain led to urban unrest, and the strangers 'provided a convenient scapegoat' for expressing that frustration in sometimes violent ways.[7]

While the usage is not perfectly consistent, Elizabethan documents widely employed the terms 'alien' and 'stranger' to refer to persons from a foreign country. The home 'country' in the second half of the sixteenth century is England plus the Principality of Wales. The Scots and the Irish are, therefore, 'aliens' along with the Continental European strangers. The term 'foreigner' referred to persons from outside the city or region being discussed or those who were not 'freemen' of the city (belonging to a guild, allowed to keep an open retail shop, possessing voting and civic representation rights). Continental aliens were usually 'foreigners' too, then, in so far as they rarely gained the freedom of the city and became 'citizens'.[8] In practice, freemen Londoners might cast themselves specifically within what the character Pleasure in Robert Wilson's *The Three Lords and Three Ladies of London* calls a 'race' of London.[9] That would set them against the provinces, such that while '"Foreign" English, needless to say, had separate interests from continental strangers', they were 'often lumped together with them by citizens' of London as general outsiders.[10] On the occasions I use 'foreigner' in this book, I generally do so in the modern sense of the term, synonymously with 'alien' and 'stranger'; I make it clear when I am talking specifically of the early modern sense of a foreigner.

In between the status of a 'true born' English man or woman and an alien was a denizen, a permanent resident with rights of residency and work in the adopted country. Denizens achieved their status through letters petitioned from the Crown. The exact privileges of any denizen were individually laid out in the letter, and it was a status that began with the date of the letter and was not inherited by the children of the alien.[11] In a state of limbo throughout the period were those whom we might consider English subjects (i.e. born to English parents) but born abroad (again, including in Scotland and Ireland) or born in England to one or two alien parents. Parliamentary debate and court cases through the reign of James I argued the national status of such persons, and the drama provides several examples of equivocally identified alien residents.[12] Aliens could also petition and pay for an Act of Parliament for naturalization, but very few took this expensive route. In fact, a surprisingly small number of aliens seem to have taken the option of the relatively inexpensive denizenship. Even before one of the primary benefits of denizenship – the right to apprentice an alien son with an English master – was removed by an Act of Common Council in 1574, the proportion of aliens taking denization was fairly low. There was also a very significant drop-off in letters of denization issued later in Elizabeth's reign: from 1,669 in the period 1558–78 to 293 in 1578–1603. Only 1 per cent of the alien population in 1593 had free denizen status.[13] This may indicate a loosening of the official attitude towards alien and native commercial contact as the alien communities became assimilated, such that aliens no longer needed letters to practise their trades with English men. It may also indicate the opposite: aliens could have become more introspective and dealt more within their own communities. There may also have been a *decreasing* commitment to permanent settlement, for aliens who could not be sure they would remain in England for long probably did not feel a strong need for denization.

ALIEN STAGES AND ALIEN CONFUSION

This book studies the ways in which English drama in the second half of the sixteenth century responded to and represented the increasingly diverse and increasingly fraught contact between alien and English men and women in London and England. From this context, I theorize the ways in which certain plays create a notion of 'Englishness' that early modern London audiences might – for better or for worse – recognize and approve of. In the preceding section, I outlined early modern categorizations of national and local identity. Below, I introduce my own terminology for the present study, and as I do so I remain aware that retrospective labelling of a period or culture can *make* or impose categories as well as *describe* them. Therefore, I base my readings of Elizabethan drama in the contexts, signs, and events of the period. At the same time, I am interested in testing the effectiveness of stepping back into our own time to use hindsight and modern theoretical and political tools to assess the desires and anxieties and hopes, the proofs and arguments and gaps in Elizabethan English understandings of regional, national, and international relations.

This section's title phrase, 'alien stages', indicates this book's concern with several aspects of the working of the Elizabethan stage. First, rather simply, I am studying plays in which physical representations of contemporary and recognizable *aliens* appear on the *stage*. Second, where the English stage shows a play set primarily in England but featuring alien characters, it becomes an *alien* stage as representations of non-Englishness essentially determine dramatic 'readings' of London, England, 'British' history, and communal identities. And third, there were two broad steps or *stages* in the dramatic representation of the alien in Elizabethan England.

In the first 'alien stage' (primarily but not exclusively in the Marian and earlier Elizabethan drama), English–alien contact is represented as causing infection, 'deformation', or corruption by the presence of real alien bodies and influences. These earlier plays appear to do what they can to dismiss or eliminate alien elements (characters, habits, professions, clothing, language). They set up Englishness *against* otherness by homogenizing the varieties of alien identity (thus all foreigners are equally 'other'; thus all 'others' are diseased, corrupt, etc.). To highlight distasteful foreign elements and make of them a common denominator against which to define Englishness is the process of national-identity-building outlined by much current criticism, and I discuss this trend below.

The second 'alien stage' is suggested and tested in late morality plays, but is only clearly manifested in the late-Elizabethan drama. In this latter stage, the plays demonstrate that the absorption of what was deemed utterly 'alien' in earlier drama is not just acceptable, but also necessary, for the rise and maintenance of what the plays set forth as a stable, strong English protagonist. 'Englishness' in the plays always requires some moral grounding that asserts its superiority to other cultures (and in Elizabethan plays specifically un-Reformed cultures), and it requires physical prowess demonstrated by strength of mind (standing one's ground in the face of adversity) and strength of body (successful judgement against evil, usurpation of positions of power, comic trickery) to secure solutions to intractable problems. 'Englishness' in these later cases combines itself with the alien and (generally rhetorically) extracts out of that fusion a reformed, expanded, revitalized, and always politically equivocal defin-ition of the English self. As we will see throughout the book, the very status of 'Englishness' as a phenomenon with an existence *prior* to alien contact is continually undermined.

The working of the second alien stage is hardly straightforward, as it argues for an Englishness that is not set *against* the alien but rather relies on the presence of that other within itself. I contend that this notion of an Englishness that incorporates the alien in all aspects of its representation would not have been too surprising to Elizabethan writers or thinkers. In his Italian–English primer, *First Fruits* (1578), John Florio has his Englishman ask an Italian what he thinks of the English language. The Italian replies:

Certis if you wyl beleeve me, it doth not like me at al, because it is a language confused, bepeesed with many tongues: it taketh many words of the latine, & mo from the French, & mo from the Italian, & many mo from the Duitch, some also from the Greeke, & from the Britaine, so that if every language had his owne wordes againe, there woulde but a fewe remaine for English men, and yet every day they adde.

[. . .]

Make the experience of it, take a booke and reade, but marke well, and you shall not reade four woordes together of true English.[14]

This sense of the English language as a hodge-podge of tongues was asserted by several writers in the period. Language becomes a vital con-cern in most of the plays that I discuss in this book, because use and avoidance of language is seen to reveal the will of characters to be incorporated into various communal bodies. I have introduced the 'mongrel' English language issue here as a symptomatic synecdoche for the state of Englishness as a whole. For what is interesting in this passage is the use of the word 'confused' to describe English a few lines before the concluding notion that there *is* such a thing as 'true English'. We are thus presented with the two basic nuances of the word *confuse*: a sense of uncertainty and disorientation on the one hand, and the process of 'con-fusing' or coming-together to form a single entity on the other. The end of the passage attempts to keep an alien–English division to stave off the fear of confused uncertainty in a mixed-up language. Yet such exclusivity of identity is already made equivocal by the passage's acknowledgement that 'confusion' in the second, literal sense lies behind the very construction of Englishness.

The passage from Florio briefly lays out the perspective of the two alien stages by keeping them both in suspension: as in the first alien stage, the speaker attempts to retain an oppositional hypothesis that the alien somehow comes along *after* the creation of an entire language of 'pure English' and invades it; however, as acknowledged in the second alien stage, the speaker has already outlined a process in which English is 'bepeesed', put together with foreign tongues – the alien is within English *as it is being formed*. The Italian speaker also notes that English 'is a language that wyl do you good in England, but passe Dover, it is woorth nothing',[15] suggesting the confusing paradox of a language made up of all the tongues from past Dover, but which is useless once outside the confines of the English borders. Englishness is an identity that only exists by containing the alien, yet it is an identity separate from other national identities.

In the second alien stage, and in the drama of the last decade of Elizabeth's reign, the search for a settled and ameliorating sense of Englishness will no longer permit simplistic tar-brushing of the alien; each alien element must instead be recognized as already involved in – *confused* with – English society or culture. As with the language that only develops into a full system by absorbing (pre-existing) alien words, the plays show the alien being absorbed and fused with the native self as that native forms and claims an 'Englishness'. The fact that such Englishness is most fully laid out by morality vices (with, as we shall see, alien origins), a Welsh king of England, and daughters of a Portuguese father in *Englishmen for My Money* lets us know that the question of origins remains at stake through the Elizabethan period, and remains unanswered. At any point a culture can look back and talk about previous incarnations of native identity, but from any point that identity can be seen as constructed from alien incorporation. This book will not resolve the question of the English chicken and the alien egg.

The second alien stage, then, gives us something beyond the traditional view of identity determined by its difference from the other: Englishness as an ideology of power built, paradoxically, around the alien that is within it, 'con-fused'. The process of alien incorporation between the first and the second alien stages is a political and rhetorical move as much as it is a representation of cosmopolitan awareness on the part of English writers and audiences, because any 'openness' to the other is necessarily also a co-option of the other. To deny the alien through a prejudicial or ignorant confusion and rejection, as in the first stage, is to leave Englishness always naive and open to surprise, attack, and deformation by alien bodies and ideas. To incorporate the alien within Englishness by productive confusion, as in the second stage, is to hybridize and strengthen Englishness for its long-term imperial presence in wider British, European, and worldwide contexts.

The drama's rhetorical constructions of and rehearsals of versions of 'English identity' embed belief in the concept's reality. If the steady intake of alien elements – foreign bodies – promotes representations of an Englishness vaccinated against 'impurity' from the outside, it should be made clear early on that such an idea of exclusive identity is a fiction. The alien remains as a slightly uncomfortable joke or as ancestry to be suppressed and recast. Here, that other rather Miltonic sense of 'confuse' as the confounding (*confundere*) of the rebel angels comes into play, whereby determination to *be oneself*, to be true to one's not-lost identity, in spite of adversity, is itself delusional – but powerfully so. Ideologies of identity do not lose their status as having material existence within societies just because their truth factor is compromised. Thus the plays can *produce* identity separately from politico-historical impositions of geographical and religious identity. I should close this section with the note that the plays engage with the two alien stages as a matter of degree rather than exclusively – one play's anxiety and rejection of the alien may overshadow a subtle awareness of the alien's potential usefulness; another play may be very interested in celebrating the alien in England and Englishness while retaining some basic prejudices against the 'other'.

'THE STAGE IS ENGLAND': CRITICAL AND DRAMATIC POSITIONS ON NATIONAL IDENTITY

Much of the critical examination of representations of English identity has remained a study of the first alien stage. We have consistently been told in cultural and literary studies of English national identity that self-identity is determined by its reaction to the other, and specifically its insistence on its difference from the other. The attraction of an antagonistic, oppositional theory of national identity formation has produced many exciting studies of exotic English–alien contact in plays set abroad, which engage forcefully with the early modern matrix of religion, ethnicity, sexuality, and commerce. Since these plays are usually travel or historical plays featuring merchants, pirates, renegades, and soldiers, the premise of Anglo-alien opposition is reasonable. But in British studies, too, we are told that 'nationality can only be imagined as a dimension of difference' from the outside world; 'England is always discovered elsewhere, defined by the encounter with the Other' (frequently for these critics, the Irish 'other'); 'Englishness and English nationality have been historically defined against non-Englishness'; '"Englishness" at this point in time is fiercely determined by a demonisation of all that is not English'; and 'not-Welshness, not-Scottishness, and certainly not-Frenchness [and] not-Spanishness ... gave the English their surest sense of national identity'.[16] One problem with these statements is that they seem to claim to know what Englishness is. I have been frequently using 'scare quotes' for the term Englishness so far to indicate the fact that 'Englishness' is not a stable concept, but one that is worked out and defined time and again in different plays and decades. Another problem is that the statements seem to place 'Englishness' only within a 'nation' of England that feels a sense of 'national identity', and they seem to assert that there is no 'Englishness' outside of England.

In his examinations of English nationhood, Richard Helgerson takes the investigation of the English search for a stable identity in a different direction. He has provided an alternative way to think of the production of a 'colonial' English self, one that brings the view closer to home in geographical terms but pushes it further away in time. He emphasizes the irony of Elizabethan writers' obligation to and desire for another set of others – the ancient colonizing Romans. The late sixteenth-century call for English rediscovery of their poetic genius did not strive for a new and different mode of expression but for a reliance on foreign examples, he argues: 'Likeness, not difference, will be the measure of success.'[17] Thus the alien invaders and their cultural legacy are indeed acknowledged as incorporated into Englishness, but this 'likeness' produces a new identity that is specifically 'English' (those Romans are gone) and therefore still set in opposition to contemporary alien bodies and cultures – this doubleness echoes John Florio's Italian speaker's representation of the English language.[18] Other scholars, such as Jodi Mikalachki, have also concentrated on the need for the English to understand themselves through classical comparison. She writes of the English 'longing on the one hand to establish historical precedent and continuity, and an equally powerful drive on the other to exorcise primitive savagery from national history and identity. The tensions between theses two imperatives inform virtually all articulations of the nation in this period.'[19] This book agrees that the English are striving for stability as they search for national identity's 'precedent and continuity', but it updates the notion in so far as the 'savagery' of the modern men and women in the plays set in contemporary England only bears a trace of the 'primitive'. The alien tendencies are just as often newfangled abhorrences as they are ancient monstrosities (although bad alien habits – for example taking tobacco – often have earlier 'primitive' lives).

Two broad points of view dominate studies of English national identity, then: one in which English identity is formed by a centrifugal, colonial activity that uses the other in foreign lands against which to define itself; the second in which the centripetal colonial activity of the distant past haunts and to some extent constrains a creation of English national identity. In contrast to these positions, *Aliens and Englishness* is concerned with an important body of sixteenth-century drama that works out Englishness by dealing not with exotic or ancient others but with European aliens of the present and relatively recent past; not by resistance and antithesis alone but by absorption and similitude; not with 'elsewhere' as a location of non-Englishness but with the here and often the now of England (and the expanded 'England' of Britain). *Aliens and Englishness* sees Elizabethans' reflections on English identity as increasingly a process of finding and absorbing alien aspects around them and less the simple phenomenon of frictionally and uncooperatively rubbing up 'against non-Englishness'. Therefore, the dramatic selection for study in this book has been guided by those plays that are set primarily in England and deal with relatively modern (i.e. not ancient) English, British, and European characters. The religious questions in *Aliens and Englishness* concern the Catholic military and ideological threat, the acceptability of immigrants' radically reformed Protestantism, the strength of supranational fellowship with Continental Protestants, and the real or imagined presence of Jews and 'Jewishness'. The ethnic and 'racial' questions are those of cultural traditions and 'difference' between European and British neighbours. In the plays this involves aliens who were significantly visible in London and a few major towns – mostly the Dutch, French and French-speaking Lowlanders (Walloon), Welsh, and also to some extent the Italians and Iberians. Questions of sexuality carry over from moral drama's overt preaching to reprise in the later Elizabethan drama as a set of reformed Christian imperatives in new, urban, mimetic contexts. Finally, the economic questions concern urban artisans and merchants and their ability to live in London and the larger provincial towns, which they felt were increasingly populated by aliens.

By studying the ways in which the plays work through perceptions of the subtle shifts in Anglo-European social and political alignment, we follow dramatic representations and creations of Englishness that were, I suggest, more 'real', present, and 'closer to home' to the Elizabethan playgoers; more essential to an English understanding of London; and more finely tuned to that audience's immediate concerns than the assertions of self and other, native and alien, 'barbarous' and 'civilized' that we find in literary representations of exotic Anglo-American, Anglo-Mediterranean, or Anglo-Eastern contact. While ethnic 'others' have been treated very seriously in literary criticism of the past thirty years, the white male and female alien to Englishness have received more attention from historians' studies of migration and labour patterns and less attention from literary scholars interested in how alien figures are represented and used in imaginative and ideological ways.

The main study texts in this book are plays set in England, and these productions force a focus on what the Elizabethan dramatists decided to represent about the incoming alien, rather than how English self-perception was challenged and changed by external alien encounters. So, while a large proportion of the English were no doubt fascinated by images and narratives of and about the New World, Africa, and Asia – and Henslowe's diary shows that this was a large part of his theatre's repertoire – such texts did not extend to fantasies of an England peopled by Americans or Africans. (This is of course in spite of such historical phenomena as the presence of a small but noticeable black community in late-Elizabethan and Jacobean London, revealed to us through expulsion orders.)[20] Caliban is not in Elizabethan drama, nor is he in England for an extended period of time – although Trinculo reminds us a decade after this study leaves off that he could have been. Literary and narrative representation of these ethnic groups probably helped prompt ideologically self-centred confirmations of national and personal superiority on the part of the English, but exotic foreigners either remain distant and among other foreigners, or they are catalysts, enhancing certain interactions between English citizens and British or European others. With this domestic dynamic in mind, we should take seriously the literal suggestiveness of the scene-setting in the list of 'The Actors Names' in *Grim the Collier of Croydon*, possibly by William Haughton, where we read that 'The Stage is *England*'. Instead of the more benign 'The scene is England', the statement suggests a stage that not only works with 'Englishness' in some ways, but is compulsory viewing in order to know England. This interestingly alters and arguably compounds Thomas

Platter's famous remark about English insularity, that 'the English pass their time, learning at the play what is happening abroad': they apparently also pass their time learning at the play what is happening *at home* and how they might want to think about themselves.[21] The concept of the stage *as* England – as alleged island (in place of Britain), as powerful space surrounded on all sides, as a place with both a fixed identity and a mutability like the English character itself – bears further examination throughout this study. This may be especially true in relation to the history plays, which must *make* the theatre England, and the London comedies, which take place in a theatre that is already part of the London topography with which they are so overtly concerned.

Aliens and Englishness' concentration on plays set in England, moreover, demonstrates that any country, before it can go out and 'overwrite' another country, creates methods and practices through which it is itself overwritten, self-edited, and reproduced both internally and on its margins. This is an ongoing, contemporary phenomenon, not just something from an ancient colonial past. The flourishing of drama in a country that came late to the colonial race happened not in general response to an outgoing English who were inventing or re-inscribing the alien, but in response to the incoming aliens (as visitors and residents). Scholarly concentration on Jacobean drama and aliens has placed the interest in foreignness abroad or in a well-developed cosmopolitan London. But *Aliens and Englishness* reveals the idea of the alien being worked out long before this, in an environment of smaller spheres of experience, where only hints of the exotic would have made their way to the majority of theatre audience members. In this sense, the present study is pre-colonial, for it shows how dramatists attempted to work with a conflicted country before the permanence of the Jamestown settlement: a country at war with Continental and domestic religious opponents and dealing with domestic unrest over class, economic and social decline, and immigration (especially into London and Norwich). But it is also a study of imperial England. For the distant history of Roman occupation, the wars and settlement in Ireland, the rhetoric of empire that confuses expansion within the 'British Isles' and expansion beyond the Atlantic archipelago, the conflicts over trading routes and the establishment of trading companies in the last three decades of the sixteenth century, the increasing importance of Elizabethan piracy and renegado activity, the reports of foreign conquests in the New World, and the endeavours of English captains were all factors promoting a patriotic and 'nationalist' surge among court advisers, the literati, and the merchant classes, who felt (or had) some direct connection with these achievements, and who were involved in promoting, suppressing, or manipulating the production and consumption of drama.

I do not pretend that the processes of alien confusion in drama or in everyday life are exclusive to England, nor that they are first experienced in the early modern period. The assessment of personal and political identity set over and against, and ultimately through, contiguous and distant neighbours is surely a worldwide, transhistorical phenomenon. *Aliens and Englishness* concerns itself with investigating a specific half-century (1550s to 1590s) within a limited location (England, primarily London) in order to encourage reassessment of the literary, political, and cultural texts that contributed to a complicated sense of Englishness in a country on the one hand insular and protective and on the other hand preoccupied with opportunities for geographical and cultural expansion. In a country defined by the Church of England and immured by seas and restless British natives, it was alien presence that split the country and aggravated tensions between duty to country(man), religious fellow, class, professional trade, and family – inevitably causing disunity on anything approaching a national level. Benedict Anderson has attempted to delineate an 'imagined community' of nationhood – with a strange juxtaposition of adjectives – as 'a deep, horizontal comradeship'. The nation comprises natives, known and unknown to each other, the unknown imagined as similar to the self in terms of one's conception of, and loyalty to, a realm. Despite class boundaries and the working of inequality in a realm, the 'imagination' could invent a single idea of nationhood.[22] The 'alien invasion' of sixteenth-century immigration into England, however, broke into any inferred horizontality of English comradeship in a very visible way; it seems to have unbalanced the community in so far as the alien bodies imposed physical barriers to the development of a perceived national society (i.e. a society of natives unified across class difference), and it scored the communality with regionally drawn lines. A play such as *Sir Thomas More*, which illuminates these alien–English and intra-English tensions, keeps us mindful of the constant fracturing or at least disturbance of very wide ideas of communal identity in the period. It also powerfully demonstrates the drama's ability to bring these very questions and conceptions of 'national' identity into focus – and dangerously so, as indicated by this play's censorship and revision.

To take the issue of regional and national community a little further, we could consider Philip Edwards' comment in *Threshold of a Nation*: 'The history plays which Shakespeare and his fellow-dramatists of the professional theatre wrote in the ten years following the Armada must have done a great deal to create a sense of national identity among Londoners and the city-dwellers of England.'[23] I want to take seriously the notion that the dramatic literature did much to *create* senses of identity. Such representations may only be related liminally to actual present politics, being more apparently entrenched in psychological and social ways of seeing oneself in a half-visible 'national' community. Moreover, a Londoner's 'sense of *national* identity' may differ markedly from that of other 'city-dwellers of England', and such differences are addressed in Chapters 3, 4, and 5. The dramatic genres covered in this book – morality, history, and city comedy – demonstrate that there *are* such things in Elizabethan England as concepts of 'national' identity; however, these understandings are always located in partial, limited, and polemical points of view. The plays understand 'Englishness' to be a shared phenomenon, but quite where this idea fits into a communal comprehension remains a question. As we shall see, some of the plays insist on class-based community, some highlight the work of gender in bringing together English society, and most of them acknowledge the underpinning of (Protestant) Christianity to their construction of Englishness. So while Anderson's 'deep, horizontal comradeship' gives us a conceptual rubric, the plays demonstrate the difficulty of defining shared community as at once geographical, religious, mythical, and 'racial'.[24]

We see issues of alien confusion raised in all manner of texts, from poems and songs to sermons and Proclamations, but Elizabethan drama explores the phenomenon most extensively and richly. Drama in the public theatres encourages improvisational popular reaction to its displays of native–alien conflict and domestic inter-class fracture. It enhances complex textual features such as irony and inconclusive relationships between characters, thus leaving the written text exposed and 'open' for further dramatic interpretation on the stage – or in the street. As a public performance, drama is unlike a book, which tentatively straddles the line between private contemplation and public offering. Play performance limns and alters urban spaces, as theatres in the period become at most little worlds, at least little cities, in which the fears and fantasies of a proud English people are rehearsed in front of and among them. Elizabethan drama puts physical bodies before the playgoers to show English characters rejecting, abusing, and finally incorporating the aliens in their midst in a process of moulding and coming to comprehend an indefinable, multiple, and dynamic 'Englishness'. Drama is rehearsed yet reinvented in every performance, rather like Englishness itself each time it faces up to the alien. And as every writer after new historicism is bound to acknowledge, drama reveals and examines the theatricality of Elizabethan England outside of the theatre buildings. Dramatic representation had to remain relevant to political life, and discussions of the alien problem kept it tied to contemporary history. Elizabethan dramatists understood the difficulty of homing in on a concept of Englishness, since it is a formulation that depends in large part on dynamic, mutable, unstable alien forces. There is no clear, stable 'other' against which to set a singular process of Englishness, and this uncertainty prompts the drama's obsessive return to the same questions of representing identity, to methods of self-scrutiny, of looking 'with inward eyes' on the road to English ideological (religious and socio-political) reform.[25]

Drama is always – among other things – *play*. As such, even as it preaches or politicizes, it also questions and ironizes. The theatre, as Louis Montrose has argued, both serves authoritarian, orthodox power and – during the process of playing, and perhaps beyond – argues with that orthodoxy to give it 'a subtle and diffuse power . . . in its very *theatricality*' (original italics).[26] Richard Helgerson sees the distance between theatre and authority leading to 'representations of England [that] are at once the most popular and, in the case of those produced by Shakespeare and the Lord Chamberlain's Men, the most exclusively monarchic that his generation has passed on to us'.[27] This view of Shakespeare's increasing exclusivity has been challenged by Jean Howard and supplemented by Aaron Landau, and the debate reveals the difficulty of assessing the politics of 'play'.[28] There may be no perfect way to remove oneself as a writer, player, critic, or playgoer from the pressures of the culture and the ideologies in which one has been raised and educated (or mis-educated), but the theatre exists in a (perhaps obvious) paradoxical relationship with authority. It has been forced to the margins and outside of central authority, into what Steven Mullaney has called a 'liminal' zone of equivocal licence. But such exclusion also gives the theatre a certain independence or authority, a view 'back in' to the centre, a view perhaps clarified by the distance.[29] The inevitable multi-vocality of plays and the equivocal position of drama's political statements troubles an entirely smooth, teleological progression between the two 'alien stages' of rejecting and incorporating the alien; and it is difficult to talk of an authoritative, native self when the self is involved in absorption, alteration, fusion, and confusion. Moreover, as I have suggested already, 'Englishness' (especially on stage) is only an *assertion* of stability, a construction of identity akin to dramatic performance. Drama always suggests the paradox of 'playing out' an 'essentialism' like identity. What is asserted in an English character's performance is often a masculinized demonstration of power with an underlying personal fragility or fear of failure. The battle for authority over one's own identity runs through all the plays studied here, and it is staked out in an uncertain field.

A central problem with the assertion of English identity lies in the early modern reputation of the English for lacking assertiveness or certainty – an issue raised by Florio's representation of the confused English language. Concentrating on the serious early modern investment in geohumoral theory, Mary Floyd-Wilson reminds us that the English were considered impressionable and changeable and that Englishness has as its essence the identity of malleability and imitation of other cultures. Put another way, 'Englishness' constitutes an absent presence, a core that is a space, a performative centre to be displayed on the surface of the dramatized body. Belief in a genuine, solid identity is ingrained by acting out cultural roles that accord with desires to be (and to be seen) a certain way.[30] Floyd-Wilson describes the problem of the English 'turning Irish' as an example of (in Spenser's Eudoxus' words) the English 'forget[ting] his owne nature', as opposed to the Irish who, says Floyd-Wilson, 'refuse to forget their nature'. 'Spenser's *View* implies, no doubt unintentionally, that an Englishman *will* forget his own nature, for to do so is a symptom of Englishness itself.'[31] This argument seems to highlight the ongoing dynamism of 'Englishness', and we can see the problem of using binary English/alien contrast if one arm of the binary does not have (or display, perform) a stable identity role. For the English cannot be forgetting their nature if their nature, as Floyd-Wilson notes, *is* to alter, to keep changing.[32] Hence the emphasis in *Aliens and Englishness* on the weaving intersections between native and alien as 'Englishness' is manipulated and asserted.

Later in her book, Floyd-Wilson discusses the concept of self-fashioning for the English. She outlines the problem of the geohumoral representation of the English as being rather slow-witted in their misty northern clime: 'For the northerner, and the English in particular, to fashion oneself as a civilized, temperate gentleman meant countering or refining one's innate disposition and inclinations. Thus, self-fashioning was self-forgetting.'[33] John Lyly's quip from 1580 that 'there is nothing in England more constant than the inconstancy of attire' is instructive here, for we can take his use of clothing as another synecdoche for Englishness itself.[34] If the innate disposition of the English is to be changeable and impressionable and if the English inclination is to 'try out' otherness, then self-fashioning quintessentially enacts the decentred centre or the elusive 'nature' that *is* Englishness. English self-forgetting is in a sense, then, impossible. Self-fashioning as deliberate show for the English man or woman at the various social levels of artisan, gentleman, lady, or aristocrat becomes the only possible way to represent the self to one's own self and others. To play at being other, to be alien, to incorporate the foreign, and to confuse the actor and the 'other' part being played is to show Englishness itself in action. 'Englishness', of course, in this reading, is always 'in action', always in a position of relativity because it is always playing itself out, performing, proving its existence. Because it does not have a definitive pre-existence, Englishness alters itself and rejects or incorporates aspects of the encountered alien as the occasion requires. This sixteenth-century history of improvisational experience serves England well as it expands its imperial influence through Britain and the known world in the seventeenth century.

I begin *Aliens and Englishness*' dramatic investigation in Chapter 2 with a discussion of three moral plays published in the 1550s, 1560s, and 1570s. The first, *Wealth and Health*, is an anonymous Marian play republished (and possibly revised in addition to the recast closing dedication) in the first year of Elizabeth's reign. This play demonstrates that the drama of the first alien stage is always under tension from hints of deeper insight about the embedded role of the alien in Englishness. Largely a discussion of the economic and moral state of the realm under Mary, the play uses financial and somatic metaphors to work out its view of an England imposed upon by Catholicism and a Spanish (albeit largely absent) 'king consort'. These metaphors 'racialize' the view of the alien in an attempt to keep Englishness 'pure', but that very process reveals shared characteristics of alien and English ideology. The republishing of the play in 1558 allows us to look at the play from both sides of the Marian–Elizabethan divide and to consider its potentially subversive messages about 'non-English' monarchy through the Marian years. The play's characters, with their 'hidden' names (Will is really 'Ill Will' and Wit is really 'Shrewd Wit', etc.), make all transactions doubtful and all notions of truth equivocal. This play introduces the first of several stock Dutch characters that appear in the 'alien' plays, and he acts here as a funnel for English class-based, nationalistic frustration. Behind the politics of the play lies the call for moral 'reformation', a term that can usefully be adapted across that 1558 border to appeal to audiences in different religious climates.

The second play discussed in this chapter is Ulpian Fulwell's popular *Like Will to Like*. This play is more entertaining and 'modern' than

Wealth and Health, but in many ways its comedy is frightening as it seems to argue for the alien as an evil presence within Englishness, directly asserting Lucifer as the force behind moral corruption in England. More precisely, however, the play shows up the English as already 'alien' in this dangerous manner. The vice figure's name, Nichol Newfangle, brings out both the comedic and serious elements of such a character: he promises his master Lucifer that he will corrupt the English with ridiculous fashion (which he does not in fact do in the play), and he represents the mistake of thinking of bad fashion as an insignificant problem in England. This chapter and others are concerned to historicize the very real early modern sense that the pride of clothing was a leading factor in the period's moral destitution. Seeing three editions between the late 1560s and the late 1580s, *Like Will to Like* was probably being played and read for several years *after* Robert Wilson's *The Three Ladies of London* (discussed in Chapter 3) was first on stage in the early 1580s. Thus we see that the shift between audience reception of drama emphasizing the first and second 'alien stage' is not locked in time. Playgoers could enjoy the older antagonistic way of looking at the alien while newer, incorporative alien plays were exciting a public eager to establish a strong sense of Englishness. That sense of overlap is strengthened if we notice the continuity between the plays and earlier morality characters such as Illwill in *Hickscorner* (1514) and New-guise and Now-a-days in *Mankind* (1465–70).

George Wapull's *The Tide Tarrieth No Man*, the last play discussed in this chapter, takes on another trope with its vice 'Courage Contagious'. The metaphor of blood circulation and the context of 'plague' were used by the playwright and other authors to create the environment within which *Wealth and Health* was performed, and in this later play notions of infection are revived to show how proper English reformed behaviour is corrupted from within by alien bodies. This play also expands on *Wealth and Health* by reprising the familiar dual-named characters (Neighbourhood is really 'No Good Neighbourhood', etc.), and Courage the vice is also 'Courage Contrarious', emphasizing his ability to mutate as necessary to do his corrupting. The English must adapt to avoid such alien infiltration, but adaptation is also an alien quality. Here we really see the line between the first and second alien stages being blurred as the very push to eliminate the alien confirms the alien nature of the Englishness being striven for. A crucial feature of this play is the multiple naming of the merchant, aka Greediness, aka Wealthiness. There seems to be no way to be both moral and wealthy. Such a view will be altered by the end of the century, but in the 1570s and 1580s this third play's combination of moral sermon and contemporary social politics pushes us towards a 'belated morality' that speaks very clearly to the fast-developing trading centre of London: Wilson's *The Three Ladies of London*. In contrast to previous work on these plays cited in Chapter 2, I argue that the most important alien characters in the plays are vaguely depicted as English. We do not see alien confusion working through a reading of the Dutch 'Hance' of either *Like Will to Like* or *Wealth and Health* so much as we find it through the discovery of unacknowledged or slowly revealed alien elements that make up the purportedly English characters.

In Chapter 3, I am interested in showing how the physicality in *The Tide Tarrieth* is brought to the fore in later plays. The moral message for Wilson is always backed up by a physical threat; moral decline will lead to physical pain. This is not a new insight, of course. In the cycle plays and late medieval moralities and miracle plays – from Noah's beatings to the lost limb in *The Croxton Play of the Sacrament* – the road to righteousness is fraught with the danger of blood, sweat, and tears. But Wilson places the dangers on the audience's doorstep and in the present. *The Three Ladies of London* has Lady Lucre 'rule the roost' in London, causing the demise of Hospitality (a centrally important concept in sixteenth- and seventeenth-century England) and the moral and physical destruction of Ladies Love and Conscience. We find that Lady Lucre and her henchmen have alien heritage, and the play makes sure to emphasize that it is foreign importing of useless products that corrupts Englishness, and the exporting of naturally 'good' English produce that enriches foreign countries and alien merchants. The Italian merchant, Mercadorus, who runs the trading business for Lady Lucre, has a comic Italian accent, which (like the comedy in the earlier plays) dramatically (but not really) hides his central role in facilitating the corruption of Englishness. The Jewish usurer, Gerontus, in spite of being a surprisingly accommodating and generous Jew, is of course also a part of the alien mill that allegedly grinds up notions of pure Englishness. The play continually places its moral problems in the context of resident aliens in England, but it simultaneously reveals the permanence and embeddedness of such figures in England, thus blurring the line between alien and English. *Three Ladies'* topicality (if not its style) clearly remained vital: it was republished in 1592, as the capital was seeing the beginning of a new wave of anti-alien sentiment. Just a year later, a 'libel', a document threatening the welfare and lives of aliens in London, was posted on the church of the Dutch community, followed shortly after by the composition of the famously censored play, *Sir Thomas More*. I demonstrate the essential connections between the libel and *Three Ladies*, particularly the relevance of the libel's Jewish reference. I then close the chapter by looking at the ways in which the play *Sir Thomas More* maintains the currency of moral behaviour – especially the issues of hospitality and citizenship – as a dramatic message by steeping it in London's class- and gender-based anxiety about aliens in its midst.

The moral plays tended to use excursions – from imagined trips around the world to alien immigration to trading ventures – to open up ideas of moral development (for better or for worse). Travel in each case changes the characters involved or the nature of the places from, through, and to which they travel. In Chapter 4, I revisit Shakespeare's much-discussed second tetralogy of history plays, and I use the trope of the journey to locate the boundaries of English–alien crossover and confusion: Mowbray and Bolingbroke's banishments and subsequent lives and Richard's military excursion to Ireland in *Richard II*; Henry's proposed pilgrimage and the rebels' travels to meet each other in *Henry IV*. Most work on these plays in British studies has been concerned with Ireland as the alien to England's 'civilized' identity; so in this chapter I challenge a notion that Wales was unequivocally a part of England in early modern perception of 'national' identity, or that Wales can simply be looked *through* as a window onto Ireland. As members of a Principality, not a separate country, the Welsh should simply be 'foreigners' to Londoners in the same way that a Cornish or Yorkshire man or woman would be foreign. With its separate language and 'British' history, however (like the foreigner from Cornwall but unlike one from Yorkshire), the Welsh identity proves trickier than this to incorporate into Englishness. The residual 'alien' in Welshness continually overpowers *and yet underpins* assertions of Englishness. Important to this chapter is the relationship of characters to the topography and geography of England, Wales, and London, and to this end, this chapter finds the work on mapping and geography in Shakespeare and early modern Wales by such scholars as Lisa Hopkins, John Gillies, Bernhard Klein, and Garrett Sullivan important. Representations of 'the kingdom' and local features within it, such as stones (*RII* 3.2.24), hilly moors (*RII* 2.3.4), rivers (*1HIV* 1.3.97, 3.1.95), and mountains (*HV* 5.1.32) literally 'ground' characters. An understanding of 'place' helps define a subject's identity within the space of a country or city, thus Mowbray complains that taking him out of his native land will silence his English tongue and Bolingbroke considers his exile a journeyman's period before he gains the freedom of a true citizen. Similarly King Richard will claim Wales as his own even as the Welsh have deserted him, and in *Henry IV* the rebels will struggle with their confusion – the Welsh and English families are cultural antitheses striving to divide their newly imagined kingdom. By *Henry V*, it takes the comedic Fluellen to confirm a tenuous connection to (and cooption of) Wales within the body of the king.

I spend time reading closely in the passages that seem to establish concrete claims about alien identity and at the same time reveal uncertainties that we saw aired less overtly or seriously in the morality plays. When the English consistently call Glyndwr 'wild', for example, they are drawing on a history of representing the western British as uncivilized and in doing so deliberately avoid having to investigate the truth value of the epithet. While Englishness produces the nature of the alien it wishes to rail against, the alien already resides within the identity that the English are building for themselves. In this chapter, I am looking out at the alien through canonical English texts, a point of view that has been a particular bone of contention in British studies. J. G. A. Pocock warned us over thirty years ago that 'the history of an increasing English domination is remarkably difficult to write in other than English terms'. David Baker concurs, worrying about the exclusion of marginal textual voices: 'If we cannot dispel this inherited ignorance, neither can we claim that we do not, willy nilly, perpetuate it.'[35] More recently, however, Willy Maley has made the line of argument that I am following – that revisiting assumptions of Englishness is a way to break down English presumption and 'blot the landscape of "this sceptered Isle"'.[36] Re-reading through the English lens does not necessitate a *perpetuation* of early modern ideology. As we will see, taking on the English point of view through English texts cannot concretely, imperviously, or reliably lay down an English law of national identity, but instead forces us to question the assumptions and presumptions that lie behind such a construction. 'English' language, foreign and related languages, gender, class, religion, race, and culture cannot isolate themselves in the ways fantasized in the earlier plays. They can only expound and build themselves up with the use of each other and by drawing on multiple notions of non-Englishness. *Aliens and Englishness* makes no claim to provide a comparative British history, which would require Irish and Welsh language texts at the least. Nor does it do more than examine the apparent intra-British, intra-archipelagic, and English-staged Anglo-foreign relationships as depicted in the Elizabethan drama. In reading this way, we closely re-examine what a few pieces of imaginative literature may have *thought* they were saying, or what they *seem to us* to have been saying about Welsh and 'British' pressures on

English identity. There will be myriad nuances of connections and divisions between actual historical border groups in the western and northern marches, and between ethnicities of Saxon and Norman stock that these readings of drama do not get through to.

In Chapter 5, I study three plays from the last few years of the sixteenth century, concentrating on two city comedies, William Haughton's *Englishmen for My Money* (1598) and Thomas Dekker's *The Shoemaker's Holiday* (1599). Two very popular plays by two important playwrights of their time, they bring together the moral issues of earlier plays in the contexts of 'race', class, and gender with the histories' emphasis on place. Both these plays work out Englishness by having their main characters 'identify with' London – its buildings, streets, traditions, demographics, and alien presence. In *Englishmen*, Pisaro is a resident alien from Portugal, who has married an Englishwoman (now dead) and had three daughters by her. These half-Portuguese women work their way into Englishness through marriage to Englishmen, with the help of the Englishman-in-French-disguise Anthony and the confusing built environment of London. As in *Sir Thomas More*, the city of London becomes a character that must be defended from alien penetration, and which can act on behalf of the English. In *The Shoemaker's Holiday*, Simon Eyre works his way up from shoemaker to Mayor of London with help from the Englishman-in-Dutch-disguise Lacy such that the city once again becomes the geographical space that promotes Englishness. Not surprisingly, all these assertions of Englishness turn out to be just that: assertions. Behind the success of the Englishmen in Haughton's play lies the constant fear of English inferiority that must be denied. The power of the English language to defeat the alien is important to the play, but as we have seen in this introduction, English language is riddled with the alien, and Haughton's clown, Frisco, jokes uncomfortably about the vulnerability of English language and English bodies to alien penetration and alteration. Pisaro's probable Jewishness connects him to another character, the English usurer Mamon of John Marston's *Jack Drum's Entertainment* (1600–1), the usurer 'with a great nose'. I include a brief discussion of this latter play to contrast its country house setting with the city plays, a romance plot with a prodigal comedy, and most pertinently the 'Englishing' of the alien figure of the usurer. In the Jacobean period the English usurer becomes familiar, gradually shedding 'Jewish' features; but at the turn of the century, he is still very much a pivotal character demonstrating the increasing acceptability of morally doubtful behaviour.

Whereas *Englishmen* circulates around gender and nationality understood in many ways as 'race' (as it was in *The Three Ladies of London*), *The Shoemaker's Holiday* seems to argue for an egalitarian London utopia where the alien influence is either peripheral and a simple tool for English advancement or something that remains abroad, like the French who must be fought with after the play leaves off. But the shoemaker Ralph's journey to war and his consequent injury, Lacy the nobleman's apparently forgivable desertion, and the ultimate overseeing of the shoemaker's holiday by the king make sure that we understand that Englishness relies on strict understandings of class rank. Wilson's morality argued that good English characters know their places in society, and for all the danger in the pseudo-heroism of Doll's death in *Sir Thomas More* and the cry of unity of the London workers, Englishness is pitched as relying on order as set down by the character of More. Further, such Englishness ends up protecting the aliens. It is only the constant alien confusion in *The Shoemaker's Holiday* that pushes the action forward and allows the English to assert their Englishness. By the time of these late comedies the first, 'Great', Armada was a decade-old bit of history; a significant resident alien population had been a familiar phenomenon for half a century and more; and sermons, pamphlets, travel and conduct books pointing out English foibles and alien dangers had come off the presses for decades. In this climate, playwrights and audiences were prepared overtly to play out the ironies of asserting pure Englishness as something opposed to the alien, while they understood (if uncomfortably) the alien footings and brickwork in the building of English identity.

CHAPTER 2

Discovering the alien in Elizabethan moral drama

The plays studied in this chapter represent various stances within the first 'alien stage' as outlined in Chapter 1. The anonymous *Wealth and Health*, Ulpian Fulwell's *Like Will to Like*, and George Wapull's *The Tide Tarrieth No Man* demonstrate the early knowledge of alien presence pervading English material and ethical culture between the late 1550s and the early 1580s. Even though the writing desires and seems to *will* a pure Englishness, the alien cannot be shaken off. For a play to talk about religious corruption at home is for it to recognize the influence of non-English practices; to discuss domestic economic problems is to engage with the relative dealings of alien merchants and craftspersons and to investigate the nature of bullion to cross borders; to question the government is to read Englishness against the examples of foreign princes and potential invaders. All these negotiations between setting up Englishness and wrestling with the alien push the boundaries of the first 'alien stage'. In one version of this stage of English–alien relationship, cracks in the make-up of a country are blamed unequivocally on alien presence; passages, scenes, or the main thrust of a play may therefore concentrate rather simply on attacking alien bodies, fashions, or habits. At points, a clearer recognition that something alien might already reside in the native self seems to surface, and the anxiety caused by this revelation necessitates a deflecting mechanism whereby overtly staged alien bodies (in our first two plays, 'Dutchmen') are located as objects of comedy or derision to partially direct attention away from the corruption of the native.

Rejection of the alien, and the ongoing attempt – in spite of all the evidence to the contrary – to assert 'Englishness' as having an existence discrete from anything alien, builds to produce another English stance in these plays, a second version of the first 'alien stage', as we see especially in *The Tide Tarrieth No Man*. Here pride, narcissism, and patriotism – a combination that creates what the period called 'security' – assure the natives of their national superiority and invincibility, while the country's identity ironically parades on the stage for the audience in the character of ideologically 'deformed' Christianity. The weaknesses of the self-assured community with aspirations toward a 'national' identity are therefore left open for the alien to see and exploit. Happening more in spots of dramatic time than through a teleological progression from play to play, this chapter's corpus of moral interludes shows London's, England's, and visiting and resident foreigners' own hybrid identities. The move from the concept of a dismissible alien body to the alien presence *within* is a frightening one, for the separate, identifiable alien person can be physically removed and eliminated, but the *alienated* individual or community must be reformed within the self or community. The longer such a state is allowed to remain, and the deeper the apparently alien influence takes hold, the more the alien must be acknowledged as a growing part of the native self, and the harder it is to get rid of through a reformation of some concept of pure Englishness. Metamorphoses of the physical alien into its abstract, internalized, and psychological manifestations are rife in sixteenth- and seventeenth-century drama, and the two coexist, symbiotically, encouraging readings – especially of course in allegorical drama – *through* physical figures to abstract or representational determinations and back again through *ideas* of the alien to tangible foreign sources.

The three plays studied in this chapter combine potent and straightforward political and social statements with highly equivocal and deeply ironic commentary on the civic and moral state of England. I want to take some time, then, to expand on Chapter 1 and enter relevant late Marian and early Elizabethan contexts. We will then be able to give nuanced responses to the plays' genres and manners of presentation and production in their times and places of performance. Elizabethan 'alien' plays were produced during decades of fear about alien presence and influence at all levels of society: working producers of raw materials and finished goods (especially those in London and provincial towns with high alien populations) feared unfair competition from a mixed immigrant population – desperate refugees and skilled artisans; conservative preachers tried to balance their dedication to loving their foreign 'brothers', protecting the English poor, and pitching an identity for 'Englishness'; noblemen had a duty to provide hospitality to their neighbours in the countryside but were drawn to the city for the lifestyle and fashionable foreign products that arrived there; merchants worked with unfavourable exchange and interest rates and juggled their privileges between London, Antwerp, and Hamburg; courtiers' jobs and lives depended on international relations, and English monarchs had to walk the line between keeping friends friendly and foes pacified in the ongoing religio-political struggles between Spain, the Holy Roman Empire's pressures out of Rome, and Reformist northern Europe. The middle and late sixteenth century also saw England worried about monarchic succession passing into foreign hands. When Edward VI and his advisers drew up laws of succession, the document apparently designed to keep the line male was underlain by another, Anglo-centric motive: Mary and Elizabeth were excluded from the lineage for fear 'that they might marry foreign princes and subject the realm to alien rule'. Mary, of course, did just as Edward had feared by marrying Philip II and provoked blunt disapproval from countrymen in England and abroad; Elizabeth's spinsterhood was no more comforting, for if the problem with Mary was her marriage to a foreigner, the problem with Elizabeth was her failure to marry with an Englishman.

Marian accession impacted the alien population in England, and the mostly Protestant Dutch and French Walloon residents began returning to the Netherlands and Flanders. A few tried to remain in London and the surrounding countryside, but by December Mass was officially restored and the emigration continued. On 17 February 1554 a Proc-lamation was issued expelling non-denizen aliens. Many more strangers left, but Andrew Pettegree argues for a significant remaining Protestant alien population, perhaps 40 per cent of those already in England, throughout the Marian years, not least, he suggests, because the expensive process of denization that they had opted to earn was not a privilege to be given up lightly.[1] When Mary married Philip of Spain in 1554, it seemed to spell doom for the Protestant sector in England, both alien and native. Although by prenuptial agreement and personal choice Philip's personal influence in England was slight (he was 'a king who had no desire to rule over heretics'[2]), Mary's own declarations that she was ruled by her hus-band did nothing to put the English at ease about the possibility of direct foreign rule, either immediately or upon her death. When, after the first of Mary's false pregnancies, the king left England in August 1555, not to return until the political situation required it in the spring and summer of 1557, there was little doubt that the match was a purely political one on Philip's part. With the failure of the second 'pregnancy' in 1557–8, the stage was once more set for conflict as the ageing Mary's throne would be left open either for Elizabeth or Philip; and out of the woodwork of exiled corners and Continental Protestant printing presses came the tracts prophesying imminent terror.

Less radically than some, Laurence Saunders' *A Trewe Mirrour or Glasse . . . of Englande* takes the form of a dramatic dialogue between two friends, the Catholic Eusebius and Protestant Theophilus, who lament the fact that intelligent friends such as they are should be split by ideology. Eusebius is curious to hear his Protestant friend's reaction to the marriage of Mary and Philip, and asks, 'I heare say ye King of Spayne shal at last be crouned kyng of England, what say you to that[?]' Theophilus attempts to reply diplomatically, 'Alas brother Eusebius what should I say to it: if god have determyned, who maye wythstande: we muste commyt it to his good pleasure and wyll'. 'But do you not thynke it a plage?' asks Eusebius, using the ubiquitous disease metaphor of alien influence in England that Jonathan Gil Harris has so ably examined, and prompting the stronger reply that he seems surprised not to have drawn the first time around:[3] 'Yes verely', Theophilus agrees, 'and an utter desolacion of Englishe bloud'.[4] But Theophilus' concerns go deeper than lambasting alien influence, and he attacks the fickleness of the Privy Councillors and court advisers, who change their allegiance to safeguard their careers rather than remaining true to any personal or national conviction: 'They have not only consented and agreed' to the queen's marriage with Philip, 'but are also chefe doers and procurers thereof'. Eusebius agrees that the authorities have been infiltrated by alien ideas and influences; and such a situation gives Philip the opportunity, 'without contradiccion [to] furnishe al the fortes of England with his owne men, for I would not thinke him wise to trust straungers so muche as his own countre men'.[5] All classes will suffer, Eusebius goes on to remind us, including those sycophantic governmental officials and nobles who are for the most part of the 'newe learnyng', and therefore most likely to de dispatched by the ruthless Catholic conqueror.[6] These inextricable issues of gender, blood, disease, infiltration of habit and identity, fear of difference, lack of trust, and power-broking enter and maintain the drama throughout the second half of the sixteenth century.

A more extreme view of the situation is laid out in the anonymous *Lamentacion of England*. Signed on 30 December 1556, and with editions in 1557 and 1558, it concentrates more on prophecy of future dangers, although it also includes valid observations about the handling of power and the assertion of status by both Philip and Mary. The author begins by quoting Hugh Latimer's speech at Westminster Palace before Edward VI in 1549, which called for the English to 'put away all pride' lest their punishment be the marriage of Mary or Elizabeth to strangers.[7] 'Oh what a plage is it', continues the author, 'to see strangers rule in this noble realme violently, wher befor time tr[e]we hartid Englishmen have governid quietly?' Moving on from this selectively amnesiac retrospective, he invokes the memory of Catherine of Aragon, implying a continuous alien presence in the royal house, which turns him to consider economic national problems. Mary, he asserts:

toke the most part off here blude and stomake off her spanish mother, and therefore from time to time ever regardid her spanish kinred, and permotid them, by geving them licensis, wherby they do cary and convay away, out of this realm, frely without paieng any custome therfore, our goudly & best comodites, as woll Tinn leade lether & c. to the great decay and ympoverishment, off the pour comons off this realm, by reaison wheroff the said comodites, be now at doble pryces, that they were before, & also pour men cannot be set a worke as they have bene.[8]

There are two problems troubling this writer. This passage claims that political and economic mismanagement are going on at home, and it is a problem the drama takes up with gusto. Favouritism and bending of the trade customs rules that should ensure native merchant advantage are eroding domestic practice. Thus inter-class tension aggravates the alien–native problem, as it will continue to do in the minds of the working classes through the 1590s. Two ideas about the alien are already in place here: first, alien bodies are already present at all levels of Englishness and the origin of the alien is difficult to determine; and second, English forces seem, ironically, to enable or motivate the alien to re-infect or deform the English.

The political point of the marriage is clear. Philip's 'spanierds have blasid abrode in other contres saieng what shall the king do with such an old bich, also affirming that she may be his mother, a yonger is more meter for him'.[9] But he will take the marriage, the author of the *Lamentacion of England* correctly predicts, to draw England into war with France again, which will impoverish the English.[10] The blatant economic motives of Philip make it 'manyfest and playnly apperyth as clere as the sone, that in mariage he sought not the quenes persone but only the rich and welthy realm of England'.[11] At exactly this time, as we shall see below, the play *Wealth and Health* personifies wealth of the realm as something to be protected from the Spanish threat, but also as something already beyond the grasp of the English. It is interesting, moreover, that in spite of the criticism of Catherine's 'blood', the author does not use ethnicity per se as a cause for rejecting her. As Eric Griffin has noticed in a study of John Foxe and other writers, the complementarity of England and Spain before the sixteenth century as co-religionists against the Eastern pagan was a strong bond to break, and writers before the Armada tended to suppress ethnicity as a focus of attacking and rejecting the alien.[12] Thus Foxe 'did not implicate the Spanish people on the basis of their ethnicity', notably avoiding the 'Black Legend of Spanish Cruelty'. But as the Reforming 'little island' of Britain saw itself more and more as a collectively elect people or 'nation', it located Jerusalem in London and identified Rome as Babel or Babylon; consequently a clear shift in focus privileges 'national' ethnic identity over international religio-cultural connections.[13] Later Elizabethan plays seem to mark the crossover between these positions. Thomas Lodge's *A Larum for London* (1600) and the anonymous *The Weakest Goeth to the Wall* (1602) are two dramatic accounts of Spanish tyranny in the Netherlands and the suffering of the people of Antwerp. Written and produced as the country wondered what would happen to it when the ageing Queen Elizabeth finally died, they at once call for sympathy for fellow Protestants in distress and warn of national or regional weakness.

Fear and control of alien behaviour in England were well-grounded in Elizabeth's reign, for the country would have been the perfect prize or partner for either Spain or France. An Anglo-Spanish league would have encircled France with Spanish allies; a permanent link with France would have placed a north–south barrier between Spain and the occupied Netherlands. The strategic status of England probably contributed to an initial coolness in the official stance toward the aliens returning after a Marian hiatus. During 1558–9 returning strangers and those surfacing from hiding did not feel particularly welcome, although there were some pockets of acceptance in towns like Sandwich, Colchester, and Norwich. Elizabeth remained wary of versions of the new religion, and petitioners for the return of the strangers' churches to their old privileges were flatly refused at first. However, manufacturing in England required alien craftspersons and skills, and the provision of patents and monopolies multiplied at this time.[14] Despite official restrictions on immigration and alien movement, the queen would not accept any disturbances against the strangers, for a significant number of them remained denizens with many of the rights of citizens, including a right to live peacefully in the adopted land. Following a report by the Lord Mayor of London, detailing a fray between Frenchmen and Englishmen, a Proclamation was issued for 13 August 1559, stating:

The Queen's Majesty commandeth all manner her subjects, of what degree soever they be, to keep the peace as they be bound, and specially towards all manner of persons of strange nations within her Majesty's city of London or elsewhere, without reproaches of words or like quarrels, and to remit the avenge of all quarrels past of late in the same city to the ordinary justicers. And the like also her Majesty commandeth to all strangers born, to be observed on their part.[15]

There is to be no more conflict, and malefactors will meet with 'her highness' determination, that no partial favour be showed to English or stranger, but that every of them shall live in the safety and protection of her laws'.

Early in her reign, Elizabeth had to worry about the practice of radical new Protestant religions, whose new stranger churches, begun in 1550, were feared as centres of resort for Englishmen dissatisfied with the Church of England. Indeed, records in the 1560s and 1570s show Englishmen being received into the alien churches. An order in 1573 was sent to both the French and Dutch churches commanding them to cease these activities, with which edict the Dutch promised to comply. The French may have been less quick to fold under pressure, however, but did officially say that they would only entertain Englishmen provided they were not attending in contempt of Church of England ceremonies.[16] New Reformed influence also led to Proclamations such as that of 1560, limiting extreme reactions against the physical remains attributed to Mary and Catholicism: it prohibited destruction 'by the means of sundry people, partly ignorant, partly malicious, or covetous . . . of certain ancient monuments . . . which were erected up as well in churches as in other public places within this realm only to show a memory to the posterity of the persons there buried, or that had been benefactors to the buildings . . . and not to nourish any kind of superstition'.[17]

In *The Tide Tarrieth No Man*, as we shall see, the character of English Christianity has a difficult time working out his own identity and the way to achieve a successful English reformation. Placing a settled Elizabethan church in between the alien extremes of Catholicism and Calvinism was no easy task, and foreigners remarked on the unclear nature of English 'reformed' churches. Patrick Collinson has written, 'One might say that when most people became, after a fashion, Protestants, real Protestants became Puritans', and these 'real' Protestants 'will have regarded the godly strangers as "brethren" in the sense that conformist, conventional English church-goers were not'.[18] Such a foregrounded separation of religious and national identity keeps the question of 'Englishness' suspended between a desire for national autonomy and an understanding of alien impact. English religion had a choice between two alien positions, then: the old, Roman one and the new, 'Germanic' one. And this hovering identity, tethered by the alien, disturbed both the English and foreigners. One upper-class visitor's notes on a service in Westminster Abbey read, 'In this beautiful church the English Ministers, who are dressed in white surplices such as the Papists wear, sang alternately, and the organ played.'[19] This priestly apparel was a particular bone of contention in 1565 when the French church was lent out for a baptism with an English minister who refused to wear the surplice. Elizabeth, upon learning who the minister was, immediately sent a substitute.[20] The temptation toward English heterodoxy had to be watched very closely as the 'popish' rituals and regalia of the English Church seemed to be a cause of English persons seeking out the new style of the Continental services; Collinson estimates that 'the ratio of godly, fully committed English Protestants to their fellow Reformed Protestants of other nations in the core membership of the stranger churches was roughly equal'.[21] One's identity as a morally upright Protestant English subject became increasingly a matter of personal conscience rather than one of a perceived national identity. The comic, moral, and historical genres of drama – from the characters Wealth and Health of a country, through Lady Conscience and Hospitality of Robert Wilson's London (Chapter 3), to Welsh and Portuguese 'English' men and women in Shakespeare and late-Elizabethan comedy (Chapters 4 and 5) – all had to deal in shifting public and personal contexts with this discovery of region through religion and conscience through country.

WEALTH AND HEALTH

Nationally marked foreign characters in these early plays would seem to be the most significant alien figures: Hance in *Wealth and Health*, Hance and Philip Fleming in *Like Will to Like*, and Mercadorus the Italian merchant in *The Three Ladies of London*. For all their potential as staged representations of the real immigrants or residents of London and England, however, these foreigners work as sounding boards or deflectors, temporarily acquiring our attention before sending us elsewhere. As we shall see, the alien more importantly lies in the plays' apparently native and rarely neutral allegorical figures. Entered in the Stationers' Register in 1557, the anonymous *Wealth and Health* is possibly a play from earlier in Mary's reign; it was also printed early in the reign of Elizabeth, however, and I read this play across the Marian–Elizabethan divide. I suppose, along with T. W. Craik, that it could have been played before Philip at court when he was in England in the winter of 1554–5, although I prefer the option of a 1557 performance, prompting the Register recording.

Unlike Craik's or A. J. Hoenselaars' views of the play as generally benign to a Spanish presence, I see clear evidence that a Marian court performance would be edgy and challenging.[22]

Wealth and Health begins with the title characters arguing over their contrasting identities and their relative worth to their country. Liberty enters to assert himself as a conceptual umbrella under which Wealth and Health go about their work, and after some refamiliarization between the characters, Wealth and Health acknowledge Liberty's importance. Illwill (presenting himself as plain 'Will') enters 'with some jest' and insinuates his way into the identities of the other characters on stage and through them to all men and women; Shrewdwit (alias Wit) joins Will as partner. The drunken Dutchman, Hance, enters with a song and the worrying claim that England is mistaken if it thinks it is a wealthy (and therefore healthy) country, for its riches are being scattered abroad. Wit and Will win places in the service of Wealth, Health, and Liberty (who do not quite cotton onto their deception), and they leave the stage just as Remedy enters lamenting the state of the realm and the need for moral reformation. Liberty, Wealth, and Health leave Remedy with assurances to come to him 'for succour' if they 'be infect in the soule or body' (C3), and Wit and Will return, only to be easily deciphered as villains by Remedy. As soon as Remedy exits, Wit and Will's employers re-enter to confirm their corruption by the 'ill' and the 'shrewd' elements of Wit and Will. Remedy meets Hance the Dutchman and unequivocally rejects him: 'fie on you aliau[n]ts al I say' (Dv). Having got rid of Hance, Remedy is faced with Health, who enters 'with a kercher on his head' (D2) because he has been 'wounded' by Wit and Will – his fellows Wealth and Liberty are 'fallen in decay' and 'kept in duraunce and captivite' (D2v). Remedy promises to help Health, and when Wit and Will re-enter, thinking they are alone and laughing at the fate of the recently exiled Dutchman, Remedy accosts them. Will comically affects a Spanish identity in an attempt to evade arrest; Remedy threatens to imprison Will, but Will insists that incarceration is hardly sufficient to keep him away from the hearts of men. Health releases Wealth and Liberty and brings them to Remedy, who concludes with an assurance to all: although Illwill and Shrewdwit will 'reygne a while, wrongfully and unjust / [Y]et truth wyll appeare and their misdedes blame / Then wronge is subdued, and good remedy tane' (D4–D4v).

Wealth and Health enter the play in harmony, 'synging together a balet of two partes' (A2), but almost immediately Wealth notices that the play's audience seems to have forgotten him. He insists that 'Welth hath ben ever in this countrey, / . . . / And here I wyll endure' (A2v), but the claim of originary residency – itself an attempt to stake out something of the identity of the nation – and the will to survive are both questioned throughout the play. Moreover, the instigators, perpetuators, and explicators of the doubt of Wealth's Englishness are the alien presences in the play and the theatre. It will be the denizen figure of the Fleming Hance, the alien presence in the vice Illwill, the influence of the Spanish–Marian court, and the foreign bodies infecting Health that will teach the English Englishness and the way to reformation.

Through the sixteenth century, 'wealth' consisted in bullion and coin, visible value. To enrich the realm, money needed to come in from abroad, because circulating money at home is simply alteration, not increase.[23] Wealth's claim that he has always been in the country, then, is trumped in the mid 1500s by his note that 'All the worlde, hyther doth resorte' (A4) because of him. This seems like a nod toward Spanish enrichment of England, but the play erodes both the possession of good wealth by England and the possibility of sustained appreciation of Spanish presence. The wealth coming to England at this time is widely marked with the spirit of the alien. Diana Wood begins her chapter on the question of defining money in medieval England with the observation that to some commentators the crosses on late-medieval English silver pennies gave them a godly identity; and in a related fashion, as M. Beer notes, it is the stamping of coin with the effigy of the monarch that is the 'spirit that giveth life', valuation, and identity to bullion.[24] It is in large part the legacy of this faith in coinage as the spirit of the country – in particular a confusion of national (or legal) and religious spirit – that leads to the concentration on currency in the late-Elizabethan city comedy, to the horror of forbidden minting of new 'life' coins in a later play like *Measure for Measure*, and even to the modern debate over adopting the euro versus retaining the British pound or to the maintenance of the motto 'In God We Trust' on US money.

The *Lamentacion of England* points out what it sees as a sophisticated piece of alien knavery that corrupts the wealth of the English realm: the assertion and imposition of royal image and name by the absent half of the monarchy. With half-justified fears of real Spanish invasion hanging in the air, an iconic invasion of England has already taken place, for Philip has his image stamped on the English coin but has not put Mary on the Spanish coinage, and his tyrannical motto reads, 'Philip R. anglie, francie, neapolis princep. hispaine'. Spanish spirit infuses the English coin to align England with France as well as Spain. Money circulates in the body of the realm like blood. A century later, Thomas Hobbes would argue that the combination of pure metallic value (undebased gold and silver coinage) and the stamp was what ensured real wealth in a realm and remained constantly available for 'concoction' – a term meaning digestion, conversion of food into blood, and a bringing to a state of perfection (often in reference to gold or precious stones); this combination provides the 'sanguification' that 'nourisheth' men of a nation.[25] In the Marian moment, Spanish blood-money is feeding the English commonwealth. Furthermore, 1550s price rises in England (which were only slowly being understood as related to the fluctuation in the value of money itself) started to be felt as a result of New World wealth that entered Spain, passed through France, and filtered to England.[26] Wapull's *The Tide Tarrieth* and Robert Wilson's *The Three Ladies of London* seem to show us earlier and later recognitions of the view of money itself as a commodity much like any other, no longer the sanguine connection between monarchic and national identity but rather the lodestone that draws 'all estates' of persons, to use Wilson's phrase, into financial contact and contract to pursue personal gain at the expense of community.

While 'wealth' is strictly money, as part of the 'commonwealth' the term indicated happiness, prosperity, spiritual well-being, and the opposite of woe, as well as monetary portliness; thus Wealth and Health should not be seriously at odds.[27] To come to this compromise conclusion, however, takes some heated dialogue between the two characters in a fashion that would have been familiar to the audience. Contemporaneously with *Wealth and Health*, Man and Money were debating the necessary but dangerous place of wealth in England in *The Bayte and Snare of Fortune*.[28] Claiming his place as 'the prince perelesse in puissaunce' (A2), Money asks 'who builded London that named was newe Troy / But I puisant peny, that eche man cloth and fede' (A3); he then goes on to list over forty other English towns and cities that would not exist but for him. Man can only argue that Money has two sides to his coin and the other is destructive, simultaneously undermining this creation of England with temptation and crime, covetousness and poverty. Interestingly, this debate remains convinced that money is controllable, containable, and can be handled to good ends if only people would choose to use it properly; but human beings were evil, jealous, and covetous before Money came into the world, as evidenced by the murder of Abel (A4, A6v).

In apparent contrast, Health takes little time to assert that 'welth is ever waverynge' and 'fugitive' (A2v–A3). The wavering quality reminds us of the stereotypical inconstancy of the English that Sara Warneke has out-lined,[29] and as such indicates a very English quality and perhaps suggests that the problem lies once again with the handler and not the goods. But Health's critique of the anthropomorphized Wealth insists that although wealth is a good thing per se, it cannot exist as a stable commodity or attribute to a native national identity, but causes domestic and inter-national rifts because of the way in which it transfers itself from person to person or realm to realm. Wealth does not seem to have a conscience or any dedication or loyalty to one being – a revelation that devastated Everyman. It is dangerous, then, for it is an unstable subject, traitorous (or at least mercenary) in that it is 'mutable', 'cruell', and 'ever waverynge' (A2v), and those very characteristics put Wealth's claim that he has always been in England into doubt. Craik notes that 'there is a satirical impli-cation that wealth was not known in England during the previous reign (of Edward VI)', and this raises further questions.[30] Where has Wealth been if not in England? Where did Wealth come from in the first place? That Wealth is also, according to Health, 'hauty and proude of name' would point the finger at the Spanish in the late-sixteenth-century English mind.

The epithet 'fugitive', too, combines many characteristics that alienate Wealth from sound Englishness: the word denotes fleeing, vagabondage, immateriality or fading away, banishment and exile. So we should not be overly surprised when Hance the Dutchman later insists that Wealth is not at court but in Flanders and later again that 'welth is lopen [walking] in an ander [another] contry' (D2). How we read such a line depends on whether we consider the play performed in Marian England, perhaps at court, or in the first year of Elizabeth's reign. From March to July of 1557 Philip was in England convincing Mary to help him in his war against France. Against the majority of her advisers, Mary joined her husband's conflict by declaring war on 7 June, and by 5 July a fleet had left England to hold the French at bay while Spanish ships traded through the Channel with the Lowlands. Prior to this engagement a significant amount of public money had been spent on refitting the navy, this in a time of dearth that spanned the two years preceding the war and an influenza epidemic that was to last until the end of the decade. Wealth could not be seen as prospering at court, then, for it had indeed, as Hance suggests, been drawn out of the realm and into hulks in the service of Spain. Moreover, wealth is being passed via Spain to Hance's Lowlands, where trade is rife. Although the name Hance/Hans for a Dutch character is conventional, there is almost certainly an allusion here to the long-standing tension between the English and resident Germano-Lowland aliens in the community of Hanseatic merchants. Forming a widespread European trading network, these merchants were active in England well before their official fourteenth-century establishment as a league; they were restricted in their social interaction with the English but possessed custom breaks and trading privileges that consistently caused protests from native merchants. The following year, Mary's humiliating second pregnancy and fatal disease prompted another question that shifted the material observation just made to an ideological one: if no heir was arriving, was this a sign from God, too, of the realm's lack of moral wealth?

The feeling of Spanish imposition in *Wealth and Health*, and the weight more generally of the alien already resident in England are early forces that encouraged the writing and more often translating of anti-Spanish tracts and plays in England in the later decades of the century.[31] If there is one concept that could not be considered part of the Spanish consciousness in these writings, it is that of Liberty. Through these tracts to the very affecting late-Elizabethan plays of the fall of Antwerp (*The Weakest Goeth to the Wall* and *A Larum for London*), it is the hidden political and religious deceptions of the Spanish (the 'ill' in their 'will'), their sexual lust, bloodthirstiness, and unwillingness to negotiate that erase liberty in the cities and lands they conquer. So when the character called Liberty enters to Wealth and Health and neither of them recognizes him, it is the loaded word 'strange' that he uses in response to his isolation: 'Absence is cause of straungnes, / What looke ye on werwhy are ye so straunge' (B); 'your strange wordes alytle did greve me' (B2). Wealth and Health, the one with a compromised national identity from the start, the other who will be corrupted by the alien in the end, are like representative book-ends, the alpha and omega of alienated Englishness within which range – and especially while Spain and England are contiguous political entities – Liberty must be a stranger. Liberty, therefore, denotes a concept of Englishness, for he has been estranged from this alienated country and will be 'kept in duraunce and captivite' by alien enforcement; or, as Health puts it, 'By wast & war' (D2v), the latter epithet the one applied to Hance the Dutchman (B4), representative as he is of the draining of the country's wealth to the Lowlands.

Such exclusion of Englishness is maintained, moreover, 'thorow yll wyll, and shrewdwit' (D2), the Spanish-tainted devil-vice and his thieving sidekick, for England cannot be harmed 'but wyth falsehod or stelth' (C3). Illwill enters as the vice 'with some jest' (B2), but he has also been summoned like a devil; Liberty has simply mentioned 'wyll' and the vice appears with 'Mar[r]y I am come at the first call' (B2). Like a devil (and like a Catholic Spaniard to the reforming Protestant English in a 1558 or later text), Will is a self-confessed 'chylde that is pas[t] grace' (B3), an epithet echoed by Remedy in his interrogation of Will and Wit, whom he calls two 'chyldren that be past grace' (C3v). Wealth notices that Will is 'very homely' (B2v), intimating not just nativity and rusticity, but also uncomeliness, a disfigurement and ugliness that tends toward a devilish identity. Health apologizes to Remedy that 'I am homely to come her[e] in your prese[n]ce thus diseased' (D2), indicating visible deformity. In the period, that outer complexion or ugliness would also lead to the suspicion of inner corruption, which Wealth expresses in his dismissive 'Dryve him away quickly' (B2v). When Will is questioned about exactly whose will he is, he claims to be everyone's and anyone's: 'I am your evyll wyll / your wil, & your will, & your will' (B2v). Liberty resorts to that word 'straunge' again and declares that 'this cannot be / For in our wyles is great diversitie / For one is not lyke another' (B2v). English Liberty finds the concept of a single, mutable 'will' 'strange' and alien, and indeed he is right, because he is talking to the vice who will corrupt Englishness. Will, however, does not claim to represent a new phenomenon: he is the alien *already within*, the image behind the pattern, and for all the diversity that Liberty claims, Will insists that the essences of 'evyll wyll', 'The maddest wyl, and the meriest' (B2v) are embedded to be brought out of native and alien alike. Will can play with this concept of being *inside* Liberty (and every other character) to emphasize the pathological trope of the alien as insidious foreign body.

As we shall see, moreover, just as Wealth of the realm is implicated in an infusion of Spanish blood into the English circulation, so Will proves to be the first of the powerful trinity of what Jonathan Gil Harris terms 'poisonous bogeys' that were the frightening, infiltrating 'foreign bodies' in sixteenth-century England: Catholics, Jews, and witches.[32] Harris points out that in the second quarter of the sixteenth century, the idea of the body politic was increasingly being understood and ideologically used in terms of national boundaries;[33] this localization substituted universality and made the concept of penetration of that body so much more available for metaphorical rhetoric and, in the case of immigrant aliens, of course, physical demonstration. Harris' study of William Averell's *Mervailous Combat of Contrareties* (1588) shows the later century's shift onto observation of those national margins and in particular an understanding of corruptive disease as something breaking in from the outside through weaknesses and 'breaches' in the body politic rather than as something inevitably embedded in the complexional model of humoral theory.[34] The 'deformation' of Christianity in *The Tide Tarrieth No Man* and the 'abomination' of Lady Conscience in *The Three Ladies of London* play out this new understanding of invasive disease. As early as *Wealth and Health*, however, the notion of internal bodily balance is being pierced by the possibility of a foreign body's invasion as Will claims that he and Liberty 'be of one consanguynitie' (B2v):

> Wyl and lybertye[ ]is, of aunciterie olde
> with out lyber[t]ye, wil[l] dare not be[ ]bolde
> And where wyl lacketh, lybertye is full colde
> Thyrfore wyl and lybertye must nedes be of kyn. (B3)

In doing this, Will is causing a mutation and a deformation of the host body. Michel Serres' theory of the parasite has shown the inevitability of foreign presences within a new structure (there are always rats at the table or in the cellar of the new-built house); and within the biological body the parasites feed off the host while keeping it alive.[35] The morality plays and interludes do not separate the physical from the moral or the personal from the communal: through *The Tide Tarrieth No Man* and *The Three Ladies of London*, physical damage to the body indicates moral corruption, and religious or ethical deformation is displayed physically; the damaging effects of one character on another are those forces that anyone in a community might encounter. As Remedy works out how difficult it will be to reform the people of the country, then, he insists on the inextricability of national identity with personal bodily and spiritual care as he outlines his 'a[u]ctoritie' over 'the comon welth, & helth both of the soule and body' (C2v–C3). In these plays of characteristic nomenclature, too, Remedy has an apt warning for all:

> Take hede in any wise exchewe yl & shrewd compani
> yf a ma[n] be never soo good & use w[ith] the[m] th[at] be unthrifti,
> He shal lese his name, & to some vice they wil him te[m]p[t];
> therfore beware of such people, & from them be exempt[.] (C3–C3v)

Even a good man might 'lese' – lose, loose, or lease – his name. To lose a good name will mean to gain a bad one or be nameless; to loose the name might be for it to roam and be degraded (like the compounds of Ill and Will or Shrewd and Wit); and to lease a name might be to lend one's name to an alternate, corrupting activity, thus staining a reputation. 'Lease' also means to glean or to gather, and thus a bad name is gained (again, an 'Ill' or a 'Shrewd') by association with the unthrifty. Serres' parasite outlines the everyday alien within that never needs to be acknowledged, diagnosed, and treated; but in the quest for representation of some inherent identity, a wealth and health based in a concept of Englishness, the ways in which that alien body manifests itself must be addressed. Will perverts the right sense of 'Liberty' to make it a 'licentiousness' – as Love will become Lust in *Three Ladies* – that allows Will to 'be bolde', dangerous, evil. His presence in turn is like the vice Courage in *The Tide Tarrieth* who 'incourages' others to act illicitly; Will turns 'colde' Liberty into hot licentiousness. Liberty should of course be a well-balanced, neutral protector of English Wealth and Health, as he claims earlier in the play (Bv–B2), and Will is upsetting Liberty's humoral balance. When he house-sits for Liberty, Will has given 'Pipe whore hop theef, every knave and drabe' (Dv) free licence for debauchery, and Liberty is at pains to insist on 'liberalitie competent', hospitality and behaviour appropriate to his standing.

This enemy of the realm, Will, reveals his national colours almost by chance. When questioned by Remedy, the only character in England that Will actually fears, Will comically enters a linguistic disguise by speaking in 'Spanish': 'Me is un spy[ ]nardo compoco parlavare' (D3). A. J. Hoenselaars reads this episode as 'a shrewd attempt to capitalize on pro-Spanish sentiments prevailing in court circles'. He writes that Illwill's 'choice of nationality suggests that, despite the anti-alien policy of Good Remedy, to be taken for a Spaniard still involved certain privileges not to be expected by other foreigners like Hance Berepot'.[36] Indeed, it could be argued that the English criminal Illwill expects the Spanish 'disguise' to protect him, either because political sensitivity of the moment gives him a kind of diplomatic immunity, or because a Spaniard would not be thought guilty of Illwill's crimes. In performance, however, the initial reaction of a playgoer to this sudden switching of identity would probably be superficially to connect Illwill – that evil influence that insinuates its way into our unwilling self – with the Spaniard. The sudden (attempted) transformation of the character suggests the closeness of the two identities he represents in these exchanges. Thus Laura Yungblut seems right in thinking of this as 'a moment of agitation' in which Illwill 'reveals his true identity',[37] for this would indeed confirm the revelation of the alien within Will. However, to read it non-ironically probably misses the point. We must remember that this character is *Ill*will, one who presents himself as Will but has ulterior motives; such deceptiveness was consistently at play in the anti-Spanish Marian tracts and in Remedy's line about foreigners' 'falsehod or stelth'.

Health's response to Will's Spanish, 'Thou folse [t]hefe is thine English tonge gone' (D3), then, becomes an ironic comment on the doubleness of English-alien identity throughout these plays. While this play does not do much with linguistic identity (an issue I address further in following chapters), this simple question highlights the impossibility of a single answer: yes, his English tongue is gone for he has always been foreign, alien, and anti-English; no, his English tongue is not gone, for he has always been the will *within* the English, a force that prompts English expression. Remedy's complaint that 'I can not tel what thou dost mene, babbler!' suggests an alignment of Spanish 'babble' with aspiring Babel and its evil will that dares to rival the heavens. Remedy's demand 'But y[o]u shalt speake English & confesse an other mater' (D3), moreover, suggests the belaboured and torturous enforcement of Englishness necessary in the process of reformation as represented in these plays. The allusion to 'confession' in Remedy's speech (and presumably 'truth', as spoken by all good English subjects) makes an interesting ripple on Remedy's waters of English superiority and purity; the Catholic babble would be the language of the group Elizabeth Hanson notes constituted 'the most visible and vocal victims of English torture', that non-judicial practice occurring between the mid 1560s and mid 1580s.[38] The protection of the realm from the alien would seem to entail making the foreign language speak, confess, expose itself; here the Spanish is, of course, an ugly outside rendering the corruption of the inner Will. By getting through to the English language, Remedy assumes he will get his confession; such an identity, though, cannot be drawn out and separated from the internal alien that remains 'free Will' after the threats of imprisonment and that apparently 'naturally' spurred Will's Spanish improvisation.

We get close to exorcism in this case: the 'homely' Illwill is physically deformed by his corruption, 'so croked, by flattery, diss[im]ulation, & such other' (D4) (Dissimulation being the character who will cause the corruption of Lady Love in *The Three Ladies of London*), and he must be examined and contained for 'the devyl and yl wyl is both of one complexion' (D4) – apparently a crooked, deceptive, dark, Spanish complexion. This latter observation builds on an ethnicized alien-Spanish-devil-pride cluster that will be more overtly presented at the end of *Like Will to Like*, where Nichol Newfangle the vice 'rideth away on the Devils back' to Spain (F). In *Enough is as Good as a Feast*, *Friar Bacon and Friar Bungay*, and *Histriomastix* the destination would be hell, but Newfangle's twist at this point is to declare 'Farwel my masters til I come again, / For now I must make a journey into spain'. The alien is ubiquitous; it is always present and it always escapes. Will's last lines in *Wealth and Health* are the defiant 'Lock us up & kepe us as fast as ye can / yet yll wyl and shrcwdwit shalbc with many a man' (D3v), the declaration of the alien presence always already within the English, but against which the English reforming Remedy, in this first alien stage, continues stubbornly to fight.

LIKE WILL TO LIKE

Ulpian Fulwell's reformist *Like Will to Like* is extant in three editions between 1568 and 1587, and like *Wealth and Health* it was possibly played at court as well as by popular troupes.[39] David Bevington writes that *Like Will to Like*'s 'tone is predominantly satiric and denunciatory rather than morally positive',[40] and as such it serves more as an entertaining warning to the popular audience than a moral judgement on ruling the realm or a political allegory of the sort we saw in *Wealth and Health*; Hoenselaars compares the two plays: '*Welth and Helth* is a sociopolitical allegory about the English nation. *Like Will to Like*, however, is best described as an amalgamation of comedy and sermon.'[41] These comments both seem apt, but I think there is a shift in the later play toward a communal responsibility for the country's political and social health. As such, the denunciation and satire that Bevington sees and the comic–sermon amalgam do indeed contribute to a positive moral appeal that is, however, becoming more sensitive to the ways in which citizens make their own urban world. Networks of social types – artisans, preachers, merchants, shopkeepers – are starting to be recognized as forces for political change, and political decisions inevitably entail moral dilemmas or imperatives. *The Tide Tarrieth No Man* and especially *The Three Ladies of London* will develop this notion of the role of professional groups in making their world. In *Like Will to Like*, the overarching appeal is to English parents. The play argues that a lack of reformed education and strict upbringing in England produces licentious youth who associate with dangerous types (like unto like) who corrupt them to the point of bringing about their deaths. These dangerous types, represented primarily by Newfangle and Tosspot, are inextricably bound – by origin and association – with the alien. Tom Tosspot ends with the reflection, 'If my parents had brought me up in vertue and learning, / I should not have had this shameful end: / But all licenciously was my up bringing, / Wherfore learn by me your faults to amend' (E2); and Cuthbert Cutpurse on the verge of being hanged appeals to 'you that Fathers and Mothers be: / Bring not up your children in to much libertie' (E4). As in *Wealth and Health*, good English Liberty is vulnerable to 'lese[ing]' his name and becoming alien licentious corruption. Wapull is so serious on this point that he has Tosspot warn bad parents that 'your meed shalbe eternall damnation' (E2).

Newfangle the vice enters with traditional bravado until Lucifer appears and gives him his orders to corrupt the world. Newfangle's friend Tom Collier enters to report on his day's dishonest dealings before dancing familiarly with Lucifer. Tom Tosspot and Rafe Roister join Newfangle, and after several bouts of comic fighting, Newfangle sets up a competition whereby Tosspot and Roister can compete for a plot of land by proving which of them is the verier knave. After some contention and proofs of knavery on both sides, Newfangle offers to divide the reward between the contestants. The Dutchman Hance enters and sings a drunken song as a figure sadly fallen from a respectable position in society; his friend Philip Fleming finds him and leads him home. Following a soliloquy in which Newfangle reveals his intent to see the destruction of Tosspot and Roister, Pierce Pickpurse and Cuthbert Cutpurse are spurred on by Newfangle to their own increased corruption and eventual executions. The tone of the play then shifts with its extended moralizing section: Virtuous Living is joined by Good Fame, God's Promises, and Honour to appeal to the audience for moral reformation. Roister and Tosspot lament their fate and call on others not to indulge as they did and to bring up their children well. Severity the judge is then fooled by Newfangle who claims that he has been robbed and hurt by Cutpurse and Pickpurse, and Hankin Hangman thanks Newfangle for sending two more victims his way. Lucifer returns to carry Newfangle away, and the play closes with Virtuous Living, Honour, and Good Fame presenting a prayer for the queen and her council.

Very little time is wasted in *Like Will to Like* before the vice in England, Nichol Newfangle, is exposed as a physical and conceptual alien. The foreignness that matters to these reforming early Elizabethan playwrights might be highlighted and entertainingly staged through characters such as *Wealth and Health*'s Dutch Hance or *Like Will to Like*'s Hance and Philip Fleming, and these characters have certainly been the focus of the few critical comments on aliens in the play to date. But those overt foreigners with a defined nationality are representative embodiments of political problems that are more insidiously manifested – and more dangerous to a construction of Englishness, because harder to see and expel – in the alien within apparent Englishness. It was easy enough for *Wealth and Health*'s Wit to boast with his scatological pun that the

Dutchman will be deported, 'The horson fleming was beshitten for feare / Because he should voyde so soone' (*W&H* D2v), and for Remedy to concentrate on Hance's ability 'w[ith] craft & subtel ti[ ]get Englishme[n]s welth away' (*W&H* Dv) with the protest, 'There is to many aliaunts in this real[m]e, but now I good remedy [/] have so provided that English men shall lyve the better dayly' (*W&H* Dv); but in the end those characters are seeing the face of an alien without but not perceiving the location of the alien within.

The perception of large-scale immigration combined with urban social problems would certainly have made comic anti-alien stage business attractive to audiences, as it has been to critics. However, to say that Hance and Philip Fleming benignly 'perform in a brief satire of drinking, swearing, and general horseplay, aimed primarily at immigrant labour from the Low Countries',[42] isolates these characters as though they represent an anti-alien blip on the play's radar of Englishness. A more extensive examination of the alien must see these foreign characters as media through which the alien already present in the English can be perceived. Thus we could not talk about *Wealth and Health*'s Hance without concentrating on Illwill, Shrewdwit, and Remedy; similarly, we will see *through* Hance and Philip Fleming to the important alien presence of Nichol Newfangle. *Like Will to Like*'s 'Dutchmen' reveal the trope of the foreigner as something to be looked beyond even more simply than in *Wealth and Health*, for they are not depicted as 'War' and immediate dangers to, or corrupters of, the country as they were in the earlier play; they seem in Fulwell's play to represent a basic economic burden on English society – an irony in a period in which Lowlanders were invited to England to spur the economy.

In fact, corruption is depicted in *Like Will to Like* as passing *into* rather than out *from* the nationally defined alien. Sitting in a chair because he can hardly stand, drinking deeply, and stammering throughout his speech, Hance the Dutchman is a pathetic, broken man who needs to wait for his friend Philip Fleming just to lead him home – but this has not always been the case. Hance is apparently telling the truth when he says 'as stameringly as may be' that he once knew Latin and could 'help the pp preest to to zay mas', because Tom Tosspot confirms:

> For he was once a scoler in good faith.
> But through my company he was *with*drawn from thence:
> Thorowe his riot and excessive expence.
> Unto this trade whiche now you doo in him se:
> So that now he is wholy addicted to followe me. (Cv)

Tom Tosspot's corruption at the hands of the foreign Newfangle has inevitably led him to corrupt Hance in a kind of reflexive re-alienation of foreigner and native. We hear finally that Hance and Philip Fleming 'lie sick of the gout . . . / . . . in a spittle house' (F), afflicted with the disease of luxury, but also, interestingly the disease of usurers and Jews, a connection that this play does nothing with. The Dutchmen in both these plays contrast with the evil and vice figures in exhibiting a significantly greater sense of attachment to the country of England. *Wealth and Health*'s Hance has lived in England for thirteen years and he 'love[s] de scone [beautiful] Englishman' (Dv). The idea of being forced to walk in another land is for him 'quade' (evil), and when Remedy asks 'from whence comest thou, and what dost thou here?', Hance, as a settled resident, does not take it as a question about his national origin. Instead, he answers at the local level and replies that he has come from 'sent Katryns' – St Katherine's Hospital, outside the walls just east of the Tower, being the location of a strong alien community.[43] It is to this 'Little Flanders' outside the walls of the English city of London that Remedy orders Hance to return, only, of course, as a station en route out of the realm completely.

At the start of *Like Will to Like* Newfangle enters laughing like a traditional vice, presents his calling card of a knave of clubs to an audience member, and claims surprise that he is not generally known – or rather that the audience *thinks* it does not know him. 'Yet you wil knowe me anone I dare jeobard [wager] a grote' (B2v), he insists and draws them into his biography:

> For first before I was borne I remember very wel:
> That my grandsire and I made a journey into hel.
> Where I was bound prentice before my nativitie,
> To Lucifer him selfe suche was my agilitie. (A2v)

Reminiscent of Illwill in presentation and bad intent, the surreal suggestion of pre-natal memory and the diabolical history of apprenticeship before birth summon the spirit-like, alien nature of Newfangle. He may be represented on the earth by outward means such as unnecessary fashions, but prideful clothing is the quintessential marker of the corrupted soul. While in hell, Lucifer taught Newfangle 'All kinde of sciences . . . / That unto the maintainance of pride might best agree', and those sciences involve the making of showy apparel, 'gownes with long sleeves and winges', 'ruffes like calves chitterlings', 'And especially breeches as big as good barels' (B2v–B3). This commonplace of pride comes up in Philoponus' words in Philip Stubbes' *Anatomie of Abuses* (1583–95):

> Pride is threefold: namely, the pride of the heart, the pride of the mouth, and the pride of apparell, the last whereof (unless I be deceived) offendeth God more then the other two. For as the pride of the hearte, and of the mouth, are not opposite to the eye, nor visible to the sight, and therefore cannot intice others to vanitie & sin (not withstanding they be grievous sins in the sight of God) so the pride of apparell which is object to the sight, as an *exemplary* of evill induceth the whole man to wickednes & sinne.[44]

In spite of Lucifer's demand that Newfangle sow 'suche pride through new facions in mens harts' (A3v) as he himself possessed when he was cast down from heaven, and that he 'Let thy new fangled fations bear suche a sway, / That a raskall be so proud as he that best may', the play does not dwell on proper dress codes or transgression in apparel. Instead, Newfangle tells the apparently ignorant Lucifer that such corruption 'is all ready brought to passe, / For a very skipjack is prouder I swear by the masse, / And seeketh to go more gayer and more brave, / Then dooth a Lord though him self be a knave' (A3v). Apparel in identity-making, disguise, class mobility, national identity, gender relations, and race receives more sustained treatment in *The Three Ladies of London*, and especially in comedies such as Dekker's *The Shoemaker's Holiday*, which I discuss in the final chapter.

This Newfangle, literally dressed to kill, informs his audience that 'Nichol Newfangle was and is, and ever shallbe' (B3). Akin to Wealth's claim to 'hath ben ever in this countrey' (*W&H* A2v) but perhaps at a deeper level aligned with Will's claim to be everyone's will and 'with many a man' (*W&H* D3v), Newfangle continues the politicized identity of the inherent, already-there alien within Englishness. Particularly striking about this alien presence for the play-world characters (who are not necessarily aware that they exist in a moral play that requires a vice) is the devilishness behind it; Newfangle's declaration is clearly a blasphemous counter to God's claim to be the beginning and the end, and it is the ancestor of Iago's similarly ungodly 'I am not what I am' (*Oth* 1.1.65). The attractive comedy of the vice only seems to enhance the uneasiness felt by an audience. Newfangle's own comic fear of Lucifer both suggests the 'reality' of the frightening play-figure whose 'name *Lucifer* must be written on his back and in his brest' (A3) and contrasts with English Tom Collier's utterly fearless dance with the devil (A4v). When Lucifer addresses Newfangle as 'myne own boy' (an appellation suggesting kinship, which he will repeat several more times), Newfangle, flustered, and 'pointing to one standing by' in the audience, blurts out: 'He speaketh to you sir I pray you come neer.' Newfangle claims to be afraid of Lucifer because 'ye didst bruse me behinde' in a fit of temper and 'I am like to cary the mark to my grave' (A3v). Lucifer's brand is seared into Newfangle's behind, evoking the common iconography of the devil with a face in his rear end. The English vice is, in his deepest identity, a hellish alien, who ends up, as I noted above, riding away on the devil's back into Spain. The audience must have felt that Spain was a fitting, hell-like hot place for the foreign-devilish vice to go, and a place, moreover, where his outrageously puffed-up fashions would be appreciated. The hellish aspect of the alien will be tempered somewhat (although it will not disappear, and will even be played with) in the plays of the later Eliza-bethan theatre where the practical politics and social tensions of urban and court life demand that the contemporary, physical, 'real' effects of the alien be foregrounded – a return to face up to and incorporate those overtly foreign-marked characters. The vice, *as vice*, then, necessitates the first alien stage's obsession with rejection and disgust; greater room opens up for a negotiation within English-alien identity in the later plays, because they comprehend the international interlacing of personal and communal identities that must occur in dramatic representations of more complex city and world pictures.

While no earthly country of nativity or citizenship is positively assigned to Newfangle, we find out that England is certainly not his homeland. Lack of immediate recognition of the vice character is not unusual, and he often has to declare himself, but Newfangle's belaboured turning from one audience member to another to insist on recognition (A2v–A3) seems to be making a significant point about his strangeness or alien identity when combined with the extended story of his early life. When Tom Tosspot first appears 'with a fether in his hat' and 'new fangled fations' (Bv), it prompts Newfangle to react, 'Me think by your apparel you have had me in regard' (B2). Tosspot, however, tells New-fangle that 'your name is quite out of my remembrance', suggesting a past break between them, leaving Tosspot's behaviour and appearance cur-rently an English phenomenon. Tosspot has not been having much luck finding others in England to accompany him in his behaviour, however, which may give a ray of hope against the corruption of the English through pride of apparel and unthrifty spending, or it may just indicate that corruption will come instead from the lesser pursuits noted in the play of theft, dice, and drinking. Newfangle does not arrive in England until after his apprenticeship in hell and a trip 'by and by the whole world about' (A3). 'At *your first comming into England* wel I wot', says Tosspot, 'You were very wel acquainted with Tom tospot' (B2, my emphasis). The vice is not English, but comes into England already of some age. It is not entirely clear whether Tosspot's second line means that Newfangle *became* acquainted with him once in England or was *already* acquainted with him by the time of his arrival. The ambiguity puts Tosspot himself on the verge of a foreign identity, and the alien newfangled fashion of Newfangle creates addicted disciples: 'tospots & ruffians' (B2).

The proverb of this play, 'Like Will to Like', is driven home to insist on the necessity for a community of like-minded reformists who will create a better England for the future, in particular through responsible child-raising. The same force that attempts to unite the godly, however, shows the threat of a unified army of unreformable types and more problematically comes close to precluding any Christian attempt at reconciliation between the two sides before reformation has been effected. Hoenselaars' observation that 'The xenophobia of *Welth and Helth* is alien to the Christian doctrine of understanding that pervades *Like Will to Like*'[45] seems to ignore the fact that the two sides (native and alien) do not at all come together in social harmony in *Like Will to Like*, and the 'Christian doctrine' shown by the vicious English characters is hardly an understanding one. What pervades *Like Will to Like* is not Christian understanding, but intra-Christian fracturing. Christ made it clear that he was available for the sinners (Matt. 11: 28), and in Christian presence would reformation be made possible. Virtuous Living preaches:

> Come unto me ye that travail (saith he)
> And suche as with sin are hevely loden:
> And of me my self refreshed you shall be,
> Repent, repent, your sinnes shalbe down troden. (D3)

However, the strictly bipartisan living shown in this play does not allow any such practice; so when Newfangle introduces himself slyly to Virtuous Living as 'your olde freend', instead of any attempt to draw the sinner into a life of repentance, Virtuous Living scornfully rejects him: 'My freend, mary I doo thee defy: / And all suche company I doo deny. / For thou art a companion for roysters and ruffians, / And not fit for any vertuous companions' (D). Just a few lines before this rejection, Virtuous Living expounded on the universal influence of God, who is 'of all men to be praysed: / Of Christians, Sarasens, Jewes, and also Turks' (C4v). So when Newfangle finally returns, singing 'trim, trim merchandise' and brandishing his 'rewards' of begging bag, bottle, and a pair of halters for his victims, the audience has been well-warned of the inevitable ending. Newfangle, as a devil-worshipper, is worse than Saracens, Jews, or Turks, who (however misguided) turn to God. Newfangle is ultimately more alien – because more ungodly – in his activity than all these 'others'. This is the bind in which the play finds itself, a constraint that hinders any tale of moral restitution. It observes the state of affairs in the realm but does not display a Christian solution so much as a conservative cleaning-up operation, as the downtrodden and vice-ridden are executed, get sick, or escape the country. The Prologue's claim that the play is like 'a glasse' to see 'The advauncement of vertue of vice the decay' (A2), then, is upheld not in a way we might like, with the virtues conquering the vices and bringing lost souls back to redemption; rather the caesura of this line (after 'vertue') marks a tough point of no return, with the already-virtuous on the one side glorifying each other with crowns and swords of God, and vices on the other causing the decay of English bodies and souls for whom it is apparently too late to repent and for whom there is no help from the 'virtuous' reformed.

I want to conclude this section with some remarks on the foreigners with named nationality. The Dutch character of Hance is our more overt indicator of social fracture and alien decay, a figure to absorb national anger and deflect the dual problem of intra-English conflict and alien incorporation within the English social strata. As well as putting forth deformed speech in an over-emphasized stammer, Hance cannot hold together a dance or even the form of his upright body. The stage direction orders that he 'daunceth as evil favoured as may be devised, and in the daunceing he falleth down, and when he riseth he must grone' (Cv). He becomes almost inhuman, a semi-linguistic, crawling figure, who has allegedly soiled himself like an uncontrollable animal: 'By the mas he hath beraid his breches me think by ye smel' (Cv) says Newfangle. The 'deformation' of Hance is not presented as something the spectators should be sympathetic about or even ambivalent over. Hance does not contribute to the value judgements of the play in the way that the major pairs of good and evil figures do, nor is he in the mould of the trinity of Virtuous Living and his two companions; most of the spectators would see his fall from scholarly grace to drunkenness in 'racial' terms, as a reversion to the nature of his national shortcomings. In case there should be any doubt, Fulwell introduces Philip Fleming, with his nationally representative name, Hance's friend and partner in drunkenness. Fleming, like Hance, enters singing, and soon recognizes a playmate, Tom Tosspot.

Newfangle remarks, 'Why now I see the olde proverb to be true: / Like wil to like bothe with Christian, Turk and Jew' (C2v). It is unclear what kind of slander this is. Which part of the proverb has this meeting just confirmed? Is it the 'Dutchman' or the 'native' who is the 'other'? Equivocation is almost certainly the point, for Newfangle has travelled around the world observing races, religions, and nationalities conform to the proverb of the play, and it is this ubiquitous coming-together of likes that suggests Christian and English similarity to all things alien, and the presence of the alien within Englishness. Fleming's association with Tosspot highlights the Englishman's name's reference to 'tossing the pot', or drinking, again insisting on an embedded corrupted domestic behaviour. Charlotte McBride has observed that there was 'a shift during the sixteenth century from perceptions of beer as a new and foreign product to its status as a defining English drink'; she goes on to connect the attitude to beer and drinking to the tension over the Protestant English requirement to be hospitable to their religious brothers while patriotically looking out for their home country's political health. Thus the figure of the refugee Dutchman in England who endangers the host country through his alcoholism places 'drunkards [as] both victims and perpetrators of crime'.[46] They both reflect and accuse the English state of alien corruption.

When Hance eventually wakes up from a deep, drink-induced sleep he relates the details of his dream, which implicate either French 'knaves' or perhaps English pirates in the traffic of the sixteenth-century immigrant burden to England:

> Me thought iche was drowned in a barel of beer.
> And by and by the barel was turned to a ship,
> Whiche me thought the winde made lively to skip.
> And iche did sail therin from Flaunders to Fraunce:
> At last iche was brought hether among a sort of knaves by chaunce. (C2v)

Bevington's observation that 'Ludicrous as they are with their dancing "as evill favoured as may be devised", Hance and Philip are harmful dissipaters of England's wealth' usefully brings out a trope of dangerous comedy that we will see in the drama of the 1580s and 1590s.[47] However, the dissipation of wealth is, as we saw, more relevant to the role of Hance in *Wealth and Health*. In *Like Will to Like*, the alien threat displays a subsequent narrative in the same destructive story: while wealth is allegedly drained from England, knavish destroyers of well-being (the fraudulent and the destitute) pour in. *Like Will to Like*'s Hance's dream of a route from Flanders to England via France emphasizes the incoming flow of 'Dutch' and French (Walloon) aliens and suggests an uncontrollable over-running of the realm with foreigners. These incoming alien figures of vice and deformation are the types of characters that playgoers would like to have seen board the barge to hell in George Wapull's *The Tide Tarrieth No Man*.

THE TIDE TARRIETH NO MAN

A 'worme' is born within a piece of wood. It then consumes its home like an ungrateful person who damages their own country through 'avaricious' and 'insacious' behaviour. So begins George Wapull's *The Tide Tarrieth No Man* (Q 1576),[48] the very first lines bringing together ideas of greediness and the insidious infection of unnatural, alien behaviour. The 'worme' evokes biological and psychological forms both larger and smaller than itself, for in the early modern period the word is used consistently for a snake or a dragon but also referred to parasitic presences in the body; the worm is a 'caterpillar' against commonwealths but also the worm of conscience in life or hell; it generally refers to a miserable creature or person and in this context specifically was applied to worldly greediness. Such a worm, also, is Wapull's vice, Courage:

> Thus may you see Corage contagious,
> And eake contrarious, both in me do rest:
> For I of kind, am always various,
> And chaunge, as to my mind seemeth best. (C3v)

'Corage contagious' infects minds and bodies with his 'insacious' 'incoraging' of immoral behaviour that has stark physical consequences; he is also 'courage contrarious', mutating according to the host to which he needs to attach himself, the sequence of bodies to whom the disease should be transmitted, and the deforming effects he desires. The worm is also the merchant (alias Greediness, alias Wealthiness) – a landlord and a usurer spurred on by Courage – who eats away at the structure of his homeland, consorting with the oppressive conceptual and literal alien bodies in England such that 'The symple ones commonly, by such are opprest' (A2). Wapull's world is a far more frightening one than Fulwell's, for the isolated (if vicious) alien-infused vices that we saw in *Like Will to Like* have spread like body-snatchers to deform and recast almost all of the community.

Following the Prologue on the 'worm', Courage the vice invites all to board his boat to hell. Courage shows himself to be behind the work of the evil trinity Hurtful Help, Painted Profit, and Feigned Furtherance.[49] The merchant Greediness confesses that he was 'moved' by a preacher's outcry against citizens' badness, and Courage dresses him down for such weakness. This merchant is also a landlord who must be bribed by No Good Neighbourhood to give up a lease that should be renewed for a faithful tenant, and Courage prompts Help and Furtherance to exercise their cunning in aid of No Good Neighbourhood. A courtier needing cash to look the part is also promised 'Help' by Courage. All this connivance comes home in a traditional but effective soliloquy by poor, old Tenant Tormented. Courage promises marriage for Wantonness, a young woman who hates the single life and abstinence, because, Courage says, it is a sin for girls older than 'xii yeares of age' (D3) to lie alone. The courtier returns, having been ruined by the fees paid for all the help given him, followed by Greediness the merchant, who is off to St Paul's to call on his debtors. Wantonness follows her new husband Wastefulness on stage and rails at him for neglecting her lusts to concentrate on making a living; in a song they are renamed Pleasantness and Pliantness as he is persuaded to disregard their wealth and indulge in young love and lust before the tide turns. A sergeant leads in a debtor arrested at St Paul's on the order of Greediness; the debtor refuses to pay a bribe for his freedom and is taken off to prison. Christianity enters 'with a sword, with a title of pollicy, but on the other syde of the tytle, must be written gods word, also a shield, wheron must be written riches, but on the other syde of the Shield must be Fayth' (F2v) and is examined by Faithful Few until he 'turneth the titles'. Faithful Few attacks the corruption of Greediness and Courage, who argue for the worldly superiority of riches over godliness. After Greediness and Courage exit, Wastefulness enters, ruined and followed by Despair 'in some ougly shape, and stand behind him' (G1v). Faithful Few gets Wastefulness to repent and pray, which causes Despair to flee. Courage enters weeping, because his friend Greediness has committed suicide at the behest of Despair. Authority and Correction finally enter to judge Courage, who has no friends left to save him.

Working relentlessly to procure a commission or fee from any transaction, the characters in *The Tide Tarrieth No Man* assemble like vultures and work with a cynical version of the ubiquitous 'disguise' of the *metic*, as discussed by Jean-Christophe Agnew.[50] In commercial meetings and exchange, persons crossing socio-political boundaries have to take on new faces, manners, and characters in order to ply their trade and impose themselves upon others. Recognition of friend and enemy, native and alien, becomes very difficult and professions of identity highly questionable as anyone, whatever his or her character or occupation, has the potential to act out their anti-self. *The Tide Tarrieth* shows this by the familiar method of compound naming that we saw in *Wealth and Health* with (Ill)Will and (Shrewd)Wit, but now the everyday citizens are widely caught in this web of politic crossings. The ubiquity of this self/alien trope makes all urban relations doubtful. Hurtful Help becomes plain 'Help', Painted Profit 'Profit', No Good Neighbourhood just 'Neighbourhood', and Feigned Furtherance puts himself out as true 'Furtherance'. The vice Courage 'incourages' the multiplication of others' identities, making the merchant inhabit greediness and wealthiness and the courtier seek out worship rather than true honour.

Courage holds the alien chain that links him to No Good Neighbourhood and Hurtful Help, who will liaise with Greediness the merchant to evict Tenant Tormented; this event will be the central demonstration of a deformed Englishness that Christianity and Faithful Few critique as the thesis of the play. The play presents proud, ambitious, selfish, complacent, 'secure', and therefore weak English characters. Already utterly corrupted by the alien, they are in communal denial, as Christianity points out when he says, 'the greater part sayeth, / I am still a christian, and so shall remayne, / My Christianity say they, no domage doth sustaine: / But alas they are deceived . . .' (F2v). The play conflates the reformation of Christian practice and a recovery of Englishness, for the inability of the community to see their way to reformed Christianity is owing to alien blinding. Through self-scrutiny, an investigation of actions and beliefs, people must break down the public disguises they have used to propel themselves toward riches at the expense of their neighbours and must reveal their true faces and their 'lese[d]' names. Only then will their mistaken creed be discovered, the creed that reads the proverb 'The tyde tarrieth no man' as a *carpe diem* trope prompting them to irreligious earthly greed ('Take time while time is, / Least that you doe misse' (A3v), warns Courage at the play's opening). It is not enough just to profess Christianity, moreover; reformation must be absolute, genuine, and effectively delineate a return to Englishness: 'For better it were unchristened to be, / Then our Christianity for to abuse: / The Jewish Infidell to God doth more agree, / Then such as Christianity do so misuse', declares Faithful Few (G4–G4v).

The unpredictability of Courage the vice makes tackling him difficult. He is a mutating virus, contagious through 'contrarious'-ness, and the demonstration that his deforming influence knows no bounds comes in the figure of inverted Christianity. The characters' hidden nomenclature indicates those aspects 'incouraged' or infused into them, and now *confused* with them and thus inextricable, only half seen, like alien bodies, parasites that incubate within an apparently healthy English host, perhaps seen in external glimpses – pustules, lesions – but infecting and corrupting him or her from the inside, remaining largely hidden and difficult to remove without some superficial (physical, financial) harm to the alienated host. It will be this final apparent impossibility of separation of the alien internality from the English character that will lead to the merchant Greediness' suicide. I will outline Tenant's tale, show how Christianity's deformed position has come about through such vicious relations, and thereby demonstrate the alien underbearing of the whole play as filtered through the character of the apparently English Greediness the merchant.

The play's clearest examination of the direct effect of alien presence on English welfare involves (No Good) Neighbourhood and (Hurtful) Help's machinations against 'Tenant Tormented', already a familiar character to the audience.[51] Paula Neuss writes that the character of Tenant is one among a few who 'are introduced not simply or mainly for the purposes of social satire, as is usually supposed, but in order to give *concrete* application to the proverb, to show what it might mean in practice for this particular audience'.[52] It is this concretizing imperative, a drive to make allegory 'felt', that really marks a shift from these earlier interludes of moral restitution to Wilson's pivotal, late 'city morality' and the very 'material' urban comedy of the 1590s. 'Whether shall I goe, or which way shall I take', asks Tenant rhetorically, 'To fynd a Christian constant and just[?]' (C4v). A fine preacher, he forecasts the view of Faithful Few exactly as he states that 'Ech man himselfe a Christian would make. / Yet few or none, that a man may trust. / But for the most parte fayned, inclined to lust.' Tenant then goes on to lament the greed of his landlord (the merchant Greediness) who threw him out, and the hostility of his deceitful neighbour (No Good) Neighbourhood, who does not play his part true to his publicized name ('My neighbour supposed, is my deadly foe'). Unlike Lady Conscience in *The Three Ladies of London*, who is also evicted at a moment's notice and succumbs to a criminal life to make ends meet, Tenant declares that he will retain his honesty and strive for salvation through Christianity. To say as much in this play is to claim to remain 'English' against alien encroachment from all sides, and Tenant's concerns about the health of Christianity prepare us for the heavier fate of English Hospitality in *The Three Ladies of London*. This is Tenant's description of his situation in a passage that declares his predicament's centrality to the reforming thesis of the play:

> Both my house and living, I must now forgoe.
> What neighbour is he, that hath served me so?
> Thus crewelly to take my house, over my head,
> Wherein these forty yeares, I have bene harbored and fed.
> And now being aged, must thus be thrust out,
> With mine impotent wife, charge, and famely:
> Now how I shall live, I stand in great dout,
> Leading and ending, my life in misery.
> But better doe so, then as they live, by theevery,
> Catching and snatching, all that ever they can,
> Because that (they say) Tyde taryeth no Man.
> But God graunt that they, in following that Tyde,
> Loose not the tyde of Gods mercy and grace:
> I doubt that from them, away it will slyde,
> If they still pursue the contrary race.
>   . . .
> I see whome I seeke, is not here to be found,
> I meane Christianity, constant and just:
> I doubte that in bondage he lyeth fast bound,
> Or else he is dead, and lyeth buryed in dust.
> But if he be living, to fynd him I trust,
> Therefore till I fynd him, I will no where stay,
> Neyther in seeking of him, I will make delay. (D–Dv)

The Christianity that Tenant seeks arrives rather late in the play, and Faithful Few remarks even later that Authority has not yet turned up to finalize control over Courage and pass him over to Correction. These absences demand resistance to alien forces by such as Tenant who determine to remain honest. The strongest call for a renewed Englishness comes from the embattled few up against terrible odds – a trope of faith and singular national identity-making that reprises in the quite different context of Shakespeare's French war of *Henry V*.

Coming to this text after *Wealth and Health* and *Like Will to Like*, we will now hardly be surprised that Tenant's distress is not simply caused by evil Englishmen, but rather by the alien in their midst. Neighbourhood wants to get the lease on a 'commodious and feate' tenement but fears that two things work against him: the 'good name and fame' of the current resident and the fact that he is 'but a straunger among them'. Help explains how Neighbourhood misperceives himself and his chances:

Marry syr it is much the better for that,
For if thou werte more straunge, and borne out of the land,
Thou shouldest sooner have it I dare take in hand,
For among us now, such is our countrey zeale,
That we love best with straungers to deale.
To sell a lease deare, whosoever that will,
At the French, or [D]utch Church let him set up his bill.
And he shall have chapmen, I warrant you good store,
Looke what an English man bids, they will give as much more.
We brokers of straungers, well know the gayne,
By them we have good rewardes for our payne.
Therefore though thou be straunge, the matter is not great,
For thy money is English, which must worke the feate. (B4v)

The stranger the better, it seems. Neighbourhood, with no foreign accent and not 'borne out of the land', might be an early modern 'foreigner', strange in so far as he comes from a different town. However, Help's last line, 'For thy money is English', suggests the non-Englishness of Neighbourhood himself, and combined with Neighbourhood's own self-appellation as a 'stranger', perhaps we are meant to think of a second-generation resident, born in England with one or both alien parents. As such, his alien male lineage would maintain his status as a 'stranger' or alien in commercial and legal transactions. Help does talk about 'strangers' as 'them', as though Neighbourhood does *not* belong to that group, but in the 1570s the audience might interpret 'them' as the new immigrants of the last decade. Later, Courage refers to Neighbourhood as 'that good man growte' (C4); it is an odd moment, but it could literally mean 'Master Large' (Dutch: *groot*), the epithet recalling the frequent joke on the fatness of Dutchmen – Vandal the Dutchman uses the word 'grote' repeatedly in *Englishmen for My Money*. Neighbourhood, then, is somewhere in the middle of a scale of strangeness that plays to his advantage. He is a kind of embodiment of the moral alien 'infection' of England, *using* his host country, doing it economic and ethical damage, but keeping it productive for his own maintenance. In this passage, we are reminded that aliens, known for their willingness to pay through the nose to rent property, are given first refusal at prime real estate.

The rhetoric of strangeness in a context where all the characters are 'estranged' from themselves by their dual names quickly becomes a means for confirming familiarity. Something similar happens when the Duke welcomes Shylock to the court in *The Merchant of Venice* with the lines ''tis thought / Thou'lt show thy mercy and remorse more strange / Than is thy strange apparent cruelty' (4.1.18–20). Shylock's 'strangeness' as a Jew is of course quite familiar to the Venetians *as strange*; for Shylock to be more strange in the way that the Duke is requesting (i.e. to show mercy) would at once be alien to both the Venetians and Shylock, but of course it would bring the Jew into a familiar Venetian-Christian sphere. In *The Tide Tarrieth*, the 'strange' is posited at first as what is different from the norm. The 'more strange' pushes the strange further away, seemingly to a greater 'otherness' (as suggested by Help's definition of 'more strange' as 'borne out of the land'). However, the 'more strange' becomes the newly familiar, the self-like. Landlords are familiar with aliens (i.e. the 'more strange'); Help identifies himself as one of a community of 'brokers of straungers'; and Courage, Help, and the rest of them are far more identifiable as non-Christian, non-English aliens than as natives. Like will to like indeed, and the residents of England with the alien in their identity deal more comfortably with the familiar aliens from abroad. The contagious Courage infects the life-blood of the country by 'incouraging' money to come in with immigrant aliens, increasing a tainted wealth of the nation that gets circulated by landlord-merchants like Greediness who practise usury as a matter of course. Help knows the subject of aliens so well because his career is that of a broker, or 'factor', for foreigners (B4v). Courage describes him as 'a broker, betweene man and man. / Whereby much deceyte thou usest now and than' (B). Brokers were disliked by a sector of the godly and economic observers because they seemed to do nothing in exchange for their wealth. Like usurers, brokers have no trade from which there is a product. They use the good works of others to make money with money; even worse than usurers, they breed money not even from money, but merely from speculation, from nothing.[53] Every action revolves around gaining money at the expense of another. There is for these characters simply and literally no commonwealth.

Tenant's determination to find the straight and righteous path of Christianity is a direct response to aliens in England and what they have done to the financial and communal health of the country. When deformed Christianity finally turns up, he observes a sink that the ethical filth of society has run into and soiled beyond recognition. Christianity arrives only just in time for reformation to be made, and Wapull seems to understand that the kind of extended moralizing we were subject to in *Like Will to Like* is neither dramatically tenable nor necessary for the ethical message he wants to locate in a contemporary, physically painful world. We recall Christianity, who on first sight holds 'a sword, with a title of pollicy, but on the other syde of the tytle, must be written gods word, also a Shield, wheron must be written riches, but on the other syde of the Shield must be Fayth' (F2v). The state of Christianity is so dire that even Faithful Few starts to doubt him. The rhetoric of 'policy' is – as Peter Happé points out, and as Marlowe knew, and reinvented it – the usual preserve of the vice, and so Christianity has some explaining to do.[54] Faithful Few says, 'Now are you deformed like a thing forlorne, / Which maketh me suspect, of me in my mind.' The deformation of Christianity infuses Faithful Few, who, believing in Christianity, must now doubt his own fidelity, his state of mind, and his very identity. Can a character called Faithful Few be what he thinks he is, or appears to be, if the object to whom he is faithful is in fact corrupted? Christianity assures Faithful Few that he is what he claims to be, and that God will reform him, but for Faithful Few the question mark remains because a corrupted Christianity would claim this, too, for the purpose of deceiving Faithful Few into following him.

Christianity's explanation of his appearance focuses on the synthesis of financial greed or avarice and selfishness in the context of commonwealth, common-health, and national community or hospitality. In doing so, he reprises the trope of the cankerous worm that begins the play and floats the image specifically of Greediness the merchant as the scum on the rising alien tide; thus Faithful Few sees the 'English' truth of Christianity lying behind 'policy' and 'riches'. The deformation of Christianity is a direct result of greediness, whose 'cruell force I may not withstand' (F2v). 'Greedy great' has caused Christianity's predicament, 'Greedy great for this cause I have named, / For that the greater part use greediness, which is to be blamed' (F2v). This behaviour has tainted the whole community, making Christianity's claim easy for Faithful Few to believe: 'Alas I lament to heare the report, / Which of us cittizens in every place is spread' (F2v), 'So that for the covetous greediness, which some cittizens use, / A shamefull ill reporte to the whole ensues' (F3). The power of this strain of greedy infection is indicated when Faithful Few first meets Christianity: he tries to turn Christianity's titles to reveal 'gods word' and 'Fayth', but he cannot yet do it (F3–F3v). Faithful Few remains determined, however. 'I know how Greediness, with the great part is used' (F3v), he declares, but '*Si Deus nobiscum, quis contra nos*, / If God be with us, who may us resist' (F3v). Ironically, of course, all are resisting. Christianity will return to God's word and faith, but Faithful Few remains just that, only a few. William Dynes argues that in the Estates Moralities and 'Moralities of Economy' from *The Tide Tarrieth*, on, there is a strong sense that the time for true reformation has already passed.[55] Individuals are still able to make the change, as we see Wastefulness repent (Gv–G2v), but this is a trickle of fresh water against the brackish waves.

Greediness the merchant's rejection of Christianity is tempered by Faithful Few's naming the merchant 'a Christyan with a canckered heart' (F4). This might suggest the possibility of the Christian country and its people being reformable despite the extent to which alien evil has insinuated itself. The merchant's conscience was touched by a preacher earlier in the play, and he was almost pulled across that line into reformation: 'His talk I confesse my conscience did nip' (B2v), he declares to Courage's disgust, 'And a thousand witnesses the conscience is' (B3). This is an interesting moment, for Greediness recognizes his evil and this was the concern of Christianity and Faithful Few – that lost souls 'cannot, or will not know, / The way to reforme me Christianity' (G). The knowledge of his evil, and the tortured conflict between earthly temptation and his conscience's objections leads to the man's desperate suicide. In the end, however, he cannot resist living in accord with the teachings of Courage, who reminds him that 'the world will thee despyse' (B3) if the merchant wilfully gives up riches. The merchant declares, 'In deede as thou sayest, it doth me behoove, / Not so rashly to lay my gayning aside, / Least so my selfe a foole I do proove' (B3). If evil or ignorant persons believe that they and other misbehavers are in fact Christians and that their evil ways are legitimate pastimes, then there is no effective way to reformation:

> Yet many there are, which in the world doth live,
> Who for Christians will needes accoumpted be:
> Though to all abhominations, their selves they doe give,
> And from no kind of vice be cleare or free.
> Covetousnesse is accoumpted no sinne,
> Usury is a science and art:
> All wayes are good, whereby we may win,
> Although it be to our neighbours smart. (Faithful Few, G)

And indeed, in the end, the merchant's 'canker' is too powerful a disease. Faithful Few berates the merchant, who, he says, 'both in word and deede, thy selfe thou doest misuse' (F4), turning 'Merchant' into 'Greediness' to make 'Wealthiness' at the expense of Christianity (and therefore care of the realm). That the merchant has become the worm is *manifest* here, and I used the word deliberately. By his own hands, he has dug his own corrupt hole deep into the bowels of his country, where English tenants are trying to survive what they see as the waves of immigration sweeping them out of their national rights; and he represents the corrupt infestation, the alienated Englishman who facilitates the eating away of his country by foreign bodies.

As Jonathan Gil Harris has demonstrated, the canker was widely envisioned as the 'eating', or 'biting' worm of usury in the early modern period, the term employed in pro- as well as anti-usury tracts.[56] The canker is also the caterpillar, the worm (*OED* 'canker' n. 4) that we saw at the opening of *The Tide Tarrieth No Man*. If money is cankered, then it is a disease in the heart-blood of the commonwealth, and a disease that always 'originates' with the alien. The mechanism of circulation of course obfuscates that very notion of origin, such that the English and alien cannot be extricated, the former 'dying' under the influence of the latter. The very character of the merchant called Greediness and Wealthiness who practices usury, then, is weighed down with a heart full of unredeemable bullion against which his minor pangs of conscience are no match. In Courage the vice's split-personality monologue/dialogue over the death of the merchant, he understands that although 'I am sure he is dead, or one in his likenesse, / For when he was buryed I stood by' (G3), he is in fact a 'foole' to think so, for 'Greediness will never dye, / So long as covetous people do live' (G3). The figure of everlasting greediness will shift to become the eternal presence of Fraud in Robert Wilson's *Three Lords and Three Ladies of London* and the later comedies. Before that, however, Wilson's *The Three Ladies of London* continues the examination of a 'cankered commonwealth'. The word 'cankered' appears four times in *The Three Ladies of London*, twice to refer to the money received by Conscience from Usury (17.75 and 97) and twice to refer to the corruption of others – the hearts of Dissimulation, Usury, Simony, and Fraud (4.179) and, ironically, the accusers of Lady Lucre (17.27). It is an apt trope – bringing together as it does the conceptual with the physical, the worm of conscience and loss of godliness with the pain of disease and financial ruin – for a play that remains highly allegorical but expands *The Tide Tarrieth*'s suggestiveness to confirm that every dramatic moral problem has its material, communal, urban, alien consequences.

CHAPTER 3

Accommodating the alien in mid-Elizabethan London plays

The previous chapter's closing notion of the push toward real, physical consequences of moral behaviour is what Robert Wilson brings home in *The Three Ladies of London*, a play he wrote a couple of years before being drafted into the new Queen's Men's company in 1583. The play opens with Lady Love and Lady Conscience lamenting their impoverished state at the hands of the despicable Lady Lucre. Dissimulation, Fraud, Simony, and Usury reveal themselves as villains before trying to gain service with Love and Conscience who reject them. All the while Simplicity is caught within his limited understanding of the world; he recognizes some villainy, but gets into trouble easily. When Lady Lucre enters, these henchmen tell narratives of their history in good vice style. The Italian merchant, Mercadorus, is insinuated into the group and assures Lady Lucre that he will serve her in his capacity as a cheating and commonwealth-ruining trader, exporting good English materials and importing foreign trinkets. Hospitality stands against them all, representing English Christian tradition and stability of the realm, and for his pains he is murdered by Usury. Indeed, in order to survive characters have to be protean and selfish. Thus Peter Pleaseman will be a preacher in whatever denomination is required, Artifex the artificer will use fraud in his craft to compete with the aliens, Creticus the Lawyer will argue any which way Lucre desires for his reward, Sir Nicholas Nemo offers hospitality and promptly disappears, and when Mercadorus refuses to repay his loan to his Turkish Jewish creditor (the honest Gerontus), he threatens to turn Turk to avoid the debt. Lady Conscience is driven to poverty and eventually convinced to run a private bawdy house for Lady Lucre; Lady Love is married to Dissimulation and grows monstrous as a result. They are both judged in the final scene and condemned to hell-like punishment, 'dying, yet never dead' (17.95) where there is 'Weeping, wailing, gnashing of teeth, and torment without end' (17.58).[1]

59

In spite of Fame's proclamation in the opening scene of the play that justice will be meted out appropriately, most of Wilson's vices do not meet with fit judgement, and his virtues fall through entrapment in the tempting and debilitating labyrinth of London. With the burgeoning market and rapidly increasing population matters of daily concern in London, the moral allegory of corrupted Conscience and lust-filled Love hits home in the theatre of the 1580s via the immanent and established experience of English–alien proximity. It is 'by the means of Lucre', states the title-page, that 'Love and Conscience is so corrupted'. But that first 'Lady of London' is, as we shall see, alien. All the allegorical figures are capable of inflicting or feeling psychological and physical pain. The play insists that trope manifests as reality and that allegory threatens English bodies; it does so by placing an inordinate weight on the problem of immigration into London and England and the presence of multiple foreign identities. Thus we should examine the historical basis for such a representation by outlining the investment of *The Three Ladies* in the patterns of immigration into London and England and the demographics of the capital city in the second half of the sixteenth century.

Whereas the nationally defined foreigners in the earlier moralities were important in themselves, they remained isolated representations of a larger presence and acted in the last instance as sounding boards for the alien-confused 'English' characters deeply involved in the corruption of a perceived Englishness and a process of socio-Protestant reformation. Wilson uses a multinational and wider-reaching foreign presence to build a claustrophobic enclosure within which we find residents of London continually exposed as alien with the concomitant corruption of the Christian Englishness of natives. For playwrights to emphasize geographically marked alien bodies in this way is a tactic based in part on the experience of cosmopolitanism in London and in part on the necessary adjustments that need to be made as the English imagination of foreignness and Englishness gets shaken up by the experience of international events in the 1570s and early 1580s – from the Paris Massacre to the sack of Antwerp, from the French Wars of Religion to invasion rumours surrounding the Spanish Armada, and from the excursions of the new Turkey Company in 1581 to the ongoing debate over intervening to protect the Netherlands from Spain. In forcing this emphasis on real alien bodies in England to broach the issue of alien confusion in England, Wilson draws on the earlier drama but clearly lays a ground for the history and comedy plays of the 1590s that mine the specificities of alien bodies for ethnic 'clues' and answers to the elusive questions about, and the quest for, Englishness. This 'event-based' reading of Wilson's casting of his plays is supported by his writing his topical 'Armada' play *The Three Lords and Three Ladies of London* (*c.* late 1588–9), as a sequel to *The Three Ladies*, clearly seen by Wilson himself as in the same mode of direct, alien-filled critique.

When Thomas Platter wrote that London is not said to be in England, but rather England to be in London,[2] he was referring to massive migration from the provinces in the late sixteenth century. But the capital also accommodated a varied non-English immigrant community. Estimates of alien population vary, but we might think, along with Nigel Goose, of a 'norm' alien population of about 8,000 for the second half of the sixteenth century. This would give an alien population percentage of between 5 and 10 per cent, as the city's general population increased rapidly to some 200,000 in 1600.[3] The major waves of immigration in the 1560s were split mostly between those from the Netherlands (about 75 per cent) and those from France (15 per cent). The Mediterranean yielded only about 6.5 per cent of aliens, in spite of the Italians' history of court-level connections in England, the position of Horatio Pallavicino as Thomas Gresham's successor, and a stable émigré community established by the early years of Elizabeth's reign.[4] A further 3.5 per cent came from other regions. Whether one-in-ten or one-in-twenty is a more accurate proportion of aliens to natives in London, strangers were apparently a very visible minority. This visibility was made all the more obvious by two phenomena: first, the clustering of the alien communities in relatively small areas, a situation revealed in both official records and popular texts that respond to immigration and the alien presence; and second, an estimated 50,000 aliens coming into Elizabethan England (30,000 in 1567–73 alone, prompted by the Duke of Alva's activities on the Continent) would have meant that, although they did not all stay, the coming-and-going alone of this number of immigrants would give a strong impression among the English of a massive influx of strangers.[5]

There are effectively three groups resident in the capital: Londoners, English 'foreigners', and aliens or strangers from abroad. The pressures brought to bear by conflicts within this uncertain triangle surfaced to cause some confusion in *The Tide Tarrieth* and does so again in *The Three Ladies*. Religious houses and mansions that had been bought up after the Reformation were converted into tenements to accommodate the new population; A. L. Beier writes, 'By 1570 the space left by the dissolution of the monasteries was filled. By 1580 slum housing reached crisis proportions, and the authorities acted to halt its further spread.'[6] Lien Luu considers overcrowding the primary reason for Anglo-alien hostility in London, 'although additional economic factors that affected several social ranks included unemployment levels, inflation, and trade deficits'.[7] The greatest migration into London was of English apprentices and 'betterment migrants', and many 'poor incomers'. Both British (English and Welsh, with some Scottish) and Continental immigrants were part of a larger single problem: Mayor Nicholas Woodrofe wrote to Lord Burghley in 1580, asking 'Ffor restrainte of the buyld*inges* and erecting of smale tenem[en]t*es* and turning of great howses into smale habitations within the liberties of London by forens ... and the strangers here comonlie unclenly people'.[8] Real estate supply and demand is working as it should – or from an anti-alien point of view, as it *shouldn't*, because it ruins the English – as Mercadorus the Italian merchant in *The Three Ladies* advises Lady Lucre how to handle her properties:

> Madonna, me tell ye vat you shall do: let dem to stranger dat are content
> To dwell in a little room, and to pay much rent,
> For you know da Frenchmans and Flemings in dis country be many,
> So dat they make shift to dwell ten houses in one very gladly,
> And be content-a for pay fifty or threescore pound a year
> For dat which da Englishmans say twenty mark is too dear. (5.72–7)

A Proclamation issued on 7 July 1580, shortly before the composition of *The Three Ladies*, had attempted to deal with the suburban overcrowding problem by forbidding just this multiple occupation of existing buildings, 'ten houses in one', and by curbing the erection of new houses within three miles of the city walls.[9]

An Act against new buildings in and around London to stem the tide of immigration and to avoid compounding the problem of overcrowding of persons with the overcrowding of buildings followed in 1592. In that same year, Q2 of the still highly topical, if old-fashioned, *The Three Ladies* was published.[10] And just one year later again, growing alien–English tension and overcrowding is recorded by John Stow:

In Billinsgate ward were one and fiftie housholds of strangers, whereof thirtie of these housholdes inhabited in the parish of saint Buttolph in the chiefe and principall houses, where they give twentie pounde the yeare for a house lately letten for foure markes: the nearer they dwell to the waterside, the more they give for houses, and within thirtie yeares before there was not in the whole warde above three Netherlanders, at which time there was within the said parish levied for the helpe of the poore, seaven and twentie pound by the yeare, but since they came so plentifully thither, there cannot bee gathered above eleven pound, for the stranger will not contribute to such charges as other Citizens doe.[11]

Particularly interesting in this observation is the fact that not only does the active alien presence cause rents to sky-rocket, implicitly evicting English tenants, but the *passive* aspect of the increased foreign population – the refusal to contribute to the poor – aggravates the problem of the dispossession they have allegedly caused and worsens the already-dire situation of the parish poor. Of course, such isolationist behaviour on the part of small immigrant communities was an inevitable result of encouraging them to remain essentially separate cultural islands through their own churches, trading halls, and home-based production and wholesaling. Moreover, there was an imbalance in poor relief expectations: while 'it was either assumed or explicitly stated in practically every place the refugees settled that they would maintain their own needy', the aliens often had to contribute to their parish's poor relief even though they were not receiving city money for the maintenance of their own poor.[12] By 1593 and the mid 1590s in general, class-aggravated anti-alien protests and threats built in London.

Lady Lucre instantly dismisses Mercadorus' suggestion and tells us that by the early 1580s, aliens were so well settled in English properties that Londoners had no choice but to pay the inflated market rate for rents; and the capital was allegedly joined in its desperate straits by a number of other towns to which aliens were attracted by direct invitation or distributed by government population policy:

> Why, Signiore Mercadore, think you not that I
> Have infinite numbers in London that my want doth supply,
> Beside in Bristol, Northampton, Norwich, Westchester, Canterbury,
> Dover, Sandwich, Rye, Portsmouth, Plymouth, and many more,
> That great rents upon little room do bestow?
> Yes, I warrant you, and truly I may thank the strangers for this,
> That they have made houses so dear, whereby I live in bliss. (5.78–84)

The exchange between Mercadorus and Lady Lucre argues that the admission of aliens has confused English and alien in the capital city. Any insistence on the 'otherness' and inferiority of the aliens is given the lie by the apparent similarity of the state of poor Londoners and their immigrant counterparts. Those 'infinite numbers in London' may be the English migrants as well as 'old' Londoners, and it is the 'strangers' who are entirely to blame for making the English strangers in their own land and whom Lucre 'may thank'.

A combination of uncertainties about the aliens in their midst and the country's place in Europe certainly made the English reactionary and less tolerant of the aliens than they might have been at a different historical moment. We must be cautious, however, of overstating the matter. Steve Rappaport and Ian Archer have (in contrasting ways) put the English situation in the context of a less stable continent,[13] and Joseph Ward and Nigel Goose have tempered the general assertion of the 'xenophobic' English. Without denying extensive, recurrent anti-alien propaganda and spates of violence in Elizabethan England (even called for directly in the drama), violent behaviour against aliens was not as widespread or long-lasting as were continuing complaints to the authorities about other socio-political issues, such as fair trade practices and relief of dearth.[14] A generally antagonistic reputation attached to the English, however. As outlined in Chapter 1, the English 'character' as combining a tough, northern fighting ability with an effeminate inconstancy is a geohumoral commonplace that strongly influenced foreign views of the English and even the ways in which the English examined and understood themselves.[15] One Antwerp merchant noticed in his 1575 visit to England that the English 'are bold, courageous, ardent, and cruel in war . . . but very inconstant, rash, vainglorious, light, and deceiving, and very suspicious, especially of foreigners, whom they despise'.[16] The English are a people rife for alien confusion, resisting the alien but subject to absorbing the habits of others, afraid of foreignness but needing (to understand or contain) the foreign to bolster and inoculate the self against what they fear.

Extant texts of foreign visitors to England tend to concentrate in a few areas of the English character: their self-sequestered and therefore xenophobic and ignorant nature; their lack of art and culture (as a result of such insularity); and their alleged idleness, passivity, corruptibility, inconstancy, and – as noted above – potential rebelliousness. Goose has recently warned us, however, of the dangers of the sources available to us to assess foreign observation of the English character. Several factors compromise extant Continental reports of English visits: national stereotyping, class prejudice in which the upper classes are represented as broad-minded and the working classes virulently xenophobic, plagiarism between writers, and simply the brevity and context of some writers' visits to London. When the Dutch physician and geohumoralist Levinus Lemnius visited England in 1560, for example, his mature age, the early date of the visit, and the class of person he is remembering probably contributed to the likelihood of a pleasant experience. He did, however, note that others 'will skarcely bee perswaded to beleeve' his good report of English learning and hospitality.[17] Late in the century the Duke of Württemberg's secretary writes by contrast of an 'extremely proud and overbearing' people who, because they 'seldom go into other countries . . . care little for foreigners, but scoff and laugh at them', especially the pugilistic 'street-boys and apprentices'.[18] Although the secretary is shocked by the lack of respect across class lines, age may be as important a factor here. If at this time the 'presence of servants and apprentices gave London's population a distinctive youthfulness: roughly 40 per cent were below age 15', then it would be virtually impossible to avoid encountering annoying teenagers in town.[19] And indeed, we might think of the troublesome tricksters and thieves of *Like Will to Like* as representing this youthful demographic.

Wilson's bringing together of a wide community of alien figures in the context of alien–English tension and intra-English class mistrust puts most pressure on his character Hospitality. If, as Daryl Palmer asserts, 'Hospitality defined life in London', then the murder of Hospitality in *The Three Ladies* is a pivotal moment, for it effectively destroys the idea of London itself, and the later play *The Three Lords* makes it clear that Wilson considers the city of London to be at the core of Englishness.[20] His death is, furthermore, of particular importance for a study of the alien confusion of Englishness because of the stated exclusivity of the character. When Conscience asks Hospitality, 'But I pray you, sir, have you invited to dinner any stranger?' the answer is an emphatic negative: 'No, sure; none but Lady Love, and three or four honest neighbours' (4.65–6). This is an English and an urban answer: it strongly suggests the rejection of any aliens from the table, but it also suggests the rejection of *any* influence that may bring corruption to the hospitable house. Three or four honest neighbours would not include an Englishman like Artifex, for example, once he is corrupted by Fraud. Even a citizen, a freeman, might end up representing anti-citizenship in this alienated city. Felicity Heal notes that civic entertainment and hospitality might invite outsiders, and some small towns made a point of celebrating their achievements of building and incorporation by inviting surrounding country gentry to town feasts; largely, however, hospitable feasts were a centripetal practice for citizens and 'neighbours'.[21] If Hospitality represents the life of the city of London, then his 'protectionism' or exclusivity is not that surprising or unusual. Once Hospitality is killed by his nemesis, Usury, London as a location for locating Englishness is lost, and that process of loss is depicted through the subsequent fall of Conscience.

As the canker of Wilson's commonwealth, 'so well settled in this country', Usury 'will pinch all, rich and poor, that come to me' (2.267–8). Connoting both financial hardship and bodily pain, 'pinching' insists on the inevitable confusion we have seen through the Elizabethan moral plays with their alien-instigated and circulated wealth on the one hand, which works through dissimulation (Illwill, Newfangle, Courage Contrarious, Dissimulation) and deprives or corrupts the native English (Liberty, Tenant, Artifex), and physical or somatic consequences on the other (deformed Christianity, spotted Conscience). Having been evicted from her house by Usury, Conscience complains that 'Both he and Lucre hath so pinched us, we know not what to do. / Were it not for Hospitality, we knew not whither to go' (5.13–14). Hospitality is the direct antidote to poverty and bodily discomfort. Lady Conscience next appears 'running apace' in response to Hospitality's cries for help. With Conscience's post-eviction declaration that Hospitality is her only hope still ringing in our ears, Usury murders Hospitality (Scene 8). Lady Conscience can find no friendly reception wherever she goes, and in her desperation, she succumbs to Lady Lucre's temptation. The play has demonstrated that the practice of usury directly eliminates hospitality, and Conscience confirms the connection: 'if we lend for reward, how can we say we are our neighbour's friend?' (10.28). Covetousness leads to the 'unsatiate' mind (10.31), and with no end to aim at in life and no heaven to believe in, endless desire for increase leaves us with characters like the merchant Greediness or the merchants and usurers of the later comedies.

When Lady Conscience complains, 'But usury is made tolerable amongst Christians as a necessary thing, / So that, going beyond the limits of our law, they extort, and many to misery bring' (10.25–6), we are thrown back to Christianity's complaint that the people claim that he is sound when he is deformed: the mistaken Christians in *The Three Ladies* apparently go '*beyond* the limits' of the 1571 Anti Usury Statute, which permitted usury at 10 per cent, yet they still call themselves Christians. Such mistaken interpretation of the self means that when a few lines later she asks 'Who bargains or chops with Conscience' (10.43), we cannot help but take the multiple connotations of that second verb into account: along with its simple meaning of market dealing, to 'chop' is to change or alter, to veer off to one side, to bandy with or change the logic of something. This question lays out the problem: 'Christianity' and now 'Conscience' are seen as ambiguous terms, interpretable, just as 'the tide tarrieth no man' should be a clear religious call to reformation but is easily 'chopped' into an earthly *carpe diem* trope. Conscience, then, carelessly announcing Lady Lucre's 'free heart and liberality' (10.71) (somewhere between a legitimate Liberty and licentiousness) is corrupted by Lucre until she 'mean[s] henceforth not to be seen' (10.120) – Conscience, neighbourhood, Christianity, Englishness disappearing from the urban landscape. She must deck her own home beautifully and make a little hospitable corner 'where few neighbours dwell, / And they be of the poorest sort' (10.94–5) for Lucre to bring her 'familiar friends, to play and pass the time in sport' (10.78). The irony of the part Conscience is forced to play – that of perverted and depraved hospitality – is palpable.[22] And the corruption of a Christian Conscience, like the deformation of Wapull's character of English Christianity, is a multilayered process that literally *incorporates* – or in Jonathan Gil Harris' study of the spotting of Conscience, overwrites on the palimpsest – the metaphorical/allegorical, the natural historical, and the economic readings of diseased English Conscience.[23] The pinch of finances is felt in physical hunger, and the worm of conscience manifests itself through the destruction of the commonwealth and the individuals in it.

   Hospitality's loss is owing to alien aggression and English ignorance. He is murdered by the Jewish-parented Usury, on the order of the Venetian-grandamed Lucre (I return to these identities below). At Hospitality's funeral we hear: 'There were many of the clergy, and many of the nobility, / And many right worshipful rich citizens, / . . . / But to see how the poor followed him, it was a wonder' (8.86–9). The cries of the poor are ineffective, the influential citizens just mumble into their sleeves, and 'none will hinder the murderer for this cruel act' (8.95). Good English Hospitality is lost because the simpletons of England have become greedy; Wapull insisted on greed as the non-Christian, non-English worm of the Commonwealth, and Wilson has Simplicity misunderstand Hospitality's apparent miserliness:

Now, God's blessing on his heart: why, 'twas time that he was dead.
He was an old churl, with never a good tooth in his head.
And he ne'er kept no good cheer that I could see;
For if one had not come at dinner time, he should have gone away hungry.
I could never get my belly full of meat;
He had nothing but beef, bread, and cheese for me to eat.
Now I would have had some pies, or bag puddings with great lumps of fat,
But, I warrant ye, he did keep my mouth well enough from that. (8.40–7)

Heal notes the modesty of urban hospitable fare, citing William Harrison's observation that country hospitality would provide 'a fat capon or plenty of beef for welcome, while in the town a cup of beer or wine and 'an "You are heartily welcome" is thought to be great entertainment'.[24] All of this, and the play's joke about the non-existent host Sir Nicholas Nemo (Scenes 4 and 8), comment on the state of what

Caleb Dalechamp called *private hospitality* in his 1632 *Christian Hospitality*. This is the type of hospitality on which Heal concentrates, and with which most of the contemporary commentators concern themselves.[25] However, Dalechamp – whose early Caroline text outlines understanding of hospitality in place in late-Elizabethan England – had another category: *public hospitality* demands that a people 'suffer strangers to come into the land ... defend them by good laws from injuries and wrongs ... give them leave to exercise their lawfull calling, [and] ... procure the relief of those that are in want and necessity'.[26] The irony that Wilson's play highlights is that the latter type of hospitality (which benefits aliens) has destroyed the former type of hospitality (which benefits the English).

But accommodation had seemed the right thing to do. Dalechamp's title is telling: hospitality is simply *Christian*, and for the moral plays through the Elizabethan settlement, proper Christianity is Englishness. The contemporary tracts and sermons on hospitality all cite the Old and New Testament stories in which Jews and heathens hosted their neighbours and strangers; how much more necessary, then, (the argument went) for a Christian country to host its needy neighbours. The seventeenth century saw an increasing number of sermons and tracts on public hospitality in response to a general English doubt about its relative benefits. Dalechamp insisted, 'Love and kindnesse we ow to all strangers which are come amongst us ... A Jew, a Turk, a Pagan, or any other infidel, deserves to be respected and relieved in his necessities, though not for his manners, yet for his manhood, for his communion and fellowship in the same nature with us.'[27] Reasons put forward for the general decline in English hospitality ranged from the massive inflation of the sixteenth century, which had increased threefold in a generation,[28] to the diversion of personal funds toward the vanity of excessive apparel and foreign fashion, to the unhealthy over-engagement in such pastimes as the expensive new leisure pursuit of smoking tobacco or even selfishly studying books, which took one's mind away from providing entertainment for others.[29] In theory, of course, to an extent all these causes of hospitality's decline could be blamed on aliens. Hadn't they encouraged the merchants to hoard goods and drive up prices? Hadn't they taught the brokers to pinch every last penny out of the London market? Hadn't they introduced the luxury cloths that made fine apparel and tempted the English beyond measure? And wasn't it an alien habit that merchant adventurers had brought home in smoking (or 'drinking') tobacco? As Jeffrey Knapp points out, tobacco, as one of the imported trifles of the

Elizabethan age, was one that specifically reminded the English of their belatedness in imperial endeavour and of their enemy, Spain, who sold it to them from their New World possessions.[30] The later Elizabethan drama would understand the paradoxical Englishness of all these alien habits, for alien confusion demonstrates that the English do not (to invert Shylock's claim) 'better the instruction' of the aliens whom they blame for bad behaviour; they are rather tutors to themselves who use the aliens as perspective glasses wherein to see their own desires for personal and communal development.

Lady Lucre's residency 'in bliss' and the permanent and successful settlement of aliens in the London of *The Three Ladies* is directly related to what is happening outside the country. Daniel Vitkus has usefully extended the notion of 'turning Turk' to examine how the burgeoning international market inevitably led to perceptions of the corruption of English subjects and the commonwealth.[31] Vitkus also notes the importance of the Italian merchant and Jew as a team involved in opening up English trade in this detrimental way. Indeed, Wilson's surprisingly 'good' Levantine Jew, Gerontus, is still a usurer, and his money is still the life-blood of Mercadorus' abetting the corruption of England. The coincidence of dates of historical events and literary texts is proof of little in singularity, but a cluster, progression, or pattern might support a connection between dramatic production in London and shifts in the wider mercantile world: the founding of the Turkey Company in 1581 coincides with the writing of *The Three Ladies*; the Venice Company is chartered in 1583, *The Three Ladies* is published in 1584; the second edition of *The Three Ladies* comes out in 1592, the year of the combined Levant Company.[32] For English merchants, the 1580s were a decade of rapid grabbing and monopolizing of trade opportunities; for moral and comic playwrights, such a climate invited the staging of both the excitement and the fear of international intercourse.

The Jew–Italian partnership in Wilson's Turkey sets up a rather obvious 'mirror' for England's Usury and Lady Lucre, since Usury received his training in Venice under Lady Lucre's 'Grandmother the old Lady Lucre' (2.216). Thus we are surely supposed to think of his heritage as Jewish. Sure enough, in Wilson's sequel play *The Three Lords*, Simony lists the aliens for Usury's benefit: ' 'Tis not our native countrie, thou knowest, I *Simony* am a Roman, *Dissimulation* a Mongrel, half an Italian, halfe a Dutchman: *Fraud* so too, halfe French, and halfe Scottish: and thy parents were both Jewes, though thou wert borne in *London*' (1439–42; F4).[33] H. S. D. Mithal questions whether Wilson put that last clause in the mouth of Simony precisely because this is slander and not the truth. But these epithets provide at least representations of alien confusion and help make the point that Usury, whatever his parentage, is a second generation English resident whereas the others (*pace* the testimony of Simony) are all new immigrants; he was born in London, served in Venice, and now has returned because 'England was such a place for Lucre to bide, / As was not in Europe and the whole world beside' (2.222–3). Usury as an international money-man, but more usefully as an allegory of human behaviour and the contemporary economic state of the nation, draws the gallimaufry of foreign bodies into circulation in England. These bodies, moreover, are unknowable, mutable identities that inevitably forsake the body within which they are accommodated: 'every man doth sue' for Lady Lucre, says Lady Conscience, 'And comes from countries strange and far of her to have a view' (1.7–8). Lady Love confirms that 'men come from Italy, Barbary, Turkey, / From Jewry: nay, the Pagan himself / Endangers his body to gape for her pelf. / They forsake mother, prince, country, religion, kiff and kin' (1.13–16).

The drawing of this foreignness to England, however, is bound up with an Englishness already tied to the alien economy. When Lucre orders Mercadorus to waste the English economy by exporting 'wheat, peas, barley, oats, and vetches, and all kind of grain, / . . . / leather, tallow, beef, bacon, bell-metal and everything, / And for these good commodities trifles to England thou must bring, / As bugles to make baubles, coloured bones, glass, beads to make bracelets withal', everything 'slight, pretty and pleasant, they care not to have it profitable' (3.40–7), this is a description of the existing state of affairs that has let in the alien rather than a plan of the future. Mercadorus replies that he has been exporting staple goods 'all tis while' and importing 'many baubles dese countrymen to beguile' (3.53–4), and the effectiveness of this anti-English practice is borne out in the decades that follow. William Harrison's *Description of England* (1587) laments the English fashion for foreign products at the expense of home-production; Robert Yarington's *Two Lamentable Tragedies* (1594) says much the same thing; and in his *A Direction for Travailers* (1592) Sir John Stradling tells how the admiration of foreign artisans in England has encouraged apprentices to learn under foreign masters instead of English.[34] Philip Stubbes seconds the fear of 'draining' the country of good product in *The Anatomie of Abuses*, while the greater part of his text suggests an increase in English 'vanity'. '[W]e are so captive in Pride', writes Stubbes, 'that if it come not from beyond the seas, it is not woorth a strawe. And thus we impoverish our selves in buying their trifling

Merchandizes, more pleasant than necessary, and inritch them, who laugh at us in their sleeves, to see our great folly in affecting of trifles, and parting with good wares for them.'[35] Some would say that the English were expending or impoverishing their very identity. John Deacon wrote in 1616 of 'Our carelesse entercourse of trafficking with the contagious corruptions, and customes of forreine nations':

so many of our English-mens minds are thus terribly Turkished with Mahometan trumperies ... thus spitefully Spanished with superfluous pride; thus fearfully Frenchized with filthy prostitutions; thus fantastically Flanderized with flaring net-works to catch English fooles; thus huffingly Hollandized with ruffian-like loome-workes, and other ladified fooleries; thus greedily Germandized with a most gluttonous manner of gormandizing; thus desperately Danished with a swine-like swilling and quaffing; thus skulkingly Scotized with Machiavillan projects; thus inconstantly Englished with every new fantasticall foolerie.[36]

That final phrase has a delightful ring to it that sounds more than one note at once. To be 'inconstantly Englished with every new fantasticall foolerie' is to be shifted around, thrown from identity to identity, ever unsure of the centre of Englishness. But if each new fashion re-Englishes at each turn, however different from the one before, then behind the bare imitation is something native about that very behaviour. This idea echoes my discussion in Chapter 1 of Mary Floyd-Wilson's work on geohumoralism and Sara Warneke's work on the foreign influence on English travellers as ways into understanding the separatist Englishness that is paradoxically built on confusion of international identities.[37] To display Englishness is to incorporate the variety of foreignness that already exists or that comes along.

If hospitality between English citizens is dead, and if Conscience consequently disappears from view in London, the remaining honest Christians like Wilson's craftsman 'Artifex', 'living hitherto with good Conscience' (3.87), can no longer survive untainted by the alien. Artifex is drawn into a scheme in which foreign goods are made poorly but dressed well and sold to the impoverishment of the honest English worker. This might already be a doubtful accusation against the aliens, who were generally known for superior knowledge and workmanship; but a significant number of immigrants were also found to be coming to England out of economic desperation. English reactions to this phenomenon included the production of the Dutch church libel of 1593, which is often discussed for its apparent allusions to Marlowe and his plays of the immediately preceding years – both 'Tamerlaine' and 'paris massacre' appear in the text. This inflammatory document was attached to the wall of London's Dutch church in Broadstreet Ward and threatened the lives of resident aliens. It was one of a number of such texts, and I discuss the climate of fear and control in which they were produced below. A small caveat and a note to keep in mind as I refer to this document: the extant text is not original or entirely contemporary, but a transcript of 1600, the provenance of which is discussed by Arthur Freeman;[38] also, the Privy Council notes in its *Acts* that among a number of libels set about the city of London 'there is some set uppon the wal of the Dutch churchyard', possibly suggesting that this was not the sole example found in that location (although some *one* libel could be implied by the word).[39]

We might now add Wilson to Marlowe and read in the Dutch church libel allusions to Mercadorus and Artifex in *The Three Ladies*, a recently revived and published play of the important Queen's Men's company, and a play more directly concerned with the complaints in the libel than anything Marlowe produced. Despite being over a decade old by the time of the libel, *The Three Ladies* could well have remained a vital touchstone for such a reactionary text. *The Three Ladies'* constant presence in the literary imagination of the rest of the sixteenth century is indicated by several events: very soon after its composition, *The Three Ladies* prompted a response, *London against the Three Ladies*; as late as 1598 Everard Guilpin's *Skialetheia* directly refers to *The Three Ladies*;[40] the play was revived with *The Three Lords* in 1590; and a second quarto was published in 1592. It is easy to see reference to *The Three Ladies* in a text already 'dramatized' by Marlovian allusion; just five lines into the fifty-four-line poem, we read:

> Your Machiavellian Marchant spoyles the state,
> Your usery doth leave us all for deade
> Your Artifex, & craftesman works our fate,
> And like the Jewes, you eate us up as bread. (lines 5–8)[41]

The proximity of these two characters in the poem and the connector of usury and Jewishness strongly suggests that the writer had Wilson's play in mind. The cunning Italian merchant, the facility of usury, and the Jewish source for the ruining of the English provide a nutshell summary of the foreign-situated influence in *The Three Ladies*.[42] 'Artifex' in the libel would seem to be an alien, but his position is closely aligned with Wilson's English Artifex. He begins as the English artificer, complaining:

> But my true working, my early rising, and my late going to bed
> Is scant able to find myself, wife and children dry bread,
> For there be such a sort of strangers in this country,
> That work fine to please the eye, though it be deceitfully,
> And that which is slight, and seems to the eye well,
> Shall sooner than a piece of good work be proffered to sell. (3.88–93)

Fraud manages very quickly to persuade Artifex to play the alien. Artifex is sick of being poor and seeing the foreign artisans succeed, so 'to be a workman to Lady Lucre' (3.101) he will work under the name of Fraud, inhospitable to his foreign neighbours, and a cheat to his English customers. When Fraud asks that 'the next piece of work that thou dost make, / Let me see how deceitful thou wilt do it for my sake' (3.110–11), the corrupted Artifex replies, 'Yes sir, I will, sir, of that be you sure, / I'll honour your name, while life doth endure' (3.112–13). Artifex pledges a life-long commitment to alien behaviour, becoming one of *them* – from the English libel's point of view, '*Your* Artifex'.

The aliens are all confirmed as part of the English establishment by the end of the play. Judge Nemo (whose name suggests impotence and absence) only has the women in his courtroom:

DILIGENCE.   . . . there are but three prisoners, so far as I know, . . .
JUDGE NEMO. No! Where is that wretch Dissimulation?
DILIGENCE.   He hath transformed himself after a strange fashion.
JUDGE NEMO. Fraud: where is he become?
DILIGENCE.   He was seen in the streets, walking in a citizen's gown.
JUDGE NEMO. What is become of Usury?
DILIGENCE.   He was seen at the Exchange very lately.
JUDGE NEMO. Tell me, when have you heard of Simony?
DILIGENCE.   He was seen this day walking in Paul's, having conference and
                 very great familiarity with some of the clergy. (17.3–12)

Dissimulation's 'strange fashion' is at once a marker of the alien (strange), yet also of the 'inconstantly Englished'. Fraud has a citizen's gown, confusing the status of London freeman and deceptive identity, and Usury and Simony are accepted in their respective social spheres with 'very great familiarity'. These 'aliens' are not so much escaping *from* English judgement as they are exposing the mistaken emphasis of a scene of judgement that sets up aliens *against* Englishness at all. Throughout the play, these characters have been acting as part of a politic web of alien presence that always relies on pre-existing English social structure and the 'character' of Englishness. They cannot be extricated from their English contexts and isolated for presentation in the courtroom. Sentencing Lady Lucre, however, has an effect on the characters in the sequel *The Three Lords*. Dissimulation and Simony have had an increasingly hard time getting by in London, although Dissimulation manages to slip back into town during the market-day at Leadenhall and into Westminster to pick up the latest news. Only Usury continues to 'livest but too wel' (613; D) in London, as he is branded with 'A litle x. standing in the midd'st of a great C' (1954; H3) to denote the maximum percentage he is allowed to take on usury by law since the Usury Act of 1571. Of course, this comedy is tempered: just as the Judge's name 'Nemo' might suggest in *The Three Ladies*, as Louis B. Wright noted, that 'the dramatist satirically showed that no judge had yet dared sentence Lucre', so the branding as *punishment* is countered by reading it as a confirmation of the *legitimacy* of Usury in London.[43] This brand declares that London *owns* Usury, or that Usury is London's adopted child. Just as the death of the merchant Greediness could not kill greediness in England at the end of *The Tide Tarrieth No Man*, so Usury, although mutilated and thwarted from his previous free-ranging character, is given a permanence, a safety to settle into London under the law that made usury a safer and therefore established practice in England.

Whether we can read this episode as showing Usury 'no longer pos[ing] a threat within the world of the play' is arguable, but Teresa Nugent seems right to emphasize that a suppression of the danger of usury in *The Three Lords* indicates not a solution to financial 'pinching' and 'biting', but an equivocal shift, whereby the new arch-enemy of a merchandising state is the trade-threatening figure of Fraud.[44] The concept of Fraud arguably almost runs the show in later Elizabethan comedy, and Wilson himself put forward this proposition in the comic episode of *The Three Lords*, where Simplicity is allowed to punish Fraud for deceiving him earlier in the play (when Fraud is playing a Frenchman, incidentally). Lord Pleasure orders that Fraud be bound to a post and Simplicity run at him, blindfolded, with a fire-brand to burn out his tongue 'that it never speake more guile' (2292–3; I3v). Over-excited at the prospect of personal revenge, Simplicity runs at 'the contrarie post' (2300; I3v) (presumably the stage posts of the public theatre) and burns that instead. While everybody watches Simplicity's comic show, Dissimulation rushes over, unbinds Fraud, and the two escape. It seems that no matter how many mistakes these 'alien' vice figures make they remain in the interstices of English behaviour, as 'London and its rulers are blind to the presence of caterpillars of the commonwealth'.[45] In the full context of their history in *The Three Ladies* and *The Three Lords*, this scene confirms the confusion of alien vice and English virtue, of the embeddedness of the alien in London. Lines like 'Dissimulation like a shadow fleetes, / And Simony is out of knowledge growen' (2239–40; I2v) seem to convey celebratory notes about the suppression of vice, meaning that Dissimulation now lives a ghostly, unreal existence, frightened of virtuous authority, and Simony no longer exists in England. But such readings contain an exact and clear counterpart: Dissimulation was *always* a shadow (that is what defines his inscrutability), and Simony is going about his business under the moral radar of the country.

Moreover, Fraud is not 'unfound in London' (2241; I2v) because he does not exist, but because he *is Fraud* and cannot be found. When Simplicity's blindfold is removed, he is convinced by Diligence that the lack of a body next to his burnt post is because he 'hast quite consumed him into nothing' (2309–10; I3v). The irony of Simplicity's naive belief in the death of Fraud – he is of course being defrauded at that moment – is the last important note in the play before the closing prayer to God and queen. It is a note that echoes the insistence of the Elizabethan moral corpus in general that these alien vices are English problems that cannot be eradicated by practical or violent means but are rather issues for the English Christian conscience – something that by now seems hard to locate or believe in. It is a note too that sounds within the public theatre announcing that the new drama of the 1590s – both history and comedy – will entertainingly but frustratingly emphasize the urban, material, physical conflict between alien and English identity. What Simplicity says is, as usual, funny but apt:

wel, al *London*, nay, al *England* is beholding to me, for putting *Fraud* out of this world . . . But let me see, I shal have much anger, for the Tanners wil misse him in their lether, the Tailors in cutting out of garments, the Shoo-maker in closing, the Tapsters in filling pots, and the verie oistermen to mingle their oisters at Billinsgate. (2313–19; I3v–I4)

English Simplicity is convinced that Fraud is dead but this puts him in a quandary. He knows that these settled 'foreign' vices are in fact an ingrained part of the English artisans' and traders' (Artifex-like) habits, and his good deeds will bring little thanks from his fellow workers.

The Three Lords that brought *The Three Ladies* back to life in 1588–90 may well have been revived in turn for a double-bill when the second extant quarto of *The Three Ladies* appeared in 1592, a print-run timed to comment on the building tension in the capital. Such a production would have coincided with the writing of another play with similar concerns that probably never reached the stage because of its scenes of political violence: *Sir Thomas More* by Anthony Munday and others.[46] Simplicity had warned in *The Three Ladies* that the playgoers were 'eating up' (8.180) the play as if it was something to be digested as they go about their business in the city. The fear was that such 'eating' could lead either to digestion and a feeding of illicit energies or to regurgitation in some foul manner. After several years of native–alien unrest in the early and mid 1590s, it was becoming common to hear protests that

Stage Plaies . . . move wholy to imitacion & not to the avoyding of those vyces which they represent, which wee verely think to bee the cheef cause, aswell of many other disorders & lewd demeanors which appeer of late in young people of all degrees . . . who wee doubt not driew their infection from these & like places.[47]

The London authorities were painfully aware of such possibilities, and the inclusion of scenes of civil unrest in the play of *Sir Thomas More* led the Master of the Revels to blue-pencil it back onto the authors' desks.[48] This study is concerned with the first two acts of the play, which outline alleged abuses of Londoners by resident aliens and dramatize the 1517 'evil May-Day' attacks on the strangers. The second act has More (un-historically) quell the unrest with speeches widely attributed to Shakespeare, after which More claims that the balance of 'My country's love, and next the city's care' (2.3.198) lay behind his action. The leaders of the unrest are sentenced to death, and Lincoln suffers execution moments before the king's pardon arrives. In Act 3 More's famous comic sense is portrayed in his meeting with Erasmus and his improvising with a troupe of travelling players. Act 4 introduces the debate over the Oath of Supremacy and Act of Succession and More's family's suffering, with Act 5 containing More's imprisonment and execution.

This play inserted itself into the fray of Elizabethan London's alien–native conflict from the not-too-safe distance of the Ill May-Day anti-alien disturbances of 1517. On 2 June 1592 the Privy Council attempted to calm both alien and native sides in the long-standing war over the London marketplace. Complaints from Dutch candle-makers that they were being threatened by English traders and defences from the English that their livelihood was being threatened by the aliens were investigated secretly, while openly the Council declared a stay of action against the alleged native malefactors.[49] The apprentices were not satisfied and gathered to rise up a week later in Southwark. But Scott McMillin's comment that 'A riot of apprentices actually broke out on 11 June', and Richard Dutton's 'there was . . . rioting led by feltmakers' apprentices', are not proved by the epistolary evidence, which seems to indicate that the 'rude tumult' was an assembly put down before it got out of hand.[50] As Barbara Freedman has reminded us, we should beware the use of words such as 'riot', whose connotations change with time, especially if the words do not appear in the relevant documents.[51] 'Riot' in the period could refer to large-scale gatherings but also to a general tendency toward ruffian-like behaviour (even sometimes mirthful revelry annoying to others) and in the street could involve as little as 'where three (at the least) or more doe some unlawful act: as to beate a man, Entre upon the possession of an other, or such like'.[52] Caused by the wrongful imprisonment of apprentices, the Southwark crowd was calmed by Mayor Webbe who had a suspicion of 'a great disorder and tumult *lyke to grow*' (my emphasis). 'Having made proclamation, & dismissed the multitude', he reports, matter-of-factly, 'I apprehended the chief doers . . . & have committed them to prison'.[53] *Sir Thomas More* repeated this story element with violent rhetoric, and the Master of the Revels' fear of the play was, quite rightly, that by using the Ill May Day riots as analogue to current unrest it sensationalized contemporary events that were not in themselves quite so serious.[54]

Having said as much, this event, with its potential for wide-scale unrest, may have been a potent prompt for beginning to write *Sir Thomas More*. McMillin believes that the play was written 'between the summer of 1592 and the summer of 1593 and that the representation of the Ill May-Day uprising was intended to reflect the crisis over aliens that was troubling the City during those months'.[55] In fact, it is not until the late spring of 1593 that we hear of significant trouble, when a libel (a threatening or illegal placard set up in a public place) seems to have sent the court itself into convulsions, and it issued a carte blanche to the arresting officer to apprehend and torture those who had threatened violence against aliens in the document.[56] On 22 April the Privy Council recorded the queen's demands against the 'disordered and factious persons' responsible, authorizing officers 'to examine by secret meanes who maie be authors of the saide libells'.[57] The letter goes on to suggest the employment in these secret investigations of strangers who might possess some intelligence concerning possible libellers; results of the search were to be reported to the queen personally. It is clear that the authorities were willing to take great risks by employing strangers. Should the native libel supporters discover the cooperation of state and

immigrants, their fears of being betrayed by the noble class could extend
to the feeling of abandonment by their government as a whole, thus
breaking down any faith in the non-alien identity of authority.[58]

The connection of alien fear and national class disunity was made on
5 May 1593 in the Dutch church libel. Its inclusion of the problem of
inter-class tension manifests in the plays either as moral and political
vacancy (the absence of Sir Nicholas in *The Three Ladies*, the corruption
of Scrope and the conspirators in *Henry V*) or as vicious, money-based
conflict (evil landlords, usurers, corrupt officials):

> With Spanish gold, you all are infected
> And with yt gould our Nobles wink at feats
> Nobles said I? nay men to be rejected,
> Upstarts yt enjoy the noblest seat*es*
> That wound their Countries brest, for lucres sake[.] (lines 45–9)

As we move on to discuss Shakespeare's second tetralogy, we will see that
the English–alien disturbances in the years leading up to these history
plays foregrounded and embedded the fusion of class and national
identity. The Dutch church libel notes, 'And our pore soules, are cleane
thrust out of dore' (line 31) by the immigrant population, with the
collusion of the upper classes who do anything 'for lucres sake'. (Incidentally, this latter phrase or its equivalent appears in *The Three Ladies*
at 5.90, 6.25, 14.24, and 14.56.) What seems to have been a stalemate
position between the 'libel' threats without significant action and the
Council's worry provided a hot-bed for any new crisis that should come
along. The potential for unrest put the Privy Councillors on the edge of
their seats, and it warned the Mayor of London that 'oftentymes it doth
fall out of soche lewde beginninges that further mischiefe doth ensue yf
in tyme it be not wyselie prevented'.[59] The authorities certainly did not
want to leave it to chance. The Friday after the appearance of the libel, 11
May 1593, the Privy Council ordered officials to enter into all houses of
suspects, and since 'of late divers lewd and malicious libells set up within
the citie of London [this] doth exceed the rest in lewdnes', the suspected
malefactors were to be put 'to the torture in Bridewel … to th'end
the aucthor of these seditious libells maie be known'.[60] If such a response
is directed against the apprentice class angry with mistreatment, it is a
dangerous move, since it could easily be interpreted as further mistreatment. This could fan the flames of inter-class tension and certainly risked
a repetition of the unrest from the wrongful imprisonment the year
before.

The frank and mimetic thrust of *Sir Thomas More* gives us an immediacy that lies right between the topical but allegorical plays by Wilson on the one hand and the 'real' and potent Shakespeare histories displaced by time and the foregrounding of theatricality on the other. The dramatic study of alien presence, it seems, required some significant 'buffering' from present anxieties if it was to question the English self. *Sir Thomas More*, for all it is nominally set seventy-five years in the past, interferes too much with the stability of the present – in particular, stability associated with a young, theatre- and game-oriented demographic. Ten years earlier the Lord Mayor of London had written to a Justice of Middlesex laying out the concerns of crowd size, place, and symbolic significance in public shows. Referring to an illegal fencing bout planned for playing at the Theatre, the Lord Mayor worried specifically about 'the danger of disorders at such assemblies, the memorie of ill May daie begon vpon a lesse occasion of like sort'.[61] The play of *Sir Thomas More*, had it been allowed, would have provided a far more direct 'occasion of like sort' in the second act: a rumour circulates of a Frenchman beating a carpenter in Cheap, and Lincoln incites a crowd assembled at St Martin's to 'fire the houses of these audacious strangers' (2.1.21–2). Doll predicts 'we'll drag the strangers out into Moorfields, and there bombast them till they stink again' (2.1.42–4), to which George Bettes adds 'Let some of us enter the strangers' houses, / And if we find them there, then bring them forth' (2.1.46–7). In an added hand intended to replace the same scene, a Clown replies to Doll's reservations with the exclamation that he is ripe for going a-raping; moreover, he will do it in the name of the god of war: 'Now Mars for thy honour, / Dutch or French, / So it be a wench, / I'll upon her' (2.1.50–3).[62] Generic and temporal contexts are all-important in these matters. The role of rape in subversive acts by men of the lower order or by powerful men against their vassals and inferiors appears frequently in male-oriented histories of nations and peoples. Jean Howard and Phyllis Rackin cite Jack Cade's warning in *2 Henry VI* that the nobility attack the lower orders with financial and physical pains, including rape of wives and daughters. By *Henry V*, rape is a military tactic of the English against foreigners.[63] Shakespeare's mode of the history genre, however, tends to allow temporal distance to mollify the potentiality of such terror. In *Sir Thomas More*, we have something with more immediacy and political power than *Henry V*. The early sixteenth-century riots were still fresh in the authorities' minds and the Clown's rapacious call is savagely imminent and primitively appropriate as it calls up the power of impregnation by the conqueror. This listing of violent acts to be performed against the aliens is the kind of rhetoric that frightened authority: a call to action in a libel and in the theatre was a call to action in the city, or at least food for poisonous thought.

Dutton has written, 'It is the depiction of the riot, and any talk of rioting, which is uppermost in his [Tilney's] mind, particularly when it is directed at foreigners: "It is hard when Englishmens pacience must be thus jetted on by straungers and they dare not revendge their owne wrongs" [1.1.25–7] is one passage specifically crossed out by him.'[64] In fact, simply gathering with *intent* to act unlawfully was itself an offence; incitement on the stage to act against strangers comes close to this line.[65] Certainly Doll preaches the incorrectness of vigilantism as she stands on the execution scaffold, but her coming to terms with death and its final justice makes her all the more the heroic martyr of the working class. This balance to be struck between the acceptable playing out of opinions against orthodoxies of state and religion on the one hand, and provoking unrest on the other, was largely what permission to stage plays in the 1580s and early 1590s depended on. The manner of depiction more than the content being depicted led Tilney to get out his censor's pen;[66] Robert Wilson's play's incorporation of the city itself, although central, remains part of a conservative socio-religious lesson, a kind of predictable text, glossed revealingly by the characters who move around within London. As Melchiori and Gabrieli have noted, *Sir Thomas More* brings in the city as a character in its own right, and maintains what Tracey Hill terms a 'topographical topicality';[67] the London comedies and the second tetralogy carry out their own versions of this 'mapping' or place-determining strategy, as we shall see in Chapters 4 and 5. Hill points out, moreover, that 'the offences done to the citizens by the strangers' in *Sir Thomas More* 'are regarded as attacks on the City itself'.[68] The English are depicted as protectors of Englishness through a protection of London *as* Englishness. And London, as character and space that needs defending from alien penetration, mingling, and confusion, takes on a somatic and gendered identity. Indeed Doll herself claims that it will fall to women to defend femininity from male alien aggression (1.1.53–74). Hill further emphasizes the determination of the play's Londoners to take the aliens outside the city boundaries, to Moorfields, and indeed the trope of expulsion or asserting native/alien boundaries in and around the city is another one that we shall see again in the London comedies of Chapter 5.

The city is of course the product of its inhabitants and, as Ian Munro has outlined, London in the 1580s and 1590s was continually identified as a centre of excessive population, one that incorporated foreigners, who 'overcharged' the city and threatened its common health. The processes of determining valuable and harmful residents and appropriate responsive actions were ones in which social class played a major role.[69] Revisions in *Sir Thomas More* show a 'dumbing down' of the anti-alien crowd, according to Hill – an apparent attempt to defuse the thoughtful (or at least arguably justifiable) anger of the riotous English. The instigators of the uprising are given crass xenophobic moments, and credibility is withdrawn from them by passages such as the Second Addition, which 'insinuates that Lincoln and his comrades identify with *apprentices* rather than citizens and merchants'.[70] Interestingly, however, as much as these alterations or alternative versions may have been attempts to dilute the controversial edge of the play (and I am not arguing that we *can* say that with any certainty), they in fact bring in further complications of alien confusion. A particularly interesting nexus in *Sir Thomas More* is the trope of food and eating, for it is one that attaches several aspects of English fear and resolution in relation to the alien. It is also a trope we have seen hinted at before in the drama, and one to which the later drama will return. The sermon Lincoln reads out to the disgruntled English worries that 'aliens and strangers eat the bread from the fatherless children' (1.2.111–12) and echoes the Dutch church libel's accusation that 'like the Jewes, you eate us up as bread' (line 8); in both texts this notion is immediately preceded or followed by lines relating the concomitant effect on craftsmen and merchants (*Sir Thomas More* lines 114 and 115; libel lines 5, 7, and 9).

Soon the play takes on the trope of eating with gusto. Early in 2.3 appears the following passage:

LINCOLN.   Our country is a great eating country, argo they eat more in our
               country than they do in their own.
CLOWN.   By a halfpenny loaf a day troy weight.
LINCOLN.   They bring in strange roots, which is merely to the undoing of
               poor prentices, for what's a sorry parsnip to a good heart?
ANOTHER.   Trash, trash! They breed sore eyes, and 'tis enough to infect the
               city with the palsy.
LINCOLN.   Nay, it has infected it with the palsy, for these bastards of dung –
               as you know they grow in dung – have infected us, and it is our
               infection will make the city shake, which partly comes through the
               eating of parsnips. (lines 7–18)

These exchanges begin with the notion that the aliens will 'acclimatize' (in geohumoral terms) and eat more not because they are greedy in themselves but because they are in England, where eating is a healthily pursued pastime. What is difficult to avoid is that these new great eaters bring alien food into the body of London. They bring 'strange roots', glossed in the next line as 'parsnip', but suggesting 'stranger stock', alien genealogy. The conflation of representative foodstuff and national identity takes on comical proportions in the scene in *Henry V* in which Pistol has the 'Welsh correction' of a leek forced down his throat by Fluellen. The trope of eating (and refusing to eat) as a marker of national identity in *Sir Thomas More* is more extensive and has been studied recently by Joan Fitzpatrick, who discusses the need for the Londoners to purge themselves of the alien 'infection' and protect their gendered identities against rape and emasculation.[71]

Most references to eating, to the body, or to the city have their counterpart connotations in each other; thus the question 'what's a sorry parsnip to a good heart?' at once asserts the insufficiency of parsnips to the English 'hearty' constitution, but 'heart' also parallels parsnip as if Lincoln is suggesting an alternative vegetable ('heart' in the period and today could refer to the good, centre section of a food (*OED* 'heart' entry 18)).[72] The good heart in the line's context refers back to the 'poor prentices', and thus suggests the malnutrition of the city, and that in turn adds to the Clown's previous reference to 'troy weight', a standard measure from French fairs, but suggesting a city standard, that of Troy the great city that was a mythical precursor to London. The unnamed 'Another' who speaks next also brings these elements together in just a few words. The word 'trash' can refer derogatively to an object or a person, and when the speaker follows the exclamation with 'They breed sore eyes', the subject of the sentence conflates the aliens with their food – strangers spawn an inferior 'race' and parsnips cause disease in the eater. This conflation of alien and food leads to the confusion of alien with native: the parsnips and the strangers have infected the city of London. The 'bastards of dung' are again primarily the root-plant parsnips but also the aliens. They constitute the illegitimate filth that has already led to the urban disease that the Londoners want to purge out in Moorfields. This contrasts with the play's insistence that Doll represents a 'true breeder' (2.1.6), a phrase Gabrieli and Melchiori gloss nicely as 'a faithful wife, not the mother of bastards'.[73] The medicinal message of 'flaming letters' (2.1.38) that Doll imagines in burning the strangers' houses might compromise the English body of London too by burning down their own houses, thus the determination to take the aliens *out* of town to 'bombast them till they stink again', i.e. to beat the shit out of them. The excremental joke is confirmed by the Clown who remarks that 'they smell for fear already' (line 45), and it echoes the punning scatology of *Wealth and Health*'s Wit, who remarked of Hance the Dutchman's eviction from the country, 'The horson fleming was beshitten for feare / Because he should voyde so soone' (D2v).

Lincoln's last sentence in the quoted passage above insists that 'it is *our* infection will make the city shake'. In other words, the alien alone is not the vital element to native destruction; it is the finding of the alien within that will make the city shake. Now, however, instead of shaking with a disease that allegedly hurts Londoners, the rioters will make the city shake with civil disturbance. This action – as More confirms in his pacifying speech – undermines the realm's health, the 'majesty of England' (2.3.79), and its direction toward visitors perverts English hospitality, which, as we have seen, is a practice that defines Englishness itself. In the end, the rioters' excessive insistence on an external, alien poisoning of London turns out to be their self-scrutiny that reveals the 'shaky' foundation of the concept of an Englishness that is definitively antithetical to, or a clearly contrasted identity to, that of the aliens.

Sir Thomas More is a wide-ranging and evocative generic animal: it moralizes on the role of English hospitality, it revamps history to prompt late-Elizabethan re-evaluation of socio-economic status, and it prompts satirical and harsh urban comedy and anti-alien action that rely on London topography and the meaning of urban space to an understanding of Englishness. The next two chapters deal with two sets of plays being performed in the late 1590s that attempt to locate Englishness in the wake of this English–alien tension. Shakespeare's second tetralogy at once extracts Englishness from ethnic, linguistic, and geopolitical British (i.e. alien) identity, and finds Britishness *within* Englishness (a tricky concept because Britishness would seem to be a larger and external body rather than an internal presence). The late-Elizabethan London comedies, by comparison, extract Englishness from religious, linguistic, and geopolitical European identity, while finding familiarity in all these 'other' elements. In both cases, the movement of bodies is important, as the physical, real presence of alien bodies I have generally insisted on continues to be central, even as the plays highlight the alien *within* Englishness more importantly than the alien as obvious 'other'. Alien–English contact at local, urban, regional, and national boundaries (from front doors of houses, workshops, and London landmarks, to the Anglo-Welsh border and Anglo-Continental divide) forces negotiation, reassessment, and assertion of the English self through continuing development of the second stage of alien confusion.

All the drama under study here is to some extent moulded by and interested in contributing to a critique of the status of London as a place of pre-eminent *Englishness*. That the leader of the crowds in *Sir Thomas More* is called John Lincoln is not an empty coincidence. The name in some way represents an alternative to London, and his speedy execution and intended (but too-late) pardon provide an appropriate equivocality to the man who paradoxically wants to recover London by destroying what London stands for. Wilson's *The Three Lords* foregrounds the battle between the old Roman capital city and the modern metropolis by having the three Lords of Lincoln compete for the London ladies (and lose). London will remain an oddly de-centred centre of power for the northern and British rebels in the *Henry IV* plays. And the tension between London's Mayor Oatley and the senior Earl of Lincoln in Dekker's *The Shoemaker's Holiday* continues to play on this sense of London as a 'character' in need of justifying, defending, and defining in terms of Englishness.

CHAPTER 4

Incorporating the alien in Shakespeare's second tetralogy

This chapter returns to the much-discussed second tetralogy of Shakespeare's history plays to read them in the context of the process of alien confusion that concerns this book. I begin with *Richard II* to show the importance of the notion of an excursion into alien territory, a journey of some sort by characters – in this case Bolingbroke and Mowbray – invested in proving (invariably competitively) their Englishness. The journey entails questioning and crossing specific borders and pulling back identity from across those zones of difference. This trope of the excursion expands on earlier versions of it that we saw in the moralities. I then argue for the importance of Welshness to a study of Englishness before going on in a longer section to examine Welshness as a continually contested presence in the tetralogy. Welshness is a prime example of the alien that is inevitably confused, revealed, and requires excursion, negotiation across borders, and even alteration of the previously conceived self to achieve a conception and display of a powerful concept of 'Englishness'. Welshness cannot be reduced to 'Great' British royal lineage, nor can it be eliminated as provincial or foreign *uncouthness* (in both the early modern and modern senses of the term). It must be represented in all its contiguity and closeness to England and Englishness (thus the importance of geography and topography), while it maintains its alien status as the other that Englishness incorporates, without destroying, to enlarge itself. A 1589 translation of a French tract thinks of 'the ancient Britains ... in the countrie of *Wales*' as people who 'agree in manners, fashions, customes, usages: yet in language they differ from the other inhabitantes of *Englande*'.[1] The second tetralogy very deliberately shows that the hurdle of 'manners, fashions, customs, usages' between Welsh and English looks far higher from the closer perspective of England, and this chapter looks at how Shakespeare's history plays negotiate that apparent obstacle to identity. I end with a brief coda on Henry V as Welshman and archetypal English king, and Shakespeare's return to Wales in *Cymbeline*.

85

All the plays studied in this book have involved journeys taken by protagonists or vices that have proved necessary to the making of the self. Bodily, spiritual, actual, and imaginary, these excursions prepare characters to assert and display the accumulation of identity into new figures of power. The moralities have vices who come to England ready to infect the population after journeys to familiarize themselves with other evildoers (Satan himself in the case of *Like Will to Like*); Lady Lucre's men in *The Three Ladies of London* have travelled to England with garnered knowledge, and Mercadorus is required to trade abroad to bring in the alien trifles that will corrupt English women; the city comedies discussed in Chapter 5 use urban and international journeys to illustrate change and English fortitude; and the histories perhaps do this work of self-discovery through an alien excursion most forthrightly. That the journey to find the *English* self is fraught with the accumulation of *alien* identity is demonstrated in Sir Thomas More's speeches to the crowd in *Sir Thomas More*, the play with which I ended the previous chapter:

> Imagine that you see the wretched strangers,
> Their babies at their backs, with their poor luggage,
> Plodding to th' ports and coasts for transportation,
> And that you sit as kings in your desires,
> Authority quite silenced by your brawl,
> And you in ruff of your opinions clothed. (2.3.80–5)

Now put yourself in the alien position, says More, and he goes on to tell the 'rioters' that if the king proves so lenient as simply to banish them for their capital crime, they would wander in Europe where 'you must needs be strangers' (line 141). Jane Kingsley-Smith reads in More's lines a kind of geographical-ideological alien confusion, the 'mingling of nationalist sentiment, expressed through the chauvinism it encourages about being anywhere other than England, with a kind of cultural empathy which works to dissolve those distinctions'.[2] More asks the English to find their own humanity by seeing the 'mountainish' (or 'momtanish') 'inhumanity' (line 151) in equivalent behaviour *by aliens*.

Of additional interest here is More's call for the English to 'imagine' themselves alien, which makes the later assertion that they 'must *needs be* strangers' a description of their state as well as a call to understand the alien. History plays emphasize the empathetic journey, one that moves beyond touching up against and thereby contrasting the self with the alien and instead has the English subject put himself or herself *in the place of* the alien to assess similarity and difference. To *be* the alien through a projection of the mind or exertion of the body is, for the characters in history plays, to comprehend being English – not simply by contrast, but by confusion and incorporation. As we revisit the plays of the second tetralogy, I want to keep in mind the fact that such an emphasis on imagination and invention demonstrates the history genre's self-awareness. Adam Hansen points out that *2 Henry IV* uses the word 'history' as a verb, suggesting its understanding of the manipulable narrative that recovers the past, and Rumour has already told us as much at the beginning of the play, giving out a 'false history' of the rebels' victory. Thus the need, argues Hansen, to move beyond the sometimes inflexible political readings of the new historicism that must read characters as either authoritative or subversive and permit the 'disguised and confused' identities and relationships within the 'Atlantic archipelago' as presented in the plays to show themselves in their multiplicity.[3] The present study is concerned to show that multiplicity itself is part of the ideology of singular Englishness in the early modern period; these *English* plays take Anglo-centric medieval history and use boundary-crossing (whether geographical, 'racial', religious, or conceptual) to incorporate, or confuse, otherness into the characters who must promote a British Englishness – an 'imperial' Englishness that claims specificity and purity by accumulating British identity and recasting it as 'English'.

   Part of the penchant for producing history plays in the 1580s and 1590s may have been the need for writing a kind of settlement of Englishness that the English could never quite believe in reality. The Queen's Men, as a prime example, set about establishing ways of seeing history as solidi-fying present problems and glories of England; and they did so touring the provinces, where the 'broken English' of domestic 'foreigners' indi-cated their separateness and the need for unification.[4] If, as John Morrill argues, the Scottish and the Welsh have to accept that in the early modern period they were always 'Scots *and* Britons or Welsh *and* Britons', then the English conception of a totalizing English state expanding over a new 'Britain' must itself come with a severe anxiety.[5] This Britishness is itself so caught up in alien territories of the north and west that it must be complicated and perhaps deliberately obfuscated (confused) as it is re-incorporated (con-fused) into a singular idea of south-eastern English-ness. This chapter moves slightly away from the others in this book in so far as it discusses the English moving outward. Such expansion into British territory and the London–provincial conflict, however, is – like the outgoing provincial and international excursions of vices, merchants, soldiers, artisans, nobility, and monarchs in all the plays – a continuing response to foreigners and aliens coming into London and the southern towns of England.

Beginning with *Richard II*, the second tetralogy examines the excursion as an essential process for 'Englishing' the self. Bolingbroke will gather his strength to claim titles both due him and above his rightful station via the enforced Continental sojourn, and Mowbray, banished from his position next to the king – a position by which he seems to know himself and be known, and without which he *seems* nothing – will find a new life (and everlasting life) in exactly the journey of Anglo-Christian crusading that his wily adversary will never achieve. Bolingbroke misrepresents his own foreign excursion as extensive and useless labour:

> Must I not serve a long apprenticehood
> To foreign passages, and in the end,
> Having my freedom, boast of nothing else
> But that I was a journeyman to grief? (1.3.256.4–7)

And this is how David Read, for example, takes it, noting that Bolingbroke's 'use of metaphor here is telling: exile is a form of servitude which does not culminate in a firmer sense of identity or purpose';[6] Aaron Landau has recently emphasized the disdain with which Bolingbroke represents his exile as a loss of social status, from potential prince to the pauperdom of apprenticeship.[7] But neither of these views is entirely accurate. Apprenticeship with the premier companies could be a route of achievement for sons of the gentle class, and if Bolingbroke is playing the class card, it is a hand he lays down knowingly. This is the man who will stoop low to the commoners (1.4.30), and this is the man whose educative journey through the margins of his personal world not only culminates in a firmer identity or purpose (since he returns a journeyman to greatness), but also paves a proleptic pathway for his errant son, Hal. Moreover, it is a trade apparently fraudulently practised, as we find out later when Hotspur complains that his father supported Bolingbroke because he promised that his return from banishment was only for the title of Lancaster and not for the crown (*1 HIV* 4.3.62–7).

The cunning Englishman understands that he must withdraw from his native or proper circle to gather a reflective sense of the self, and to gain a knowledge of home from peripheral perspectives. The personal wealth gained from the alien experience fuses with common wealth won by a redefinition of Englishness. The process of alien confusion can remain close to home but requires some real foreign presence, in the shapes of geographical, human, magical, or imaginatively formed bodies. It is remarkable, then, that Bolingbroke as Henry IV, having taken his own journey of alien confusion and amelioration, does not himself comprehend the comparable activity in his son's excursion out of courtly life and language, for it is a process that seems inevitable – if variously approached and represented – on the road to stable Englishness. Lisa Hopkins is right to say that Henry's angry tirade against his son's crown-taking in 4.3 is 'a final ironic testimony to Henry IV's failure ever to understand his son . . . for it is what Hal has been doing all along'. But she sees what Hal has been doing as 'veering . . . erratically', whereas I argue that his incorporating of the various figures and experiences through his princely and into his kingly life draws a map of alien confusion, coherent if complicated identity-making on its way toward a profession of Englishness.[8] My own use of metaphors of mapping is not accidental, for we shall continue to see the importance of local chorography and larger mappings to the definition, creation, and imposition of identity throughout this chapter. Moreover, as Bernhard Klein's analysis has it, there are three 'conceptual stages' of mapping: measuring, visualization, and narration.[9] Shakespeare's histories play out this tripartite scheme of empirical observation and delineation, imagination and comprehension, and finally explication and (always biased) history-telling.

While it is true, as I have outlined above and other commentators note, that 'Bolingbroke cleverly makes his very exile an opportunity to proclaim his Englishness' and that 'Bolingbroke's usurpation is *facilitated* by banishment',[10] Bolingbroke's conceit of himself as the icon of Englishness and ruler over Englishness does not *begin* with the fact of exile. In these plays of alien incorporation imposed or voluntary excursions come into (the) play as inevitable consequences of the desire to determine one's own identity and the identity of a community over which one rules. Whether forced or voluntary exile, educational travel, merchandising journey, or ambassadorial trip, the alien excursion *supports* and *confirms* rather than instigates self-scrutiny, self-discovery, and the subsequent assertion of Englishness. However, this doesn't preclude the possibility of finding alien elements behind or prior to the Englishness the characters assume they are investigating. Moreover, even the 'involuntary' journeys of exile are given volition by the representations of the characters, who imagine them as life-altering or realm-changing experiences. 'Throughout this scene', observes Jane Kingsley-Smith, 'Bolingbroke has denied the efficacy of imagination' to temper physical suffering.[11] But if this is what Bolingbroke says, he is mistaken. Projections of imagined locations and lives quintessentially comprise historical drama and understandings of Englishness. We have just seen that More's insistence on the English imagining the self as alien alleviates the suffering of the immigrants and of the city of London itself; very similar are the calls to imagination by *Henry V*'s Chorus.

The experience of theatre is in many ways one of non-experience, of being presented with what is not there, what is lost and can only be retold in metaphor, with figures out of their time, and in language that is often insufficient. As a multimedia experience, however, the dramatic production goes some way toward *being* what it represents – a stage space for a location, a few armed men for an army. But *Henry V*'s Chorus still feels the need to draw us into this realm of the 'not-there' with his consistent calls for 'imagination'. In the Chorus' five speeches, he uses 'imagine', 'imagined', or 'imaginary' four times, and he calls for the playgoers to 'see' things in their 'minds' and 'thoughts' an additional eleven times.[12] He makes further requests for imagination using different terms. The words 'imagin/e/ed/ary/ation' appear nowhere else in the whole of the play, indicating the determination of the main text to deny its own falsity. The play proper insists on remaining within the 'wooden O', while the Chorus raises the very problem of containment to tell us that we can only '[s]uppose' (1 Pro. 19) such parameters, and that the theatre *requires* its audience to imagine and invent the play outside of the theatre walls.[13] To emphasize this imagination is far from rehearsing a Romantic desire for a 'pure' Shakespeare that avoids the material contingency of the stage – the opposite in fact.[14] It is to instate the very *presence* of the stage as a place of wood and plaster, within the theatre, within London. But such *English* embeddedness makes the call to imagination and the alien excursion all the more *alien* and profound. Part of the dramatic weight of Bolingbroke and Mowbray's professions of losing status, language, and life lies in the strikingly modern absurdist fact of them being banished from the stage-as-life; they are in danger of entering the impossible 'alternative world' of Tom Stoppard's Rosencrantz and Guildenstern, and therefore of being 'dead'.

The Chorus' request a few lines later to 'Into a thousand parts divide one man' (1 Pro. 24) asks the audience to imagine an army when they see one soldier, and in doing so it calls for imagining *another* representation, one that cannot be portrayed within the history or play currently being presented. This kaleidoscopic division of 'one thing entire to many objects' (*RII* 2.2.17) recalls the debate surrounding Queen Isabel's disturbed 'soul' and the insistence that true visions of alien presence come from looking 'awry' and effectively writing another imagined plot outside of the present story. King Henry V does similar rewriting by imagining the Act 2 conspiracy metatheatrically, so that he can dismiss its problems from the story of *Henry V*. Because the conspirators Scrope, Cambridge, and Grey cannot be incorporated into *Henry V*'s present notion of honest, noble Englishness, Henry reimagines the situation as a morality play in which 'Treason and murder ever kept together, / As two yoke-devils sworn to either's purpose, / . . . / But thou, 'gainst all proportion, didst bring in / Wonder to wait on treason and murder' (2.2.102–3, 106–7). The lords are already corrupted in the manner of the earlier drama's unreformable characters. They are 'English monsters' fed with foreign money, corrupted by the devilish and unknown, uncouth congruence of Wonder with Treason and Murder. This imagined scene recasts the deformity of Scrope and his accomplices in the mode of corrupted English vices such as Nichol Newfangle in *Like Will to Like* and Courage in *The Tide Tarrieth No Man*. It dismisses them to an earlier time, to another genre, and finally through execution to another world. But that very process of *rejecting* the alien-corrupted individual characters is done to *incorporate* their story of rejection – and thus confuse their alien excursion – into *Henry V*'s central story of the making of the English King.

My brief 'excursion' here through *Henry V* has been simply to demonstrate the inevitability of the power of the imagination in drama to work in two conflicting ways. On the one hand the character who imagines or re-tells a narrative displaces essentialist notions of characters as existing in a 'real', immanent world; on the other hand the same process of imaginative *invention*, of believing in the self and in the existence of a storyline into the future, aligns characters' activity with that of the audience members. Thus 'in the end', Bolingbroke's 'freedom' does not at all deal with ten, or even six, years of physical exile. The journey is real, but offstage, and his imagined return from imagined exile shortens his banishment and brings him back to power to consolidate and confirm an Englishness he has been accumulating all along. This accumulation is all the more bound for success since it is aimed against a king who is already failing: as Kingsley-Smith points out, banishment should be a tool with which the monarch keeps the commonwealth healthy and 'common', but in the case of Richard 'banishment becomes an expression of ruthless solipsism', making him 'a kind of anathema to Englishness'.[15]

On the other side of the tilt stands Mowbray, and in direct contrast to Bolingbroke, he has no labour to perform – or at least it seems so. But his present situation (the duel) has arrived at the point of silence when no more can be uttered. When the language of argument or negotiation reaches stalemate, action (usually military) begins. Hence the duel and hence Mowbray's end. If Mowbray's tongue is unstrung, then he must continue as a man of arms, silently cutting down the heathen, unheard of at home until his own breath really does leave him. The Bishop of Carlisle finally speaks for him:

> Many a time hath banished Norfolk fought
> For Jesu Christ in glorious Christian field,
> Streaming the ensign of the Christian cross
> Against black pagans, Turks, and Saracens;
> And, toiled with the works of war, retired himself
> To Italy, and there at Venice gave
> His body to that pleasant country's earth,
> And his pure soul unto his captain, Christ,
> Under whose colours he had fought so long. (4.1.83–91)

By this point in the play, the mislabelled 'isle' of England is God's equivocally generous and fickle gift, in danger of mistaking its king and favouring rebellion. Banished Mowbray has enacted Bolingbroke's politic and calculated ideological desire of conflating Englishness and godliness in a version of an anachronistic desire to make exile 'an abandoning of worldly pleasure for the sake of eternal life'.[16] If banishment from the presence of the monarch is effectively banishment from the world,[17] then Mowbray shifts into spirituality with abandon; he has, after all, been rejected by the god-instituted power for whom he has sinned, and he seems to have no option but to fight for the eventual saving of his own soul. The new Henry IV's gestures toward spirituality and pilgrimage will appropriately evade him. His determination (imagination) that 'Forthwith a power of English we shall levy, / Whose arms were moulded in their mothers' womb / To chase these pagans in those holy fields' (1.1.22–4), never happens, but Mowbray (whom the Bishop still refers to by his title of Norfolk) ex-patriotically fights just like 'a power of English' with mother-moulded arms would be expected to.

'GOD FOR HARRY! ENGLAND AND SAINT DAVID!': ESSENTIAL WELSHNESS

Having set up the trope of the alien excursion and the related role of imagination as representative of present and possible 'reality' in historical drama, this chapter moves on to discuss the place of Wales and Welshness in the 'making' of Englishness; in doing so, I am concerned to emphasize that this road into Wales is not simply the one to Ireland half-travelled. Christopher Highley's important and rewarding 1997 book, *Shakespeare, Spenser, and the Crisis in Ireland*, contains seminal readings of Ireland through Wales (and France), against which I want to set up the place of Wales in the current study. His argument is compelling in so far as the alleged blood connection between Welsh Glyndwr and Irish Tyrone and the presence of Welsh soldiers in reports of Tyrone's armies set up a chain reaction for recognizing the latter in the former's behaviour.[18] Indeed, *The Calendar of State Papers, Ireland* reveals a belief in the Earl of Tyrone's descendancy from Owen Glyndwr, which, in addition to similarities between the rebellions of Glyndwr and Tyrone, argues Highley, 'prompts an interpretation of Glendower and his part in the Percy rebellion as a displaced representation of Tyrone's contemporaneous rebellion in Ireland'.[19] This, coupled with the rebellion's organization and ideology, he continues, 'must have appeared uncannily similar to those of his precursor Glendower some two centuries earlier'. Mortimer's 'going native' is also an echo of the same fear for Irish settlers.[20] But for all its historical pertinence, Highley's methodology obliterates Wales, which ends up merely as 'a screen for obliquely registering and imaginatively negotiating the current crisis in Ireland'; Wales provides a 'veiled dispute about Ireland', because Shakespeare's texts 'invariably point through Wales to Ireland', thus Wales 'offer[ed] writers an expedient means of obliquely engaging the subject of Ireland'. Moreover, Shakespeare and Peele 'both use past Anglo-Welsh conflict as a screen onto which misgivings, anxieties, and fantasies about the English presence in Ireland are projected and interrogated', thus the Welsh conflict is a 'displaced representation' of contemporary events in Ireland.[21]

While the connection by supposed descent between Glyndwr in fourteenth-century Wales and Tyrone in sixteenth-century Ireland is one example of reading Ireland in Wales that seems essential and useful both for a reading of Ireland and for a reading of Wales, Highley reads all elements – historical and dramatic – of the character of Glyndwr as not *really* about the Welshman, but about Tyrone. Thus the ambivalent introductions to him before we see him are like the competing reports of Tyrone (but it is also, of course, just good dramatic suspense for the Welsh warrior-magician figure); Glyndwr's English court training means that an audience '*could have* recalled' the contemporary (and arguable) belief that Tyrone spent time cultivating himself in England (but it is also, as we shall see below, an essential part of Glyndwr's verbal battle – *as Welshman* – with Hotspur). Highley's sequence of positive comparisons is then complemented by *contrasts* between Glyndwr and Tyrone that are there 'to disarm the threat of the rebellious Celtic chieftain and of the Earl of Tyrone in particular'; for example, the representation of effeminacy in Glyndwr 'helps to manage the pervasive English recognition of Tyrone's enviable toughness and virility'. Thus in Highley's analysis, similarities and differences both point through to Tyrone in equal measure. And in a third relational position between Glyndwr and Tyrone, the former does not simply remind the audience of the latter, but *creates* a future for him, thus Glyndwr's absence from the battle at Shrewsbury as a result of his prophecies 'predict[s] the failure' of the cause of the allegedly equally superstitious Irish.[22] In such a critical environment, Wales *as Wales* is lost.

Philip Jenkins similarly positions Wales not as the closest British neighbour to England in its own right, but as a half-way region between the catastrophe that was the Irish colonization and the success of limited independence and identity that was the Scottish experience.[23] It does not seem politically appropriate, and it does not seem from a literary-historical standpoint fully possible, to recover Ireland at the expense of Wales, or to use Wales as the palimpsest upon which a new understanding of Ireland gets written. To do so further entails the danger of concretizing the 1536 Act of 'Anglicization' of Wales. While it might be difficult or impossible to recover an authentic and wholly unironic Welsh voice through the play of an early modern English writer, the history of Welsh national pride (to which I will return in a moment) suggests that we can read Welsh resistances in English texts. Sensitivity to this possibility will at least make sure that we do not read Wales practically and politically as solely a region of England without independent character (and independent characters).

The second tetralogy's texts talk more about English working-out and manipulation of their own identity through Wales and the north than they do about Ireland, especially after *Richard II*. Ireland is a powerful buzz-word that hints at the play's future, and of course that future is the resonant present for late-Elizabethan playgoers. However, the plays themselves work at the level of a combined British fusion with Englishness, which insists that we balance the prioritization of the Irish experience in the drama with the fact that 'Welshness and its concerns throb with no less powerful, if occluded pulse in the vasty deep of these plays'.[24]

We might pause to compare this powerful presence of Wales as the important alien with what we saw working in the morality plays: that the obvious aliens marked as either dangerous or uncivilized 'others' were touchstones for understanding the confused, embodied alien 'closer to home'. Closer in geographical and ethno-cultural terms, the alienated 'English' characters of the moralities parallel the Welsh (and idea of Welshness) in the histories. To illustrate the tetralogy's determination to have Wales itself influence and even *enact* the creation and loss of *English* identity, we need to read closely in these plays, and in the process redress the critical balance in favour of a Welshness that the plays foreground. All the readings that 'use' Wales to read Ireland are useful to an examination of the British question, but they are seeing some corrective measures in the recent work of Lisa Hopkins, Terence Hawkes, Philip Schwyzer, and others; these latter scholars are shifting the focus back to Wales as a place for consideration in more depth and on its own terms.

None of this is to deny the appropriate primacy of Ireland as the prevailing 'British' and 'colonial' touchstone, especially in the 1590s and early Jacobean period, and especially with re-readings of Spenser and the casting of Ireland as itself a staging ground and dramatic perspective glass for visions of New World expansion. Bringing Scotland and Wales back into the mix, however, is useful to a study of the overarching manner of colonial geographical incorporation, as England attempts to woo the lowland Scots and makes 'internal colonies' out of the western reaches of Britain. The 'Welsh problem' within the 'British question' necessarily involves Mark Netzloff's concerns in discussing 'internal colonialism', the deliberate separation and oppression of a segment of the domestic population for the purpose of perpetuating a hegemony. The official status of Wales as part of England 'undermines the typical association of colonialism with geographic and cultural distance' and 'blurs the boundaries imposed between seemingly domestic interests and foreign relations'.[25] Thus Glyndwr is introduced 'as an external menace to the nation . . . But when he appears in person, it is as a kind of troublesome insider'.[26] Similarly, 'justification of the conquest [of Ireland] meant that Ireland had also to be redefined as a recalcitrant part of the nation, an errant province to be "subdued" rather than a foreign land to be sub-jugated', and to that end, Michael Neill reminds us, 33 Henry VIII nominated Henry 'King' of Ireland, instead of 'Lord'.[27] This is a necessary process for the confusion of the racially different British aliens into the ruling identity of a supposedly singular Englishness. We can see how this process works as a kind of (semi-understood) training ground for later global imperialism and, even at this stage in English history, it is hard to dismiss the idea of empire. As Willy Maley puts it:

The subordination of the non-English nations of the emerging British state is posited as an essential prerequisite of Empire rather than an act of Empire in itself. The British Empire is first and foremost the British state ... England is substituted for the British state, and the Empire is exoticised, oriented elsewhere, made foreign, represented as being otherwise occupied than with, say, Ireland, or Scotland, or Wales. The use of 'Empire' to mean extra-British activity overlooks the imperialism implicit in Britishness itself.[28]

The reason for the success of this process of the English cooption of Britishness without giving it its name lies in the convenience of being unable to locate originary Englishness. Philip Schwyzer reminds us that 'Of the three virtues which Tudor writers cherished most highly in their nation – insularity, antiquity, imperiality – not one was properly English. For the sense of national belonging that found expression in Tudor England, there is no term readily available but *Britishness*' (original italics).[29]

WELSHNESS IN *RICHARD II*: ENGLISH AND/OR ALIEN

From the start of 2.4, *Richard II*'s first scene in Wales, communal identity – and in particular the understanding of the relation of English and Welsh identity – is made equivocal by the language of self-representation. The Welsh Captain uses the first-person plural pronoun three times and the first-person plural possessive once in the scene's opening four lines:

> My lord of Salisbury, *we* have stayed ten days,
> And hardly kept *our* countrymen together,
> And yet *we* hear no tidings from the King.
> Therefore *we* will disperse ourselves. Farewell. (2.4.1–4, my emphasis)

Perhaps because we as readers imagine a 'coalition force' of two armies fighting side-by-side rather than integrated (a notion that has altered by *Henry V*), our immediate reading of the first two lines' 'we' and 'our' is probably limited to the Welshmen (the 'our' referring to several Welsh officers). But this perception is instantly overwritten by the simple fact that the Welshman is addressing an Englishman, using the first-person plural *to* him, and describing their *mutual* experience: they have both waited ten days and they have had trouble keeping the *English* and the Welsh together – 'our [respective] countrymen'. By the third line, 'we' hear no tidings seems to refer to the Welsh, as the line is setting up their reasons for withdrawal, but once again it must include Salisbury, who has not heard anything either. Only by the fourth line is there a definitive split as the Welsh Captain follows the determination to disperse with 'Farewell'. But this is not the end of the confusion of national identity or numbers of soldiers present and absent. 'We will not stay', says the Welsh Captain at line 7, and, after listing the evil omens in 'our country', confirms that 'Our countrymen are gone and fled, / As well assured Richard their king is dead' (16–17). If the Welsh Captain is not talking to Salisbury about a joint Welsh–English force of 'our countrymen', then he must be referring to the Welsh leaders when he says 'We will not stay', for the rank and file soldiers have apparently *already* deserted. How we read the appeal from Salisbury, then, 'Stay yet another day, thou trusty Welshman' (line 5), depends on whether he knows that the larger part of the Welsh army have already left; if so, he is asking for the Welsh leaders to show solidarity even without a significant Welsh force; either way, the Welsh Captain's speech is not a negotiation or reasoning for his own order to withdraw but rather a bush-beating approach to telling Salisbury what has already happened. Welshness is draining out of the 'British' vessel that Richard thinks he holds, but it is impossible to comprehend this Welsh diminution without the concomitant English reduction. The story of the retreating Welsh troops confirms the dependence of Englishness upon Welshness *within* its identity of power.

This fusion, confusion, and breaching of Welsh and English identity dwells on the frustration of an idea of Englishness that is still trying to incorporate a British whole on the mainland, one that wants to explain (away) Gaunt's claim that *England* is an island, but one that constantly finds itself up against the 'walls' of the marches (as Canterbury calls them in *Henry V*), the barriers of belief, language, historical loyalty, power, and 'race'. The historical drama is working through residual resistance to alien incorporation into English identity by emphasizing the effects of border definition and transgression. From the defensive English point of view, the marches should provide a safety buffer between England and its restless neighbours, but such 'walls' also raise an obstacle to effective incorporation. Indeed, these 'walls' are everywhere, which stand between imagined national incorporation or painless comprehension of identity and the achievement of those mythical histories and difficult or impossible prophecies. We perhaps should not make too much of the fact that 'Wales' was frequently spelt 'Wallia' or 'Walles' in early modern texts (and probably pronounced as a soft two-syllable word), but we might just use it as a step to recall the fact that walls were commonly imagined in Shakespeare and elsewhere as physical, psychological, and magical markers, enclosures, and protectors of personal, racial, and national identity as much as they were constructions of mud, brick, or stone. For Gaunt, 'the silver sea, / . . . serves ['England'] in the office of a wall' (2.1.46–7) before he corrects himself, 'Or as a moat defensive' (48); for Richard, in 3.2, flesh 'walls about our life' (163) and unlike 'brass impregnable' (166), the necromantic fantasy of Robert Greene's Friar Bacon (and Dr Faustus in Germany), it cannot withstand the 'little pin' that 'Bores through his castle wall' (165–6); and Canterbury's assurance is that 'They of the marches, gracious sovereign, / Shall be a wall sufficient to defend / Our inland from the pilfering borderers' (*HV* 1.2.140–2). This latter notion of a human wall against attack is reprised in the one instance we have in the second tetralogy of the word 'wall' actually used to mean a literal wall (*HV* 3.1.2), but even here Henry imagines the wall of the castle of Harfleur as a gap plugged with corpses, and, as Andrew Gurr points out, the 'Once more' tells us that previous attacks have failed, and the breach is presumably already at least partially filled with the English dead.[30] Walls in the second tetralogy do not just enclose local spaces; they delimit lived experience, hold one in servitude to one's own subject identity and the fate that follows from that social positioning; they highlight the inside from the outside, the blessed from the cursed, the 'here' from the 'there', the cultured from the barbarian. And they do so by the insistence that 'walls' to Wales, to France, and to any enlargement of English 'imperial' identity must be looked *at*, encountered, crossed over, and even *embodied* like the wall at Harfleur, like the Anglo-Welsh fusion of Mortimer and Glyndwr's daughter, like the fraught negotiations over the rebels' map in *1 Henry IV*, or like the union of Henry V and Katherine. Such breaching of boundaries does not necessarily take us toward Ireland or expansion into newer worlds, for the plays insist on the notion of *returning* to England time and again. Characters in *Richard II*, *Henry IV*, and *Henry V* stretch or cross the boundaries of their country to enable a physical, psychological, and political re-placement in England as a process to locate a foundational *meaning* for Britain-based Englishness.

When Richard lands on the coast of Wales in 3.2, he enforces its difference from 'antipode[an]' Ireland, the distant place of potential death, by calling it home. This may be his wishful thinking – as Maley argues all claims of unified Britishness are in this period[31] – but it is designed to emphasize the fantasy of a peculiarly Welsh-based Britishness, one that the English would like to assume is somehow obvious, unstated, at least since Henry VIII's annexation of Wales and English law extension Acts of 1536 and 1543. Richard's sense of alienation by asking for confirmation that he is at Harlech Castle is balanced by his insistence that this odd place is 'my kingdom' (3.2.5), and he lays claim to a pathetic recognition by, and reciprocal relationship with, this land upon which he kneels:

> Mock not my senseless conjuration, lords.
> This earth shall have a feeling, and these stones
> Prove armed soldiers, ere her native king
> Shall falter under foul rebellion's arms. (3.2.23–6)

Titus' comparable intercourse with the stones of Rome (*Tit* 3.1) has him unequivocally within the walls of his native city, but things are not so clear for Richard, in spite of his claim to be the Welsh/British earth's 'native king'. In order for the land he is touching to be 'mother' earth with a 'feeling' for Richard, he must have come *from* that land in the first place.[32] But birthright is a sticky point in each Henry play of the second tetralogy, and it is exactly the question raised by Gaunt about Richard in the play *Thomas of Woodstock*:

> His native country, why that is France my lords;
> At Bordeaux was he born, which place allures
> And ties his deep affections still to France.
> Richard is English blood, not English born.[33]

Whether Richard is native English or not, his language is still at odds with Welsh. The text's pun on 'senselessness' (the nonsensical appeal and the inanimate ground) is enriched, therefore, by the suggestion that he cannot be heard in the west of Wales. Richard's scrambling for authority is undermined by the connections between the rule of language, the rule of law, and the matter of 'race' that Paula Blank articulates in her study, *Broken English*;[34] his statements should be unequivocal, performative, and universally 'felt', but as a man doubly alienated (by birth and language) from the land he is currently standing or kneeling on, he wields very little *English* state power.

Moreover, if Richard at this moment is kneeling to his kingdom, such a gesture enacts Jacqueline Vanhoutte's note that Gaunt's 'sceptered isle' speech 'imparts sovereignty to the land' rather than the king himself.[35] The lands of Britain have a power to rule over and determine those who are trying to contain them. From Richard's claim of nativity to the *1 Henry IV* rebels' battle over river borders, knowledgeable mapping and coverage of the land are essential elements for successful advancement. So Wales is an unfamiliar, adopted place for Richard, whether we consider him a Frenchman or an Englishman. In spite of the strangeness of this land, the king persists with Welsh–English conflation, for he laments that 'rebels wound thee with their horses' hoofs' when the rebels have not yet entered Wales. In one sense, however, Richard is unwittingly close to the truth in his unionizing of a British England, for if the Welsh have evacuated Wales and gone to the rebels, then what is Wales but his own empty, surrounded retreat? A confused alien–English balance is struck again, for what is the difference between the state of 'Britishness' of a group of monarchists (with a French-born king) in Wales and a group of Welshmen and provincial rebels in England?

The confusion of Welsh and English, Wales and England, king and rebels continues with a paradoxical representation here of the rebellion not as fracturing, but as a uniting force. When Richard complains later in the scene that the rebels are 'measur[ing] our confines with such peaceful steps' (3.2.121), we are faced with an utterance that has multiple meanings bearing upon a consideration of identity and place. The enemy's measurement is chorographic work, mapping in particular the borderlands, their distances and topographical nature; to measure is to moderate, regulate, limit, restrict, assess, and weigh – all tasks of the crown's administration, and parts of a royal progress' work of national security. To measure the confines, then – confines meaning not just 'Boundaries . . . frontiers, [and] borders' but also 'the inhabitants of adjacent regions, neighbours', be they friends or 'Walha' (strangers, foreigners – the source word for 'Wales') – is already in some way to usurp the authority and the privileged knowledge of the king, to beat the bounds and claim precedence over the area covered.

The rebels' geographical usurpation or 'ur-offensive' (a real threat empowered even more by Richard's rhetorical exposition and legitimation of its danger) is highlighted, moreover, by Richard's sense that they are measuring 'our' confines, at once the confines of the realm of 'England', the confines specifically of Wales, and – with the royal 'we' – the confines of Richard's personal world. Richard is clearly penned in with overdetermination. His own belief in and reliance on the divine protection of kings keeps him held within himself, the rebels in the marches and major English border towns keep him in Wales, his own lamentable resignation takes him from Harlech to Flint Castle, and from that point forth the king experiences physical and psychological confinement into smaller and smaller spaces of his kingdom of 'Britain'. Even the 'peaceful steps' of the line are ominously ambivalent. This peace is the calm before the storm, a peace that seems to flow one way, toward the rebels who are given peace to travel but are preparing for war. At the same time – like that British King Lear in his hovel and his touchingly 'British/ Welsh' transference from 'peace' to 'piece of toasted cheese' (4.6.88–9) – we hear the word 'piece-ful'. Thus the play radically has Richard describing the rebels' steps as (1) preparing to put the tyrannous rule to peaceful rest, and (2) 'piecing' the nation back together. Before the Richard–Bolingbroke face-off in 3.3, the abdication in 4.1, or the murder in 5.5, the play sets up the paradox of internal strife as mender of England's identity, and arbitrator of negotiation among its neighbour countries. Bolingbroke is consistently identified as an alien body at once attacking the host but also pushing it toward a singular, fused, stable Englishness that Henry V will endeavour to confirm as he figures Anglo-Welsh identity.

Power, then, relates closely to the command of land and space, areas available for enclosure, breaching, excursion, and returning to; and the map becomes a centrally important, but in the end contestatory and impotent, tool for representing that human power of possession. In its widespread metaphorical uses, such as to 'map' the face of Richard II or visages in the sonnets, 'mapping' is represented as failing to provide satisfactory delineation of present states of affairs.[36] The 'real' map does not work much better: for all the mapping and heated negotiation of the rebels, we should remind ourselves that the Trent is never turned, for the map delineates what *might be* after all, not what *is*. The map shows what the rebels lack. It is the frustrating nature of maps, like any text (and, as I mentioned before, like the theatre itself), to figure the absent. As the performatives of banishment uttered by King Richard prompted Bolingbroke and Mowbray's imagined future lives, so the map indicates the existence of a reorganized space brought into being only by a desire for it from specific perspectives. Such a problem had already been dramatically presented by Marlowe. In *Tamburlaine, Part 1*, Tamburlaine wants to redraw the tripartite T in O maps of the world to install a new, missing, fourth region with places called 'Tamburlaine' and 'Zenocrate'; and in *Part 2* he strives toward alien territory, pursuing the (arguable, hollow) identity-building journey of cunning, material power, and ideology until death.[37]

Mowbray fights to the death in these foreign fields, which are both better charted and less known by the Elizabethan period – more inscribed into textual and political history and less acknowledged as the direction for religious concentration. Henry IV sketches the path to Jerusalem with the aim of simultaneously erasing the problematic lines of his own claims to the Western region of Christendom, England, and Britain, and he too pursues an *idea* of this mapped relation to take up the place of his English 'Jerusalem' at death. And Richard, in between these figures, attempts to exaggerate and define distances between outlying Britain (Ireland, 'the Antipodes') and the western mainland (Wales, 'my kingdom', with the Welsh who consider him 'their king') so that he can claim ownership of something Anglo-British and reject *alien* (albeit *English*) rebellion. However, the present facts 'on the ground' resist his delineations and reveal the absences, lack, spaces in the grand argument of spatial possession. His nationalistic isolation, perpetrated under the name of divinity, is always invaded by the alien, from the returning usurper to the 'little pin' of Death. And that alien – divided as it is in *Richard II* into an anti-English king and anti-monarchic Englishman – is not a new figure, but a pervasive domestic one, a parasite like an antithetical mirror to a figure like Death, who has always been sitting there, some neglected and forgotten shadow of otherness within the self, waiting to be discovered and to react. It is brought into the light (as we see in the case of Queen Isabel in 2.2) through the 'perspectives' gained by looking awry, to one side as one moves through the world, as one travels out of one's immediate and familiar circle.

HENRY IV: ABSORBING THE BRITISH ALIEN

By *1 Henry IV* the inter- and intra-national Anglo-Welsh 'conversation' is staged so much more overtly as a 'British question' pertaining to the late sixteenth century. David Armitage reminds us that the first phase of empire – the expansion of 'England' into Celtic borderlands – remains an *Anglo*-British phenomenon. Armitage points out that concepts of and language for 'Britishness' and 'empire' were available to sixteenth-century writers, thinkers, and policy-makers, but their combination – a 'British empire' conceived as a consolidated force with the means to conquer outside of the Atlantic archipelago – would only be realized by the late seventeenth and eighteenth centuries.[38] This placement of English understanding of Britishness and empire in a position of grasping the elements but not the larger (global) implications of their fusion articulates other scholars' senses of the history plays as historical documents of political awareness; thus Matthew Greenfield writes 'Shakespeare wrote the second play of the tetralogy, I suggest, at a moment when it was still possible to imagine a history that did not move teleologically toward the development of the modern nation state – or toward his own *Henry V'*.[39] I would say that even *Henry V*, caught as it is in the dramatically imaginative limbo between the early-fifteenth and late-sixteenth centuries of setting and staging, can only gesture towards British unity and in the end still relentlessly Anglicizes the expansion of England into the larger 'empire' that includes British lands and northern France.

In line with Armitage's sense of English priority, I want to suggest at the same time that there is in fact no other point of view available to the Elizabethan English writer. Andrew Hadfield and Willy Maley write that 'an expanding territorial "Englishness" went hand in hand with a con-tracting cultural notion of "Englishness"', and I am suggesting that the contracting cultural notion of Englishness is the catalyst for the Elizabethan English idea of Britishness.[40] The cooption of alien space involves confirming but confining the English subject's distinct identity. As Englishness ventures further and further afield into 'Britain', alien confusion binds and restricts it, revealing how little foundation the concept of 'Englishness' really has. At the same time, such delimitation of English identity necessitates opening it up to a cosmopolitan comprehension of others. This incorporation of the alien into *Englishness* to expand its asserted legitimacy in non-English territory creates the *English sense* of *Britishness*. Looked at another way, Britishness is always placed within Englishness in the Anglo-centric legacy. The process of alien confusion in the expression of 'Englishness' across geographical and conceptual space, then, is at once English-isolationist and British-expansionist.

Englishness in Tudor England requires a route into and through Wales – geographically, in the case of Henry Tudor, who arrived through Milford Haven and marched toward Bosworth Field in 1485; concep-tually, through ideological narratives of British origins, or in the case of Fluellen's half-baked claim for Henry's blood-line and their discussion of leek-wearing. So, when Henry V calls to his many-'nationed' soldiers in terminology that according to Janette Dillon relentlessly 'erase[s] this difference under the banner of a uniting Englishness',[41] while there is no doubt that the marginal British are being pulled toward the English centre, that Englishness is already suffused with the margin that is Wales. And an Englishness that is suffused with Welshness, guided by Roman culture, stocked by Norman bastardy, and populated by northern households and Continental spouses cannot help but be careful and conflicted when it comes face to face with non-Englishness with which it has to negotiate difference, continuity, and superiority. 'Englishness' needs to pull away from Britishness in its rhetoric even as it incorporates

Britishness in practice; thus, in contrast to Dillon, Claire McEachern argues that 'Henry punctiliously insists on differences among his "dear friends"' in his speeches to the soldiers (3.1) and listing of the dead. 'The play is as vigilant in limiting the scope of common feeling as it is in encouraging it.'[42] These two views are not entirely contradictory in the context of the plays. MacMorris objects to the distinction of his 'nation', suggesting a desire for communality, while the friction between the British captains arguably demonstrates that 'the notion that the Welsh, the English, and the Scots were racially homogenous found almost no supporters at the time'.[43] Similarly, Henry V's rallying cries at 3.1 and 4.3 purport to recognize common identity only to insist at the same time on residual difference through the Anglicizing of the British army.

For the rest of this study of Englishness in *1 Henry IV*, I want to set this bifurcated Englishness on the edge of 'England'. Englishness is an ideology in Louis Althusser's definition, a fact of life with material reality not because it has a good foundation in existential 'truth', but because it is socially and politically effective. This ideology of Englishness hovers simultaneously over the far west of a medieval 'Britain' and over the new borders of a sixteenth-century Welsh province. So how is the English–Welsh border – whether physically present or imagined by the antagonistic allies of the rebellion – 'played out' in this *English* Britain of the second tetralogy? Wales can be read as a fairy or dream land of effeminacy, and Glyndwr as its feminized representative: he is, after all, the sole parent, magus-like father (and mother) who prefigures Prospero in suggestive ways, as he brings up a female child into education but also into a certain 'silence' and (pre)determination. There is, however, a residual resistance in Welshness. The Welsh language of Glyndwr's daughter keeps the English audience at bay, and Glyndwr's military history against the English is hardly an 'effeminate' one.[44] Highley notes, moreover, that there was a concomitant fear of the wild and manly Celt, and 'if the "uncivilized" connoted vitality and "hardness", the "civilized" could suggest an undesirable passivity and "softness", the very qualities that Hotspur rails against in the foppish messenger sent by the king to demand his prisoners'.[45] But Hotspur's own loss of manly control is an ironic response to such a fear. By disturbing Glyndwr's delicate temper, 'Hotspur urges Glendower to play the role of the Welshman.'[46] The hyperbole of the Welsh figure, though, seems to be at least partly self-conscious acting, for Glyndwr is the one who acquiesces to the turning of the Trent, compromising his apparent steadfastness for the sake of the rebel coalition. Glyndwr here takes on the role of the typical angry patriarch, and Hotspur is the petulant, daughter-like railer whose own father, Worcester, has to calm him/her down. Mortimer is effeminized by Welsh Kate and Hotspur is effeminized by his passions. If Hotspur should be manly, we see the breakdown of such identity as he displays an uncommon affection for his brother-in-law, Mortimer, and his Coriolanus-like 'mouthèd wounds' (1.3.96); neither, as we have seen, can he hold his tongue, revealing his 'woman's mood' (1.3.235), which leads Worcester to cast him in a mould that recalls Richard II's queen's feminine instinct: 'He apprehends a world of figures here, / But not the form of what he should attend' (1.3.207–8). Hotspur is at once feminized and confused with the Welshman whose imaginations he has been mocking.

This joint gendering and international aligning of the scene is set up earlier in the play when, in declaiming Mortimer, the king refers to 'that great magician, damned Glyndwr' (*1 HIV* 1.3.82). The king's suggested belief in the Welshman's magic is in contrast to Hotspur's disdainful dismissal, and it allows Henry to elaborate on the revolting seduction of Mortimer at the hands of Glyndwr's daughter. Glanmor Williams finds that '[T]here remained a vast area of Welsh life, not confined by any means to the illiterate, in which older beliefs in superstition, magic, witchcraft, and supernatural forces of every kind continued to flourish, with scarcely diminished currency, well into the eighteenth and nineteenth centuries.'[47] It seems that the playgoers would have easily believed in the Welsh wizard's power to seduce English victims, a power frequently associated with feminine seduction of nationally defined males: Spenser's Acrasia in the Bower of Bliss, the figure of Circe, or the mermaids calling for Odysseus. When Henry rejects the idea of ransoming Mortimer with the cry, 'No, on the barren mountains let him starve' (1.3.88), he unwittingly prophesies the death of Glyndwr himself, thus aligning the 'revolted Mortimer' who has 'turned Welsh' with the wild Welshman his father-in-law. While that line seems fairly clearly to refer to Mortimer, the grammar of the following lines makes the pleader of ransom (i.e. Hotspur) the subject of the speech: 'For I shall never hold that man my friend / Whose tongue shall ask me for one penny cost / To ransom home revolted Mortimer –' (1.3.89–91). According to Henry's logic, all these rebels are drawn into Glyndwr's magical circle, which lies on the other side of a line 'between "law" and "lore"' that Terence Hawkes claims we see in this English–Welsh face-off.[48]

With all the confusion and overlapping of identities suggested here, we might expect the significance of any border between England and Wales to fade in 3.1 – especially since we have a British coalition regionally defined against the south-east. But instead the border is maintained: we get the comic sense that Glyndwr and Hotspur are arguing with each other across an invisible but palpable Welsh–English line, Mortimer and Kate are draped together and lying across it, and Worcester jumps back and forth in a sort of arbitrating, peace-keeping jig. In fact, the combination of fiery male blood; pouting, female passion; and flapping tongues forces us to have suspended in front of us the double notion of a border that cannot be erased and a pressing desire to violate that line of difference. As Hawkes points out, the 'Act of Union' to incorporate Wales as a principality into 'England' is at once a metaphor and a statement of national and sexual significance.[49] And we are not off the mark in reminding ourselves of the fluidity of the joining of the two bodies of England and Wales, from the Severn River to the tears of Glyndwr's daughter. Patricia Parker, for one, provides an extended reading of the uncontainability, incontinence, and dangerous openings of Wales and the world of *Henry V* that would threaten male Englishness, and Lisa Hopkins' essay 'Fluellen's Name' examines in some detail the inescapable sexual incontinence and hereditary untrustworthiness of the historical women represented throughout the tetralogy.[50] This is a coupling that brings together men at the border in war continually striving to comprehend their own English or Welsh manhood: Hotspur, like Cordelia, denying the tenets of the father's law as written into his map; Falstaff (that False Taff, Oldcastle) with the notorious stab in the dead Hotspur's thigh (the displaced sexual location of rupture also for the ill-fated Adonis); Mortimer and Glyndwr bleeding into the Severn River together. Wales itself, for the Tudor line and Elizabethan playgoers, represented a penetrable and adaptable field of activity affecting its iconic status as 'British' and anti-English. On the one hand it let in Henry Tudor at Milford Haven, and on the other hand the 'haven' port at Milford could permit another aggressive entry – that of invading French or Spanish, who might find some level of sympathy in Wales.[51]

Notions of gendered space, threats and expectations across lines of difference are taken up in Hopkins' *Shakespeare on the Edge*, where she expands on the notion of watery borders associated with Wales, especially comparing them with the hard boundaries of fences and walls on which England relies.[52] Part of the outcome of the fluidity of the passages to and within Wales is the already-noted sense of the region as marginal, magical, and dream-like. Report from Wales is not certain, thus we do not know whom to believe between Hotspur's report of Mortimer's fight with Glyndwr and Henry's rejection of that version of events.[53] The uncertainty, however, feeds into the availability of multiple and con- current views of Wales for the building of Anglo-British stature; if the fight never happened in history, it happened in Hotspur's relation and therefore it happened in this 'history' play. Such reports are not very different from the calls to believe in the shifts of place and consequences of events made by *Henry V*'s Chorus. Just as utterances *make* characters on the stage, so they make events as well. The detailed atrocities of the Welsh women on slaughtered male bodies, never part of the play text, are now so engrained in the collective critical psyche by reiterated quotation taken from the chronicles, that we have lost something of this mythical, evasive quality of the fears that Wales holds for the English in *Henry IV*. Like the mysterious content within the stage directions, 'The lady speaks in Welsh', the Welshwomen episode as supplied by Shakespeare consti- tutes a deliberate textual breach that has been filled up by critics with those mutilated English dead. Hopkins' subtle reading of these moments of Welsh vagueness leads her to conclude the illusoriness of a Welsh threat, and for the Tudor regime, this was basically true.[54] All dramatic activity takes place upon report, however. Truth and falsehood get played out on the wooden 'field' of duel and battle, and Glyndwr outlasts Hotspur, albeit to his own withering end. Richard II's relation of the bounds-beating rebels brought the fact to life, and Henry feels the need to contradict and suppress something that he asserts only exists as report: Hotspur's relation of the battle of Mortimer. Henry's refusal to believe Hotspur casts suspicion on Hotspur and Mortimer's loyalty, thus pos- itioning *them* on the confusing fringe of a 'pure' English identity; this of course is entirely at odds with Hotspur's own sense of his very English position in contrast to his strange comrade/antagonist Glyndwr. While King Henry resists Hotspur's apparent rehearsal of the king's own coming-to-power, Hotspur himself attempts to recast Glyndwr outside the realm of Britishness that ambitious nobility sees as central to defining, winning, and maintaining *English* identity. Henry's action is not simply an affront to Hotspur's honesty or military knowledge, but to his willed masculine ability to *fix* events within a narrative of his own preferring, one that confirms his role in the reforming of a Welsh-bolstered English identity. We have seen, however, that Hotspur lacks something to make his desire for power a reality. If that map in *1 Henry IV* (as well as the one in *King Lear*) is supposed to be a settled agreement, not a text for alteration and manipulation,[55] then it is Hotspur who fails to align with the men of the British kingdoms of the past and present. Both fathers, and both British rulers, Glyndwr and Lear are astonished at the younger generation's ability to flout this concreteness. The maps in both cases are, for the older generation, not there to be redrawn or discussed, but to show the fixity of things, decisions that have been made.

This masculinized desire for fixity relates to the audience's expectations at the theatre. As students of drama, we like to remind ourselves often of the drama's free play, improvisation, surprise, and disorder – perhaps, arguably, its liquidity and femininity. But the predictability of theatre space, textual form, character relation, and moral structure has to inhere sufficiently in an established system of generic and practical laws for drama to be useful as an object or event for interpretation (i.e. one needs to understand the basics of the language before one can begin to translate or interpret effectively). When such fixity or reliability is thrown into question, a character like *Henry V*'s Chorus is there to direct the spectators how to 'imagine' what they see (or, rather, *don't* see). Without and within the plays, this battle for definition goes on, this contested balance between the work of the (feminine) imagination and supposition on the one hand and the necessity for a (masculine) curbed and well-defined identity or sense of place and 'truth' on the other hand. So when Hotspur comes to Henry with his narrative of battle, it is not just individual reputation that is on the line, but the very meaning and place of Englishness and Britishness as articulated in the dramatic play of power.

Hotspur evokes the Anglo-Welsh border to place his narrative of Mortimer and Glyndwr. Mortimer the Englishman leads the men of the border Marches in Herefordshire against the Welshman Glyndwr who captures Mortimer. There is a relentless pull westward here that, as we have seen, Hotspur asks Henry to reverse and that Henry refuses to believe:

> . . . the noble Mortimer,
> Leading the men of Herefordshire to fight
> Against the irregular and wild Glyndwr,
> Was by the rude hands of that Welshman taken[.] (1.1.38–41)

To call Glyndwr 'irregular' reveals Hotspur's anxiety about the Welshman's authority and his unorthodox magical powers.[56] Jean Howard suggests that the term refers to Glyndwr's guerrilla war tactics, but the word hints rather at an attempt to pre-empt and deny the *regularity* of the man: the courtly, orthodox English upbringing of which he reminds us later.[57] He is, asserts Hotspur, not aligned with *regula*, that is, he is unruly. Such a view enacts the 'law'/'lore' contrast that Hawkes placed each side of the English–Welsh border, but which is seriously questioned as Glyndwr demonstrates his commitment to *right* ways of doing things – maintenance of the family, of native identity, of the map of geological and fluvial fact. His alleged 'wild[ness]' is arguably proven by his protestations of outrageous powers, but is this any more alarming than the outbursts of the passionate Hotspur? Moreover, the word surely recalls more immediately the traditional country 'wild man', again a characteristic radically at odds with what we see in the play.[58] Such a 'wild' man would have 'rude hands', unfit to manhandle 'noble Mortimer', but while Glyndwr may well have rough, soldier's hands, they have raised and loved a daughter who enchants English Mortimer, and they perhaps 'framèd [themselves] to the harp' (3.1.120), a point of civility I return to below. This play keeps compromising extremes in Welshness and Englishness, or it sets up black/white English/Welsh contrast from one point of view to have it made grey by another. We saw that it does not repeat the full chronicle history's dwelling on the Welsh women's atrocities that so fascinate new historicists, nor does it tell the story of Glyndwr's 'wild' ending in the mountains. *1 Henry IV* kindles the latent heat of nationalism and xenophobia, only to dampen it again when there is the potential of a flare-up. Instead of the wild alien invader, we have a strong, angry, sympathetic, quite odd, intelligent, 'Anglicized' but very Welsh man defending land that he respects and loves as his life.

This play simultaneously relates Hotspur to the 'outlandish' position of Glyndwr and sets him up as a compare-and-contrast foil for Hal; but these positionings relative to other characters do not eliminate Hotspur's essential isolation. It may be that medieval 'Welshness was bleakly defined by the shared experience of resisting the English',[59] but from the play's Anglo-centric point of view, Glyndwr's identity as alien *because Welsh* is motivated or brought into being by the fact of his being alien *because a rebel* (compare him with friendly Fluellen). Either way, Hotspur and Mortimer are pulled into that rebel/Welsh cluster that lies across the English–Welsh distinction, for they too resist the centre of Englishness as represented by the king. The logical end of this thinking of course draws Henry IV into the mix as past rebel against Richard II, and even Richard II himself has the dual alien–English identity as a native Frenchman and breaker of English tradition in denying Lancaster's inheritance. For all this web of close connectors, however, Harry Percy is the 'hotspur' because he cannot settle down. Part of Hotspur's uneasiness lies in his own failure to go through an excursion of 'finding himself' and finding *in himself* a stable identity. John Michael Archer calls him 'the complete provincial', opposed to a citizen identity that Bolingbroke incorporated in his rise to kingship.[60] From what I have said in this paragraph, we can add that this does not just place him in opposition to London, but in a limbo between Henry's and Glyndwr's states of confident power. In his isolation (and his inability to engage in the kind of empathy called for by Sir Thomas More or voiced by the duellists in *Richard II*) Hotspur cannot fully accept the strange, court-trained Glyndwr. Without being able to 'take sides' in the battle, Hotspur is not just the antagonist to Prince Hal but is very much the individual, rash, solipsistic, determined-but-doomed reminder of Henry IV's enemy, King Richard. He can thus never gather together an essential English identity in the way that Henry did from excursive and familial experience, or in the way Hal does from his multiple empathetic excursions into the citizenry and underworld, or at court where he takes the crown ahead of his time (*2 HIV* 4.3).

If Hotspur is an unsettled character, Glyndwr knows himself very well, and his is a self of confident incorporation. He is the incomparable Welshman who can insist to Hotspur 'I can speak English, Lord, as well as you' (3.1.118). This may have got a laugh from a London audience, since a Welshman attacking the English of a northener is 'the pot calling the kettle black'. In spite of that, Glyndwr is certainly an extraordinary man, for, as Glanmor Williams writes of the Reformation period to follow much later than the play's setting, 'Only in the towns, and partly Anglicized areas like south Pembrokeshire, the Vale of Glamorgan, and parts of the eastern border, were there many who spoke English', and they would have been the gentry, professional men, and higher clergy.[61] Glyndwr's English is not a sign of weakness, even if part of a colonial Anglicization, but rather it displays precisely the politic intelligence we accord English Hal in *2 Henry IV*. As spectators, we already understand what Warwick confirms: 'The Prince but studies his companions / Like a strange tongue' 'to be known and hated' (*2 HIV* 4.3.68–9, 73). We already know this not least because it is hardly a new activity – it is what Bolingbroke and Mowbray were forced to do through banishment, thus finding their own true callings. Glyndwr also learns in order to compete with and outdo his teachers and adversaries. This is in fact a Shakespearean commonplace, which we hear in Shylock's claim that he 'will better the instruction' of his Christian oppressors (*Mer* 3.1.61) and witness in Othello's ability to *be* a *Venetian* general. Learning the foreign 'language' (linguistic and behavioural) is political savviness rather than weakness, whether the authority learns from the subject or the colonized from the colonizer. Glyndwr's proud assertion of his linguistic fluency is in direct response to Hotspur's provocation; it is a skill he is using *against* the English overlords, and it is not one that has compromised or replaced his own originary Welsh identity or knowledge. If Anglicization is 'the process by which English forms began to infiltrate foreign languages abroad', then Glyndwr protects Welshness *in Wales*, and his daughter's Welsh avoids the 'broken English' of Fluellen and other comic second-language speakers, which would have diluted her potency.[62] Glyndwr is no Caliban, who represents the oppressed with no other useful language and only impotently curses his master. Glyndwr has a fully formed Welsh identity, he has gathered his Anglicized strength from behind enemy lines, and his infiltration has the potential to pay off.

Glyndwr extends his claim to the power of language in a passage that insists on the penetration of Englishness by the Welsh alien. Addressing Hotspur, he remarks that he learned his English 'in the English court, / Where, being but young, I framèd to the harp / Many an English ditty lovely well, / And gave the tongue a helpful ornament – / A virtue that was never seen in you' (3.1.119–23). While this is generally glossed as meaning that Glyndwr's musical skill made the ditties sound all the lovelier, the subject of the phrase seems to be his English ditty (i.e. words and singing). Megan Lloyd has argued that 'The wild Welshwomen, along with the rebel magician Glendower and vocalist Lady Mortimer construct Wales as a place of voices in *1 Henry IV*', although we have just seen that Glyndwr's voice was nurtured and grew in England.[63] After this educational excursion, his vocal skill has been transplanted to Wales and is now making its way back into Englishness. The alien infusion is again something inherently English – resisted but irresistible; held at bay with language and overt action, but already within. Glyndwr claims that his Welsh voice improves 'the tongue' of Englishness; Hotspur's riposte to Glyndwr's accusing 'A virtue that was never seen in you' (123) rejects not musical composition, but 'metre ballad-mongers' and 'mincing poetry' (126, 130). Thus it is the challenge of language that these two take on, and it is the assertion that Welshness pervades Englishness and ameliorates it that Hotspur cannot – for all his disdain – in the end reject. Behind this anxiety lies the debate over the qualities of the English language as a part of English self-definition. On the one hand, English was a flexible, poetic language to be proud of; on the other, it was a mish-mash of colonizers' lexicons and grammars: Germanic, Latin, French. Hotspur's rejection of Welsh as worse than a bitch-dog howling in Irish in such a historical context, then, is in part a displacing of the fear of what Steven Mullaney calls the 'barbaros' in the English throat, a continued denying of the alien within.[64]

Hawkes points out that 'For English speakers, to hear Welsh is fundamentally disconcerting. In a sense it is to experience the phenomenon of "language" itself, as an unmediated, inexplicable system of signs', and David Steinsaltz concurs, noting that the Welsh is not written out because 'the Welsh language was genuinely alien'.[65] (Alien enough, I suspect, to prohibit Shakespeare from writing the lines even if he had wanted to.) The contiguity and imbrication of Anglo-Welsh cultural and religious aspirations in tension with the radical language division lies behind England's policy of language suppression and enforcement in sixteenth-century Wales. 'For all the endemic disorder', argues Peter Roberts, 'Wales in the mid-1530s was not considered by the regime to be a frontier society, where attachment to the indigenous culture and language fostered a disaffected separatism which might resist the changes of the Reformation. If anything, the linguistic difference was believed to inhibit the spread of dissent and disobedience.'[66] Thus the apparently oppressive 27 Henry VIII, *c*.26 (1536) 'Act of Union' making English the official language of the law courts and administration was followed by 5 Elizabeth I, *c*.28 (1563) ordering Welsh vernacular bibles and prayer books.[67] This sequence should not be considered points on a line of 'a consistent and single-minded "Tudor policy towards Wales"', although the latter Act 'helped sustain the Protestant Reformation and the Welsh language in ways that did not develop in other Celtic speaking regions'.[68] The Welsh translating project was particularly useful as a tool against Catholicism after the Council of Trent in 1546 'had declared the Vulgate alone must be used for public readings, sermons and disputations ... [T]he Privy Council regarded the vernacular Scriptures as a potent weapon in the campaign to implement the Elizabethan settlement of the church.'[69]

The use of language as a tool of conquest, by example of the Romans, is an important notion with regard to Wales. The mid-sixteenth-century official recognition by the English state of the need to permit Welsh for religious education in Welsh-speaking parts of Wales both aided the Protestant Reformation and allowed a distance or resistance to English power. Post-Reformation Wales remained strongly nationalist and its counter-Reformation sympathies fought for primacy with its Welshness. Thus non-Welsh counter-Reformation clerics (and even those who left Wales for seminaries abroad and returned) found it hard to ingratiate themselves with the Welsh.[70] The religious free-verse poet, Rhys Prichard, saw the need to draw the populace to the Word of God through popular means. In a reflection of the English desire to be *like* the Roman colonizer while retaining the *difference* of their own language and rising cultural promise, Prichard and others attempted to draw the Welsh commoners toward greater Welsh literacy by comparing their back-wardness with the better-educated English.[71] Glyndwr anachronistically but powerfully emerges from this controlled but semi-independent Wales as representative of a confused, advanced Welshman: the alien located within a nascent Britain that was increasingly being incorporated by an ideology of expansive 'Englishness'.

HENRY V AND *CYMBELINE*: THE WELSH CORRECTION AND THE BRITISH COMPLEXION

King Henry V gradually absorbs a 'Britishness' into his identity that he recasts as 'English' until the joyful Fluellen–Henry exchange that employs questionable premises and analogy to stabilize a macsculine but morally acceptable identity for the king. The fact that Welsh must be *in* English is most strikingly played out when Fluellen beats pistol and forces him to eat the leek. Captain Gower – the Englishman with a very 'British' name – gets the conclusive judging line for Pistol: 'let a Welsh correction teach you a good English condition' (5.1.69–70), and indeed the play has demonstrated Welsh 'cor-rection' (a leading, a straightening out) of the English 'con-dition' (what comes together, is *spoken* for).[72] Pistol's rejection of Fluellen's leek involves an important prejudice: 'Not for Cadwaller and all his goats' (5.1.25), he retorts, because 'for Pistol the Welsh are foreigners with a distinct history'.[73] Pistol represents the English 'old guard' of resistance to British and other foreign confusion. His epithet for Fluellen, 'base Trojan', is footnoted in editions of the play variously as 'rascal' and 'villain', but this is Pistol using a term that cannot be so easily extracted from its embedded sense of Britishness. Fluellen is ancient Welsh, from Trojan stock according to the legend of Brutus' landing in Albion, and Pistol attempts to separate his English-ness from that legacy by reiterating the term.[74] While Pistol's sense of Englishness uncomfortably rejects Welshness, his attitude acts as a kind of foil against which we see highlighted the king, who represents the nation and must incorporate that Welsh history into a greater whole.

Pistol must eat the leek and allow the literally distasteful lesson of Welshness to enter his body. In the fifteenth and sixteenth centuries, the leek was used in comparative phrases to indicate something of little value, and this is a kind of debased communion that once again couches vital moments of identity formation in edgy comedy. The concentration on the insignificant 'Welsh onion' is at once rather disproportionate to the significance of the 'correction' at hand, just as other vital attempts to define identity are based around seemingly minor quarrels in *Henry V.* Consider the English soldier who mistakes Harry in the night. He is a reflective means to articulate Hal's own fears of consciousness and national responsibility, and we should no longer be surprised that this shadowy figure of resistance, correction, and conditioning is given the common Welsh name, Williams. The Old-English-Irish Macmorris' complaint that Fluellen misrepresents Ireland as another 'nation' high-lights the process of Anglo-Welsh conditioning and confusion that privileges England against all Celtic countries.[75] Jamy, Macmorris, and even the arguably naive Fluellen are there to play the part of countries' representatives, but the *English* play forces them to 'act' as regional pieces of a British puzzle that feeds the British king of England's desire to represent the British coalition *as English*. Such a force is powerful enough to keep criticism talking about this scene in terms of 'regional rivalries'.[76]

There is no end to the formation of Englishness, of course. Henry V's rejection of Falstaff at the end of *2 Henry IV*, for all its sense of finality, did not confirm the king's identity so much as set him on the path to finding it. If at this point Hal is denying the alien part of himself, the unruly daemon, and a Rabelaisian excess, he is also through that very rejection revealing the recognition of a reliance on that alien element in his pursuit of quintessential Englishness. Claire McEachern notes that the usual view of Henry V's movement from 'fellowship to estrangement' in his rejection of Falstaff needs to be reread from Henry IV's point of view, in which Hal's 'tavern-founded fellowship' is itself 'personal wilfulness' that must be left alone to provide for the 'corporate welfare' assigned to kingship.[77] I have been arguing that these two processes are not so much alternatives as immanent and public correlatives. Queen Isabel's personal vision reveals public terror; Bolingbroke's wilful return incorporates a release from Richard's tyranny; Mowbray's personal plight benefits the international cause of Christendom. Hal's English self requires the interchange with the tavern friends, and his social process of rising through the English ranks from familiar prince to unequivocal king separates him from the bodies of knowledge that he now thoroughly owns and rules over. At the same time, his personal self-discovery (through recognition of the alien elements in and around London's human bodies, the city's and the country's topographical features, and the presence of Welshness all around – and of course within – him) is one that leads him through the self-serving pseudo-camaraderie of the tavern gang and into his role of synthesized, alien-English, British leader who goes under the name of King of England.

That Henry is not simply rejecting the alien but instead working through alien elements as he needs them to maintain his Englishness is confirmed in the manner in which he perceives Katherine and France. When the French King notes that Harry sees the towns of France 'perspectively' in Katherine, there is a little more going on than 'simply a shift in perspective, the transformation of an object from one set of dimensions into another, as in a map'.[78] For something at once expansive and contracting occurs in this moment. Henry is faced with a combination of a looking glass and a perspective glass, seeing himself and his possessions in Katherine to confirm his English power, and *through* her seeing the greater dimension of France as another alien aspect that builds Englishness into the future. Self-confirmation, reproduction, and imagination come together. The possession of real estate and the body of Katherine feed Henry's promotion of Englishness; the absorption of France that he sees 'perspectively' builds the empire that Henry calls English (although, as Schwyzer points out, 'Henry can never quite bring himself to declare unambiguously that he is English').[79] It is the empire that Fluellen shows is Anglo-Welsh, and the emerging empire is one that Elizabethan England will have to re-present awkwardly as alternately a pure England and a settled Britain.

When Shakespeare 'returns' to Wales in *Cymbeline*, he is working in a new political climate and writing about ancient alien problems. Early Jacobean drama examines the turning point in a colonized country forging an 'empire state', the new British England now at the helm of what Maley refers to as 'a repetition of the colonial project' that brought them into being.[80] *Cymbeline* certainly seems to be addressing this combined anxiety and desire about the past and the future. Where Maley has Shakespeare's England *copying* the colonial past, however, I have been arguing in this book that any alien heritage is incorporated and re-worked.[81] It is not there to be copied so much as recovered, even performed; and part of the impetus for the English work of alien confusion lies in the plays' contemporary context of alien presence. Maley claims that modern critics duplicate the early modern tendency to project alien contexts into the past, thereby allowing them to be made familiar.[82] But *Aliens and Englishness* has been examining plays that recognize the *currency* of the alien and wrestle with the very strangeness that is confused with the native self. Some scholarship recognizes such a dynamic. Avraham

Oz, for example, reads 'nations' in *Cymbeline* as characters in negotiation with each other to find themselves, not prioritizing a narrative of conquest and exclusion of one by the other, but instead one of 'learning and experience'. There remains, however, 'racial' and national friction of the kind we saw on the Welsh coast and Anglo-Welsh borders in *Richard II* and *Henry IV*.[83] Such face-offs between uncertain groups lead McEachern to predicate her 1996 study of English nationhood on the premise that understandings of nation and religion are not finally understood by absolute separation of apparent antitheses but by the more difficult 'ever-threatened union with an opposite, one both desired and abhorred'.[84]

Jodi Mikalachki has usefully put this tension of attraction and repulsion in gendered terms. The Roman Lucius landing at Milford Haven 'gives [Imogen] a new identity', she writes, although 'the nature of this new identity remains unclear'. 'Obedience and subordination ... love and mastery' are the poles between which Imogen's identity is uncertainly poised in her relation to the imperial representative.[85] A similar lack of clarity attends the focuses given to women in the *Henry IV* and *Henry V* plays; women are at once necessary and obstructive to the male-driven expansion of England into its British and imperial margins. The Welsh Lady literally cannot be drawn into the conversation of rebellious national delineation, and France's Katherine remains the translucency through which Henry sees his new terrain. These female markers are aliens to authority (especially in their resistances to being understood), but they are essentially 'good'. Here *Aliens and Englishness* disagrees with the alien–authority relationship outlined by Stephen Greenblatt.[86] His alien is produced or exaggerated by authority only to be suppressed and branded as dangerous. His alien therefore only has 'real' existence in its creation and magnification by an authority always to some extent 'in the know' or in charge of things. To be sure, this bears some relation to the first alien stage of antithesis and rejection of the 'other'; but the alien as I have delineated it, and as it is understood in the second alien stage, comes into existence before, and without, the power of Englishness as overlord. If Englishness as an authority *discovers* that alien, it is in the same way that new lands are 'discovered' (not *made* but *found* and recast). The idea of Englishness finds the alien, and then makes its power felt by seeing the alien as always-already in Englishness' formative 'native' DNA; Englishness thus celebrates its new-found (but not newly *created*) alien as part of its hybridity. If we talk of the *creation* of the alien, it is only in this sense of finding out the thing that was already there but not seen. English characters representing this process assert their new-found identity variously: with an ironic solipsism, with aggressive celebration, or with defensive uncertainty. King Henry V exhibits all three of these modes when faced with Katherine. She, as the alien with a strange familiarity, evokes anxiety and desire, forces the man to *act* (to be manly and to play parts – as in Henry V's role as wooer), and is taken into the identity that Henry casts as expanded Englishness. '[T]each you our Princess English?' asks Burgundy (5.2.261–2), unwittingly giving her away with a new title 'Princess English'. She is betrothed to and confused with the language that denotes a people ignorant of others (unable to speak French, unable to speak Welsh), yet from the 'start' of its self-knowledge a people full of alien elements.

We have seen throughout this chapter, then, that the incorporation of the edges, or the hidden past, of English identity, especially as processed through Wales and Welshness, works through alien confusion. So while the name of Wales (Wallia) is supposed to have been instituted by the English to connote 'strangeness' in general and thus demonstrate the place of the 'abhorred' alien (to return to McEachern's language), the revisiting of Wales in *Cymbeline* promotes the 'desired' recovery of its magical space. Jacobean England is shadowed in two directions, for it constitutes an age of post-Britain (aware of Roman history) and pre-Britain (for the desired Union is still a wish to be fulfilled). It may be just this tension between colonized subject and imperially minded power that needs to revisit the first alien stage, the old insistence on rejecting the alien to define an English self.[87] To return to a naming of England *as* Britain is to remould Gaunt's concept of the 'sceptered isle', and in such a context Sullivan notes the contemporary fear of England's threatened 'eradication of a distinctive Welsh identity'.[88] Having worked through the weighty incorporation of the various aliens surrounding Englishness in Elizabethan drama, I would suggest that this 'eradication' cannot finally be enacted, a play like *Cymbeline* indicating, rather, an ongoing discomfort with the inevitability of alien confusion. It recasts 'Britishness' as a 'natural' return to origins, but has some trouble working out the shifting nature of hybrid identity. The contesting triumphs of Cloten and Cymbeline, writes Huw Griffiths, 'produce the Celtic margins as alien, but also as a source of legitimacy, locating Britain not in the island but in a constant shift of emphasis *within* the island'.[89] The body politic and the geographical realm are here envisioned as constituting an expansive view of this book's investigations of the personal and communal interactions with the alien. England cannot simply overrun its borders and British neighbour lands; the English must negotiate strangeness 'close to home' and the familiarity of alien elements in 'wild' regions both of the self and of the realm. Set at some historical distance from their dates of performance, these plays perhaps provide some breathing room for an audience working through their relationship to English authority and identity in the difficult 1590s. When playwrights isolate contemporary London as the centre of concern, the 'shift[s] of emphasis' between the strange self and the familiar alien all happen in much closer proximity and with a tense immediacy. That new environment is the subject of the next chapter.

CHAPTER 5

Being the alien in late-Elizabethan London plays

Jean Howard has noted that 'city comedy is an interesting successor to the history plays' of the 1590s, for it shifts the focus of national identity-building from its concentration on the monarch to a negotiation between communal imperatives. In her study of *Westward Ho*, Howard promotes the new genre's concentration on the subject's 'relationship to certain places, values, customs, and institutions that could . . . lead to new understandings of what constitutes Englishness'.[1] Such 'new understandings' would be in part characters – in addition to a monarch or everyman/everywoman figure – finding a certain individuality, autonomy, or independence from older communal ideas of identity, even as urban community and unity are simultaneously trumpeted. The first play I look at in this chapter, William Haughton's *Englishmen for My Money* (1598), does indeed follow the shift away from the monarch and into the valorization of English subjects in urban spaces. Thomas Dekker's *The Shoemaker's Holiday* (1599), which I discuss later, however, uses and adjusts elements from the earlier genres to show that the new 'city comedy' does not entail a clean break from the dramatic past. It enacts a surprising return to the history genre's central iconic delineation of the monarch as the touchstone of Englishness; in doing so it also reminds us of an urban history play like *Sir Thomas More*, in which city matters are in the last instance determined by the will of the king. This tether of the English city history to the monarch remains in place: one play that has received a significant amount of recent criticism because of a resurgent interest in matters of finance and citizen status in early modern representations is Thomas Heywood's *2 If You Know Not Me, You Know Nobody*, which looks back at the Elizabethan age from the perspective of the early seventeenth century. In the play, the modern self-made man Sir Thomas Gresham, founder of the London Exchange, remains invested in maintaining social hierarchy as a marker of true 'Englishness'. Gresham buys an inordinately expensive pearl only to grind it into his drink and quaff it down with a toast to Elizabeth; thus his 'wealth enables him to express his love of his monarch and his city. He has become rich to serve his queen, not to serve himself.'[2] Dekker's Simon Eyre similarly displays his new-found wealth, but diverts (enough of) it into communal service by instigating a holiday feast.

Just as important for a study of dramatic representations and development of ideas of Englishness is the fact that not only Haughton and Dekker's plays, but also the third play studied in this chapter, John Marston's *Jack Drum's Entertainment* (1600–1), are in significant ways new morality plays. The protagonist usurer, Pisaro, in *Englishmen for My Money* and the ubiquity of the moneylender through the Jacobean city comedies suggest a continuing, if at times innocuous, moral debate about the inevitability of corruption attending money. *The Shoemaker's Holiday* revives earlier dramatic tropes and concerns when, as Peter McCluskey notices, it reinvents the comic Dutchmen that we saw in *Wealth and Health* and *Like Will to Like*.[3] And Andrew Fleck points out the play's forward-looking investment in the nascent shift of sensibility that accepted credit, wealth, personal enrichment, and even Simon Eyre's fraudulence over earlier tract and dramatic moral objections to selfish monetary gain and deception.[4] Another adaptation of the moral play here is the inversion of *Wealth and Health*'s concern that English wealth has been drained abroad at the hands of aliens. *The Shoemaker's Holiday* instead shows the enriching of English citizens through alien presence; furthermore, it is precisely the importation of luxury goods so railed against by the moral tracts and Wilson's *The Three Ladies of London* that now *benefits* native welfare. Marston's play employs the new comedy of inter-generational sexual antagonism to bring back the dangerous alien that penetrates Englishness and to reinstate a definitive purpose of moral judgement.

But *why* the late 1590s shifts (in plays set in England) from history to comedy or hybrid comic forms, from 'national' to local urban study, and from the monarch to the subject as location of Englishness? I suggest that one important impetus for these moves was the presence of resident aliens in late-Elizabethan London and in particular the increasingly common English–alien interactions and constant (if unevenly expressed) antagonism between Londoners, domestic foreigners, and aliens. In 1596, Thomas Johnson asked rhetorically, '[w]hat countrie or nation in the world is there at this presente that nourisheth so manie Aliens from all parts of the world as England doth?'[5] In fact, both English and foreign merchants and travellers had noted for decades that London lagged behind other cosmopolitan port towns and trading centres. Johnson's perception of England's 'nourishing' of aliens (in many historical and dramatic minds to the wasting of English men and women), however, is important, for it suggests the topicality of the alien play in this decade. The three romantic comedies studied in this chapter take us deeper into the paradoxical 'second stage' of the alien trope as something invasive yet inherent in native identity with a combination of novelty and tradition. Robert Wilson's streets of London are 'mapped out', and the diminution of allegory brings the characters into closer view for the playgoers, for they are now mimetic representations of the troublesome aliens in London and the suburbs rather than allusive representations of moral conditions. The pathological and practical fears of the plays the between 1550s and 1580s are newly embodied and embedded in the material city to re-examine the alien as it gets into personal and public interstices, invades the marketplace, the bedroom, human orifices, language, economic currency, the court, the workshop, the household, and the country around London.

ENGLISHMEN FOR MY MONEY: THREE MORE
LADIES OF LONDON

It is only initially and briefly surprising that a comic mode of alien representation should emerge in the wake of the anti-alien unrest in the capital that I outlined in Chapter 3, for comedy is a familiar psychological cover for anxiety. It is a flexible mode, as we shall see, for making representations of identity equivocal – self-serving as well as self-scrutinizing; moreover, comic drama dealing with potent contemporary issues could perhaps escape the censorship problems attendant upon a play like *Sir Thomas More*. In Haughton's *Englishmen for My Money*, we find the Portuguese merchant and usurer, Pisaro, living comfortably in London. He is the widower of an English wife who attempts to secure matches in marriage for his three daughters with three foreign merchants: Delion the Frenchman, Alvaro the Italian, and Vandal the Dutchman. The women themselves do their best to elope with their true English loves – three men who are in debt to Pisaro and held financially captive through bonds on their property. The Englishmen triumph over the foreigners, and with a little help from their friends (through feats of disguise, practical joking, and feigned sickness) marry the daughters and win back their property. Pisaro, in a scene of capitulation that by this time has become de rigueur in 'prodigal child' plays, accepts defeat, and the marriages are celebrated with a feast at his house.

The 'Portingale' Pisaro, we suppose, learned his trade of usury from the Jews of Portugal; but the question of whether Pisaro is himself a Jew is a vexed one. The greatest Jewish contact with England in the sixteenth century was from the Portuguese-Jewish merchants and 'Marrano' escapees travelling between Portugal and the Low Countries, but no precise background is presented for Pisaro.[6] The emphasis in the play on the fact that Pisaro lives in Crutched Friars seems important, since it was the quarter of town where the Jews mostly resided in the late-sixteenth century.[7] Thomas Coryate further records meeting an English Jew in Constantinople: 'Master William Pearch . . . invited mee . . . to the house of a certaine English Jew, called Amis, borne in Crootched Friers in London, who hath two sisters more of his owne Jewish Religion . . . who were likewise borne in the same place.'[8] Pisaro, then, could be a Jew by the circumstantial evidence of geographical history. It should be noted, however, that Crutched Friars also housed a number of the Huguenot community and other non-Jewish immigrants. To be sure Pisaro is a mixed bag of characteristics: his 'snout, / [is] Able to shadow Paul's, it is so great' (1.2.15–16), and he suffers from gout.[9] Often read as indications of his Jewishness, in the drama these are features of the usurer more generally, in spite of the former's origination in physiological/racial observation.[10] The play seems to revel in its suggestiveness and equivocation, for it continues to touch on the religio-racial identity of Pisaro and his daughters: Delion threatens to eat up Pisaro's bacon (1.3.21), Pisaro swears 'by'r lady' (1.3.8; 4.1.299; 4.3.43; 5.1.89), and Marina (Pisaro's daughter) swears 'I'll be no nun' (1.1.103) when she considers the austerity of philosophy.[11] In addition, behavioural evidence comes into play. Pisaro's challenge to Walgrave, 'I am a fox with you? Well, Jack Sauce, / Beware, lest for a goose I prey on you' (4.1.147–8) recalls both Barabas' 'We Jews can fawn like spaniels when we please, / And when we grin, we bite; yet are our looks / As innocent and harmless as a lamb's' (*The Jew of Malta* 2.3.20–2), and Shylock's 'Thou call'st me dog before thou hadst a cause, / But since I am a dog, beware my fangs' (*Mer* 3.3.6–7). Pisaro echoes Barabas further in a sudden, vicious aside, where he appears to be blessing his daughter's betrothal to Harvey: 'God give you joy, / And bless you [*Aside*] not a day to live together' (5.1.130–1).

While the evidence for reading Pisaro as a Jew is strong, then, it could easily have been made definitive. It seems clear that Haughton deliberately makes him 'Jew-ish', a character with a 'Jewishness' within him, which causes him to practise the downfall of others through usury.

'Jewishness' in this sense is the term that the judge in Wilson's *The Three Ladies of London* uses to describe the Christian merchant Mercadorus, with his evasive and damnable behaviour (14.48–9). Anti-usury tracts – both intellectual and popular – had proliferated in England, and provide a rich context for this and the many other usury plays on the Elizabethan and Jacobean stage.[12] So by the time Philip Henslowe paid twenty shillings for the new book entitled 'a womon will have her wille' (the published subtitle to *Englishmen for My Money*), usury was old, bad news.[13] And if we are to approximate the contemporary opinion of possible playgoers, it is this concept of 'Jewish' behaviour coupled with the ever-more-common and ever-more-acceptable sin of usury that should be applied to Pisaro. While the fact of usury here might be an inevitable counterpart to the dramatic figure of a Jew-like and merchant character, we have, as Laura Stevenson notes, moved on from the role of usury as the driving force of depravation and degradation that it was in the morality plays. However, that does not mean we can dismiss usury as a blip on the protagonists' radars of love as they seek out their female targets; for all that the late-Elizabethan years and early-seventeenth century constitute 'a time when everyone from knights to scriveners was lending at interest', this very fact, while making usury run-of-the-mill as a topic, shows it to be an ongoing problem in cultural history.[14]

The vague crossover between 'Jew' and 'Jew-ish usurer' is a deliberate ploy that continues the dramatic tradition of using ethnicity, religious identity, and national identity loosely for political ends. We saw this in Chapter 3: the Dutch church libel elided Protestant refugees with Jews, and in the play of *Sir Thomas More*, apparently too-inciteful terms like 'stranger', 'Frenchman', and 'saucy alien' were replaced by Master of the Revels Edmund Tilney with 'Lombard'. This was a viable substitution because, as James Shapiro notes, 'After the expulsion of the Jews from England, the Lombards had assumed the role of moneylenders and, by extension, the reputation of extortionate usurers.'[15] Anti-alien tension can be eased through Jewish channels while the Jew is conversely made less specific, as another alien; the river can be made to run both ways, depending on the political current of the day. Such re-directing was useful for desensitizing (or inflaming) subject matter in the early and mid 1590s, when the tide of English–alien tension was running high. The moralities had also talked of the loss of England's wealth as a result of Continental foreigners and the Catholic troubles. If anything, Jews were generally thought of as bringing wealth *to* a nation, although they also had the general alien reputation of dealing with each other rather than with the natives of their adopted land. As we will see, *Englishmen for My Money* begins a process that *The Shoemaker's Holiday* advances whereby the wealth-draining problem of the moralities' Hance characters, and of Usury, Mercadorus, Gerontus, and Lucre in *The Three Ladies* turns into alien *support* for the commonwealth of England and the stability of a notion of Englishness.

By the late 1590s, we might read some calming in domestic and international affairs. The satirist can perhaps choose to make use of Continental foreign figures in a way that mocks the Englishman because those foreigners are members of 'beaten' nations, apparently no longer a threat to the cultural or ideological fabric of England. However, the Irish problem was getting worse rather than better, and the triple relationship with the Netherlands, France, and Spain remained tense as the queen aged. Through the 'crisis' of the 1590s, which involved terrible winters, bad harvests, overcrowding, and poverty in the capital, the drama had a romantic-patriotic moment, perhaps in part in reaction precisely to domestic difficulties.[16] By 1598 the main Armadas, including the unexpected third, had been defeated, and the anti-alien disturbances of mid-decade had quietened. Alvaro's report in *Englishmen for My Money* that bad weather scuppered the Spanish pirates' attempt to raid Pisaro's ships (1.3.244–9) may be a reference to ongoing privateering activity in the 1590s and probably would have been recognized as a joke about the failure of the Armadas in general.

The aliens, then, are usually read here by critics as part of a tame comedy, and presumably the English playgoers felt they could laugh at their own weaknesses because the English political and social infrastructure could withstand such shocks to the ego-system. 'Haughton's play marks a shift', writes A. J. Hoenselaars, because it uses this sense of patriotic confidence to represent characters that have moved on from 'fear and hatred' so that the 'inferior' aliens 'can be ridiculed or derided in a carefree, comic fashion'.[17] This is no doubt the play's 'sales pitch', for it is a funny play in spite of its dismissal for jingoism by politically sensitive critics. But such comedy is spurred both by the current situation in London and England and the climate for plays in the Henslowe syndicate – adventure, comedy, foreign affairs. At stake in all cases of competition – international, domestic, or personal; comic or tragic – is pride. And pride is what some drama can trumpet with impunity, even as in other drama and in the non-dramatic world pride of the English is catching up with them. Thomas Lodge and Robert Greene had presented the stage in 1590 with a dramatic warning against pride in their

A Looking Glass for London and England. For the late-Elizabethan audience, it is all comic to watch, but serious to contemplate. Where Haughton's play really marks a shift is in bringing the problem of national pride so comically into the local spaces of the contemporary city. *Englishmen for My Money* literally brings home the chink in the armour of pride, for the decline in the potency of the foreigners is a narrative inscribed on the palimpsest of the weakness and unguardedness of the English. Blinkered pride does not see corruption creeping up on it, such as the insuppressible activity of usury (and by association alien influence in general), which has put down roots and flowered in England. Almost three decades after the Statute against Usury, and almost two decades after the semi-native character Usury of *The Three Ladies of London*, the practice has become established and 'Englished'. Lending at interest among the gentle class is widespread, and the Jacobean city comedies of monetary intrigue will almost exclusively concentrate on English rather than foreign usury. For all its mundane presentation, usury lies behind the relationships of the characters in *Englishmen for My Money* as the play begins. Moneylending and trading, moreover, thrive or wane according to the social status and native language of the practitioners. Thus English language and Englishness are privileged media in financial, mercantile, and – for the romantic comedy of prodigal play – sexual intercourse. The linguistic trope as a synecdoche for Englishness will explicate the spaces of London as *English* spaces and reveal the gendered nature of the battle between men to penetrate and possess those physical and symbolic holes in the urban and human fabric.

The urgency of the Englishmen's quest for Pisaro's daughters is born of three dams: romantic love is one, we assume (although not all commentators will agree); reclaiming their lands pawned to Pisaro is another; and Anglicizing the half-foreign women is the third. In the scheme of things (social, economic, and political) the latter two have wider-reaching importance. The combination of the father's usury (the 'Jewishness') and the daughters' mixed birth (the foreignness) must be conquered for the play to remain in the realm of comedy. The scenes involving comic foreigners reveal national political issues on the one hand and earnest combat with the serious danger of usury on the other. Haughton is clearly representing a London more afraid of incorporating the alien than is the population of Dekker's later play. Part of the reason for this is gendered. *The Shoemaker's Holiday* is a play ruled by men, from journeyman to mayor to king. In contrast, and although the first edition of Haughton's play calls it *Englishmen for My Money* in 1616, Henslowe for one thought the play's thesis was 'A Woman Will Have Her Will'; that is the title he put in the diary when it was written eighteen years earlier, and it is the title finally used on the 1631 (Q3) edition title-page.[18] Phrases that evoke the women's 'will' echo throughout the play, appearing more than ten times, whereas the phrase 'Englishmen for my money' is never uttered; Frisco only once uses the related saying 'for my money' at all, and that is in reference to the Frenchman. What we have here, then, are three more ladies of London, upon whom the men of London are focused and the economic and moral parameters of the city are traced. The women become the final focus of familiar tropes of language, sexuality, and topography that build up throughout the play.[19] Language and sexuality hardly separate here, and we should highlight some of the workings of these issues before returning to the women specifically.

Proper 'English' (language, behaviour, expectation) is the central concept of *Englishmen for My Money*, and it is a concept worried, manipulated, and proved through attacks on English 'purity'. Hoenselaars comments on the efforts of two English characters to imitate foreigners:

One interesting aspect of Anthony's case is that his lack of French is the crucial flaw in his disguise. Frisco, too, only manages with an immense effort to produce some broken Dutch. To a modern reader, both characters' defective foreign-language skills provide an ironic counterpoint to the foreign merchants' ultimately disastrous inability to speak proper English. The play itself does not elaborate or comment on this irony. Haughton unwittingly adopts a double standard, providing the play with that flaw by which patriotism thrives – namely, a blindness to one's own national weakness.[20]

This needs comment because it does not seem right to say that Haughton 'unwittingly adopts a double standard'. Patriotism in this play comes from a recognition of the importance of the native tongue, and English victory in war has made the English language a powerful tool of social, sexual, and hierarchical politics. The Englishmen's inability to speak foreign languages is the play's proof of such skills' lack of worth.[21] If England is the ideological conqueror, then English prevails. The play's characters do dismiss foreign language easily and through ignorance, but we should not confuse the 'unwitting' behaviour of the play's narrow-sighted characters with the level of awareness of the author himself.

When Frisco dismisses French as the pig's language that goes 'awee, awee' (1.1.170), he makes clear the view that the foreign language is something that could not be incorporated into the higher order of 'humane' Englishness, but can only be a debasing, corrupting influence. Even without the animalizing trope, foreign language destroys English, as we see when Pisaro's servant Frisco gives Heigham, one of the English suitors, his summation of the Frenchman:

> I am seeking a needle in a bottle of hay, a monster in the likeness of a man. One that instead of good morrow, asketh what porridge you have to dinner, *parley vous signiour*? One that never washes his fingers, but licks them clean with kisses, a clipper of the King's English, and to conclude, an eternal enemy to all good language. (1.2.76–81)

As a 'monster', the Frenchman is deformed, like *The Tide Tarrieth*'s Christianity and like *The Three Ladies*' Lady Love as Lust. As 'a clipper of the King's English', an alien (according to Frisco) is a deformed debaser of the realm's ubiquitous currency, the English language – it is the one binding common denominator of Englishness and prone to forgeries. And much of the play's action depends on the vulnerability and finally the survival of the English language against fraudulent non-English assaults. This problem revisits the growing concern with fraud, which Teresa Nugent noticed in *The Three Lords* at the beginning of the decade and *Measure for Measure* at the beginning of the Jacobean era;[22] it is a nice coincidence that Fraud in *The Three Lords* reveals that he is half-French. But this fear of fraudulence and debasement is also a continuation of the myth of purity in language and therefore national identity that I discussed in Chapter 1, with John Florio's notion of English as a 'language confused', and expanded in Chapter 4, with the defence of English against Welsh. Such perpetuation of the national 'purity' myth is of course deeply ironic in a play about the 'Englishing' of half-foreign women.

The failure of Vandal, Delion, and Alvaro's 'forgeries' of language as they stand below the sisters' window and impersonate the Englishmen to woo the women is a sign of the weakness of foreign linguistic currency. 'Ah, gentlemen', Frisco pleads, 'do not suffer a litter of languages to spring up amongst us' (1.2.104–5).[23] Just as coin currency is bred illegally by 'cutting' or 'biting' usury (as the period's terminology would have it), so the linguistic currency is debased with breeding of aliens in England. Pisaro's daughters emphasize the importance of preserving their Englishness through breeding and language: 'Though I am Portingale by the father's side ... I have so much English by the mother', says Mathea, 'That no base, slavering French shall make me stoop' (4.1.42, 45–6).[24] Edmund Campos suggests a difference between Haughton's play and the other two 1590s 'Jew plays', *The Jew of Malta* and *The Merchant of Venice*, in so far as the eminently convertible 'Jewish' daughters in *Englishmen* do not need to move away from paternal religion or 'race', but instead from the Portuguese national identity.[25] Such a distinction is hard to make in the drama, however. This play deliberately obfuscates 'Jewish' identity, somaticizes language, and continues the Tudor coding of money as the circulating life-blood of the body of the commonwealth (see the discussion of *Wealth and Health* in Chapter 2). Mathea's use of 'French' in the last quotation, for example, conflates the man and the language – bodily alien force is felt through the infiltration of the French language that could 'litter' a barbarous, mongrel version of English if not looked to. Frisco exclaims, moreover: 'O, the generation of languages that our house will bring forth! Why, every bed will have a proper speech to himself and have the founder's name written upon it in faire capital letters, "HERE LAY –", and so forth' (4.3.98–102). Language is generated by 'racial' procreation and in turn determines 'racial' categories. The 'Here lay' on the bedstead represents a gravestone with the 'founder's name' for the sexual 'death' of the alien. The alien's non-English linguistic prodigy is not Dutch, not French, and not Italian, but a 'proper speech', a monster in the likeness of a language, unique to that bed's combination of national identities. Frisco's prophecy must be avoided, then, for its fulfilment would increase the foreignness of the Pisaro household, intimating the simultaneous death of Englishness. Contemporary writers on the hybridized English language, however, would notice that such new speech is in fact 'proper' to English, even as the commercial, comic play resists access to that reading.

As much as the romantic comedy purports to be about connecting the lovers, these women hold a threefold store of wealth for English identity, and here again the individual experience that requires engagement with and confusion of the alien leads to the public, communal effect that promotes an ongoing sense of Englishness. The return of the Englishmen's land depends on marrying the daughters; reproduction with them determines whether they perpetuate the Englishness of their mother or the foreignness of their father; and their ability to resist penetration by the foreign incomers avoids the infecting of the realm's currency – overtly linguistic, but also economic and cultural currency. The daughters are determined to incorporate themselves into the English body politic. They can perform the apparent sin of prodigality and anti-patriarchy, disobeying their father, because they are rejecting (or rather working *through and beyond*) the alien. In the same way that *The Merchant of Venice*'s ostensibly Venetian/Christian point of view can forgive Jessica her escape from and rejection of Shylock, so we are encouraged to forgive the daughters for their escape from and rejection of Pisaro from the English/ Christian (anti-usury, anti-Jewish) point of view. The women's hybrid national identity brings with it the understanding of alien status as they ensure the restoration of English land and money to the Englishmen and the accumulation of foreign money in the form of dowries and income that Pisaro has got through foreign trade and transactions. Thus they are the embodiment of the alien within Englishness, and their determination is to be (re)producers of Englishness.

Diane Cady has argued that 'The play configures women as the vulnerable orifice in the body politic through which diseased language enters the nation', and she aligns foreign language with femininity as a continual threat to the male body politic of England.[26] It is true that the impotence and ineffectualness of the foreigners is enhanced by their overbearing foreign language, but the women's mother as 'vulnerable orifice' apparently bred three very English daughters, and these three women seem to act more as enclosures processing the alien to *protect* male Englishness and English language than as any vulnerable space. They are assumed to be the breach in the national wall by their own father, and in a way he is right. They *are* the proper focus for an alien attack. However, that attack will be contained within a fuller understanding of the privileging of Englishness. These three ladies of London have infiltrated the troubled male English world, which is impoverished through 'English'/'Christian' prodigality. Their potential danger as breaches for the entry of the alien, however, proves to be another necessary somatic penetration to relieve the pressure of the alien threat – in this case Pisaro's significant presence and power in London – and inoculate the English against the somewhat less worrying foreign bodies of Alvaro, Delion, and Vandal. The women offer themselves up for English impregnation, and this process, already begun before the play ends, confirms the circulations of blood, money, and national bodies that the residency of the alien in England and within (male) Englishness catalyses and sustains. Such protectors of the realm are in stark contrast to Brabant Senior's wife in John Marston's harsh romantic comedy *Jack Drum's Entertainment*, whose story fits Cady's thesis. The Englishman with a suggestively Lowlandish name, Brabant Senior, decides to play a joke by presenting his wife to the Frenchman, John fo de King, as a courtesan. Brabant bets on his wife's fidelity to him, but fo de King manages to seduce her. John fo de King is bald from venereal ('French') disease, and makes the joke of teaching his prospective wenches French; in other words he will talk to them in French and give them the clap. At the end of *Jack Drum's Entertainment*, fo de King triumphantly returns, post-coitus, among the Englishmen and offers to teach Brabant Senior French 'to t'end of the vorlde' (I3) for his help to a wench. This is a double confirmation of infection: Brabant will now get the French disease if he sleeps with his own wife and he has been made a non-English bawd. The name, Brabant, however, as the geographical region running across modern Belgium and the southern Netherlands, already suggests a contiguity to French identity and thus the lurking alien in Englishness.

London comedies are of course specifically interested in talking about the capital city *as* England and Londoners *as* English, thus the protection of the realm is brought into focus as the protection and ownership of the gendered and nationally marked city of London. The titles of scholarly studies of London comedy, such as *The City Staged* and *Theater of a City*, highlight the fact that these plays work symbiotically with the city itself, putting the theatre into the urban landscape and drawing London's topographical features into the theatrical world.[27] In *Englishmen for My Money*, the city structure is a catacomb-like 'open prison' or rat-run for aliens.[28] Almost as a response to the earlier drama's ongoing complaints about the 'alienation' of London through overcrowding and 'eating out' of Londoners by the French and Dutch 'like Jews', Haughton has the English take charge of the city and keep the aliens unsettled and uncertain of their place. For example, when the Frenchman, Delion, asks for directions to Crutched Friars where he hopes to find his English love, Heigham gives the deceptive reply, 'Marry, this is Fenchurch Street, and the best way to Crutched Friars is to follow your nose' (3.2.95–6). Delion is already in Crutched Friars, as he suspects, and 'following his nose' would take him through the poor Jewry to Aldgate. In fact, even if he were truly in Fenchurch Street the stranger would still find himself leaving the city by Aldgate.

The wily words to the Frenchman may seem like a simple piece of fun, but they contain two greater resonances. First, there seems to be a joke on the meaning that one's nose can be followed to Crutched Friars, because the area smells of aliens, Jews, and usurers. In Thomas Nashe's *The Unfortunate Traveller* Zadoch the Jew reveals the potency of the Jew's smell as he conspires with his accomplice to commit murder: 'Ile come and deliver her a supplication, and breathe upon her. I knowe my breath stinkes so alredie, that it is within halfe a degree of poison.'[29] Frisco also makes the most of using his nose to find the way to Crutched Friars on a dark night (3.3.40–5), and at the very beginning of the play we are warned of the potency of Pisaro's pots of stew, which give off a 'precious Vapour! – let but a wench come near them with a painted face, and you should see the paint drop and curdle her cheeks, like a piece of dry Essex cheese toasted at the fire' (1.1.158–60). Second, the turning out of the city, the dramatic attempt at expulsion and expurgation is a cultural response to 'otherness' in general that we saw in the interludes, and that concerns these later playwrights (of *Sir Thomas More* and *Jack Drum's Entertainment*, for instance) who continue to represent resistance to the inevitable incorporation of the alien. Below, I discuss the level of success and the meaning of these actions in the context of alien confusion in Dekker and Marston's plays.

Englishmen for My Money's interest in London topography allows for further enclosure of the alien. If London is now used as an alien prison, the theatre structure itself can emphasize the comical punishment meted out to the foreigners. In a night-time escapade, the mischievous Frisco loses the Dutchman, Vandal, in the dark streets of London and slips away with the foreigner's cloak. Frisco warns Vandal at one point, 'Take heed, sir, here's a post' (3.1.2–3), opening the way for simple rough-and-tumble physical comedy with characters running into stage-posts. Andrew Gurr has noticed that the identification by Frisco of the stage-posts as maypoles (3.3.50–1) implies

that they were set in enough open space to allow dancing around them. But there might also be a joke built into the visuals in this play, if the characters blundering blindly through the London streets are seen coming dangerously close to the edge of the stage when they encounter the posts.[30]

Making the theatre building the structure *of* London as well as simply *in* London constitutes part of the 'shift' I talked about in this play, bringing the action and its dangers into literally closer proximity to the spectators than did the dramatic histories of *Thomas More*, *Henry IV*, or *Henry V*. The comic alien-bashing continues as we hear from the Italian, Alvaro, 'I hit my hed by de way – dare may be de voer spouts' between Leadenhall and Crutched Friars (3.2.60–1),[31] and Vandal complains 'Ik go and hit my nose op dit post, and ik go and hit my nose op d'andere post' (3.4.1–2) (probably wandering back and forth hitting each of the stage-posts).

As stage-posts indicate the largely invisible border between stage space and audience space, so they represent ideological limits and the edges of the Englishmen's control. They are used as punishing 'weapons' by the English as they give the aliens the runaround, knocking it home to them that they are *not* at home. John Orrell has reminded us that the history of the pillars and posts in the theatre includes their confused connection to the columns that represented enslaved, dismembered, and encumbered foreign bodies in the 'caryatids and atlantes of ancient buildings'. The architectural Term (or column) was linked to these carved depictions of defeated enemies, set up to public display in literal support of the conquerors' edifices of power.[32] It is a sound mechanism adopted by Haughton, therefore, to have the Englishmen inflict pain on, and embarrass, the aliens through the use of this feature of the structure of the public theatre. If this is to read too far into architectural history and strain the possible meanings of the play, we can simply stay with the idea of the posts as the primary support for the English stage against aliens; we might also remind ourselves that a stage-post may well have been used when Simplicity tried (and failed) to tie up and burn foreign Fraud at the end of Wilson's *The Three Lords and Three Ladies of London* (see Chapter 3, pp. 74–5).

It is important for the punishment of the aliens to remain comic, for it is aligned with the aliens' own depiction as less than effective. Dekker will follow Haughton who follows Wilson in raising stereotypical views of national character within a context that allows the stereotypes' debunking. Haughton, for instance, has his English suitor, Harvey, feign fatal sickness in a ruse to win the hand of Marina. Harvey's Italian counterpart in the wooing competition assures Pisaro that 'If he will no die' from the sickness, 'I sal give him sush a drinck, sush a potion sal mak him give de *bonos noches* to all de world' (5.1.98–100). Alleged Italian skill at poisoning was well known. Marlowe's assassin Lightborne in *Edward II* learned his murderous cunning in Naples, and if we return again to that great text of prejudicial comic horror, *The Unfortunate Traveller*, we find that 'If thou dost but lend half a looke to a *Romans* or *Italians* wife, thy porredge shalbe prepared for thee, and cost thee nothing but thy lyfe.'[33] But when Harvey does not die, Alvaro denies any knowledge in the art of poisoning before the devastated Pisaro. Throughout this play viewpoints are shifted subtly; the prejudices of the Englishman against aliens are also the prejudices of one stranger against another of a different nationality. The English faction remains a team, whereas the foreign one fractures. Such English 'group identity' implies stable self-understanding, but the play makes sure to have the English men improvise their way uncertainly toward incorporation of the half-alien women.

Punishment of 'real' aliens bleeds over into punishment of 'fake' aliens, for there seems to be less and less difference between a 'real' foreign character and one national character disguised as another. This is a basic theatrical joke, of course, since all stage foreigners are 'fake' and in costumed disguise. But within the fiction of the play, mistaken national identity has ideological as well as practical repercussions. When Pisaro threatens to commit the slippery English schoolmaster, Anthony, to Bridewell for deceiving him in the process of marrying off his three daughters, he thinks the disguised Anthony is a Frenchman and says that he will make Anthony 'sing at Bridewell for this trick' (5.1.218).[34] As well as being a prison and a workhouse for the idle poor, Bridewell was a place for torture. Torture is designed to produce sound, to make the victim 'utter' (the most commonly used word in relation to torture at Bridewell in the *Acts of the Privy Council*); that extracted utterance is made in the victim's own language and reveals his own identity and fate. Bridewell was also used for something else, less notoriously, and that was holding foreign prisoners. Such a place is precisely the enclosure to 'out' someone like Anthony, to make him utter the truth in his own language. Anthony's own language, ironically, is English, and such a confession should expose the weakness of the Englishman who behaves in a non-English manner. Anthony's alien behaviour in both situations, therefore (in or out of prison) would support a revelation and continuity of Englishness as confused with the alien. He either helps his friends to English-perpetuating marriages, or he reveals himself as an English agent using foreignness to gain success.

THE SHOEMAKER'S HOLIDAY: CRAFTY ENGLISHMEN CRAFTING THE ALIEN

Alien confusion makes *The Shoemaker's Holiday* work. Acts of estrangement enable refamiliarization as characters that should remain in the country go abroad, those who should leave remain, and the returns and re-meetings after these excursions or sojourns enable confirmations of English stability through recognition of the alien. An Englishman plays a Dutchman; Simon Eyre moves out of his trade to bring himself and his wife to great estate; characters dress outlandishly, taking on foreign fashion and mis-fitting their apparel; and alien–native relations withdraw characters from familiar circles of society through their disguises of shape (bodily change through injury), of language (Lacy speaking Dutch), and of apparel (class mobility and/or transgression).

Dekker's fantasy version of London strangely sets itself in the past (Eyre was Lord Mayor of London in 1445, making the unnamed king

Henry VI), yet remains dependent on social systems of the present. The dynamism of an invented (nostalgic) past feeding the vigorously indi- viduated subjects of the present attempts to grab the best of both those worlds. The conflated historical moment inexorably pushes (through some domestic and professional conflict) toward the celebration, holiday, and apparent class resolution that charms many commentators. This aura of charm focuses on the boisterous Eyre, often easily (if arguably) com- pared with another class-crossing hero-rogue, Falstaff. Indeed, the play runs on these tracks, but I also want to suggest that it contains a number of equivocal sections that – especially in performance – question the moral values lying behind London, guild, and family life; moreover, these sections work through the alien to find answers. Dekker incorporates the alien powerfully, even though there are no major alien characters in the *The Shoemaker's Holiday*, the minor Dutch skipper being the only stranger. Andrew Fleck usefully insists that the infusion of the play with alien elements is not so much to talk about the alien but to provide 'a distorted mirror' in which to see 'the values, the hopes, and the fears of early modern English audiences'; he goes on to say, 'Dekker shapes the foreign matter of his London to create English unity and identity.' Both of Fleck's metaphors seem appropriate for the present study, for to look at the English self as in 'a distorted mirror' is to find what is alien within, to see the self *strangely*. But for a playwright to convey that alien content into Englishness takes some artistic 'shap[ing]'.[35]

The Shoemaker's Holiday seems to suggest that, despite contemporary socio-political unrest, the fantasy of communal, if not national unity is still available to the playgoers. But a conservative social hierarchy is still reinforced (as in Dekker's later, daring play, *The Roaring Girl*).[36] Ronda Arab's sense that the play 'subtly disrupts' 'a dominant discourse of civic and national authority' does not fully account for Eyre's rise *in service of* the city or the king's upper hand in the closing scenes.[37] Both these elements are something of a throwback to earlier dramatic modes: Eyre's 'property' in the play entails his traditional membership in civic com- munities as well denoting his personal possessions, and the centrality of the monarch as touchstone of Englishness is a presumption of the history genre.[38] The king gives permission for Eyre's boisterous behaviour, and the king controls the futures of the London and Lincoln families and the nation. Thus, if we see this play as a general celebration of Englishness, we should keep in mind its ending: the nation is rhetorically and prac- tically unified around feasting and the beautiful labour of the gentle craft, but it *needs* unity because of a daunting prospect concerning aliens: the king reminds Eyre and the shoemakers, 'When all our sports and banquetings are done, / Wars must right wrongs which Frenchmen have begun' (21.193–4).[39] This 'right[ing]' will not happen, of course, because, as *Henry V*'s Chorus reminds us, Henry VI's councillors 'made his England bleed' (*HV* Epi., line 12).

PUTTING ON EYRES

The monarch-led ending does other work, too. Its (masculine) 'writing' of events makes necessity the mother of invention. Lacy must be drawn back into the noble force of the king's fighting men and is therefore forgiven his desertion and awarded his bride by a king who over-rules the increasingly comic bitter fathers. Eyre's questionable route to wealth and status is absorbed into the need for a stable capital city that avoids the inter-class tensions we have seen throughout the urban texts studied in this book. In the roles of *The Shoemaker's Holiday*'s Eyre and Lacy/Hans, and the second tetralogy's Prince Hal, deceit and prodigality enable the socio-political and economic rise of Englishness (the securing of the commonwealth), and the alien nature of this deceit and prodigality is exposed to be absorbed by Englishness. With such crafty shaping of events, even the most heinous crime, treason, is mitigated by national need: 'I am a handicrafts man, yet my heart is without craft' (21.10–11), pleads Lacy to the king in defending himself after his military desertion. Of course, his heart *is* with craft, but such cunning is the paradoxical alien process (akin to Hal's tavern behaviour) that ensures the triumph of Englishness. Eyre's equivocal 'alien' behaviour also gets recast in the mould of Englishness. His role as a factor, an agent, a middleman for the Dutch skipper would have troubled a Protestant reformed audience whose parents (or who themselves) had been brought up on moralities that damned such a profession of making money from nothing, and generally assigned such activity to aliens and vice figures.[40] There is little doubt that Eyre's alderman's outfit is a disguise, and that when he dons his cloak to transact business with the Dutch skipper he is involved in a bit of intrigue. Dekker thereby deliberately puts us on the edge between on the one hand the strong moral question of impersonation as blasphemy, contradicting God-given identity, and on the other the cunning and commendable initiative of the Englishman using the alien to improve his and his community's status.

Simon Eyre understands and uses the importance of apparel in his rapidly shifting, overlapping stage-world of late-medieval estate boundedness and late-Elizabethan 'class' opportunity. When the shoe-maker becomes sheriff and then mayor, both he and his wife Margery drool over the new sartorial possibilities: 'Silk and satin, you mad Philistines! Silk and satin!' (7.108), Eyre shouts,[41] and Margery asks 'How shall I look in a hood, I wonder?' (10.36–8). Very soon afterwards, as sheriff, Eyre brings her the hood: 'See here, my Maggy. A chain, a gold chain for Simon Eyre. I shall make thee a lady. Here's a French hood for thee – on with it, on with it! Dress thy brows with this flap of a shoulder of mutton to make thee look lovely' (10.139–42).[42] Eyre reminds Margery that he brought her from the gutter to a decent living, and now he shall raise her further to a lady. The status is defined first by a 'French' fashion, and a few lines later Eyre orders her, 'on with your trinkets'. The latter are presumably the foreign baubles that traders like Mercadorus in Wilson's *The Three Ladies* bring into England. In Dekker's time, they were still deemed destructive, but Dekker does some 'shaping' so that now they simply adorn and serve an Englishness depicted as 'owning' the alien.

With the dressing-up of Simon Eyre the shoemaker as sheriff and then mayor, a change of status unequivocally follows upon the change of clothing. Or rather, endowment of status upon Eyre in decree (a text, spoken or written) allows or demands his change in apparel, which in turn effects (puts into practice, into reality) that change of status in the public eye. City government ennobles commoners, and men may take on ill-fitting outward appearance. In fact, as Robert Tittler argues, it is essential that they do so in the way that Eyre demonstrates, convincing themselves and others of the legitimacy of their illusion of power.[43] The lack of a significant difference between legitimate apparel of status necessary to carry out one's civic role on the one hand and inappropriate overdressing or disguise that gets a private job done on the other hand further encourages the playgoer to excuse Eyre's deceptive use of the Alderman's outfit.[44] Acting roles in disguise in *Englishmen for My Money* delineated the constructedness of alien national identity within the play world and the imagined incorporation of those roles into the larger performance of Englishness. In the romantic comedies, or 'prodigal plays', the development of Englishness is in the service of a competition for women and money, which is designed to demonstrate English superiority in building and confirming identity and wealth. English actors can undermine alien intervention because the strangeness of the character is only acted on terms laid down within an English theatre. 'Eyre's sumptuary pretence is also testimony to the entrepreneurial "skill" of acting, in which costly properties function not only as signs of social status, but also as collateral for its acquisition.'[45] The skill of acting that Eyre shows is an ability to step out of the self and recreate one's identity. Such skill requires appropriate *props* – at once properties of the self, owned, native and acquired, brought in, alienated from former owners or craftspersons. These props in turn act as principal investment, prompting the interest in playing out Englishness. The moral problem of Eyre's deception is then read as an alien importation, confused with the Englishman for the greater good of himself, his city, and his country.

WORKING WITH YOUR HANS

Julia Gasper reads *The Shoemaker's Holiday* as Dekker's militantly Protestant pedagogy, which casts Hans primarily as a religious 'brother'; thus 'The hospitality shown by Simon Eyre's household towards the Dutchman is handsomely rewarded.'[46] Such hospitality, she writes, is a 'specifically Protestant' act.[47] I argued in Chapters 2 and 3 that such an act is also, therefore, from the Anglo-centric point of view, a specifically *English* act. To make this English act of international relations, however, is to acknowledge the *brotherhood*, the *kinship*, not just of religion, but of the alien with the native. We saw Hospitality murdered in Wilson's *The Three Ladies*, illustrating the destruction by aliens of private hospitality – where the English exclusively take care of each other. The seriousness of the old moral code's exclusivity is avoided by Dekker, as instead of parading the *problems* of the alien, as every other writer has done, Dekker suppresses the spectre of the alien (of moral questionability in English characters) before they are manifested. Thus, in addition to the Dutchman *not* really being a Dutchman, Lacy/Hans is employed and accommodated immediately as a *useful* immigrant member of the commonwealth. In spite of entering with a 'drinking song', by which he is recognized as 'Dutch', Lacy/Hans is not directly and overtly a drunkard or a realm-drainer like the earlier Dutch characters of the moralities; instead, he is involved in the short term in making English products and in the long term in making *Englishness* a product of that work.

Gasper emphasizes that two Deloney stories provided Dekker with 'Haunce' a Dutchman and the tale of Saints Crispin and Crispianus taking shelter from religious persecution. 'By combining them', she writes, 'Dekker reminds his audience that the Dutch immigrants in contemporary London are also to be seen as refugees from religious persecution'.[48] Joseph Ward concurs, writing that 'even in the highly competitive economic environment of the late 16th century there was also sympathy among the non-elite for their plight as religious refugees'.[49] I would add that genre is important, however, and there is no avoiding the dramatic lineage of the dangerous 'Hances' of *Wealth and Health* and *Like Will to Like*. Any personal goodness in such a character does not make up entirely for the detrimental public effect of that character's actions, and the difference between the two has to be accounted for if the character is English. For comparison, we might recall the 'good' usurer Gerontus in Wilson's *The Three Ladies*. Just as Gerontus' usury – for all his personal honesty – enables Mercadorus' trade of baubles into England, so Lacy/Hans is the cipher for the importation of unnecessary 'civet, almonds, cambric, end alle dingen' (7.2–3), which enrich Eyre. As I have argued in expanding Fleck's observations, Dekker then has to 'shape' this material by having the foreign goods highlight Margery's social improvement and by having Eyre's celebratory feast paid for from the foreign gains in order to 'create English unity and identity'.

Dekker seems to be having fun by not permitting the audience a settled view on the fake alien, even as the play's nominal medieval historical setting tempers the inflammatory contemporary question of the legit-imacy of alien residents who were not religious refugees. Lacy's Dutch song prompts Firk's response that 'He's some uplandish workman; hire him, good master, that I may learn some gibble-gabble' (4.47–9). Although the word 'uplandish' is glossed by Russell Fraser and Norman Rabkin as 'provincial' ('foreign' in the early modern sense), the word also means 'outlandish' or alien (*OED* 'uplandish', entry 4);[50] as Anthony Parr's edition notes, the word's other sense of referring to highland dis-tricts of a country may be Firk's ironic joke, since he thinks he knows that the journeyman comes from the *low* countries of the Netherlands (4.47 n.). Firk's amusing hospitality is also patronizing and effacing, as he turns 'Hans' into a turkey who can only 'gibble-gabble', and alienates him as 'uplandish' from both the southern city of London and the Lowlands. As pro-alien representation, the facts that 'Hans' is the Englishman Lacy and that Firk the clown is the primary mocker of the 'Dutchman' perhaps deliberately undermine the expression of stereotypes in the play.[51] However much 'Hans' is displaced and ridiculed, he is, first, a shoemaker and is incorporated into Eyre's shop (initially by the workers, not the master) for that reason – and he is given hospitality as a fellow Protestant. Against those readings lies the possibility that the very falseness of the alien identity 'threatens to undermine [the] unpreced-ented and idealised vision' of an Anglo-Dutch workshop.[52] Moreover, a class statement might be articulated here to suggest that the lowly Firk is naive in his (humorously biased) acceptance of the alien while the world-savvy Eyre, with whom the audience might want to identify, expresses his doubts. The whole play is constantly involved in a multiple process of excusing, excoriating, refashioning, and manipulating the alien elements of London life to understand them *as* the life of London and Englishness, and class is the clearest context that the play uses to do this work.

In the character of Lacy/Hans, national identity and class identity are never severed. Late in the play, for example, each phase of Roger Oatley's tirade of anti-alien abuse against 'Hans' is brought back to a comment on native class. Gerald Porter, like most commentators, privileges the class references:

Dekker makes it clear that the rhetoric of the master shoemaker, Simon Eyre, about his 'gentleman shoemakers' – that 'none but the livery of my company shall in their satin hoods wait upon the trencher of my sovereign' ... – is illusory. The Lord Mayor of London's comment about 'a foul drunken lubber, a swill-belly, A shoemaker' in the same play ... is a cool reminder of their actual place within that system.[53]

Now, Mayor Oatley is not calling Lacy a 'drunken' 'swill-belly' because he is a shoemaker, but because Oatley thinks Lacy is a Dutchman. At 16.42–5, Oatley lets loose: 'A Fleming butter-box, a shoemaker! / ... / ... Scorned she young Hammon / To love a honnikin, a needy knave?' Again, there are two separate prejudices in each instant of abuse, the former against national origin and the latter afterthought against the trade – or rather, national difference is being encoded in terms of class difference. Oatley privileges his bias against the supposed Dutchman, proverbially fat, a 'honnikin' (a nonsense, Dutch-sounding diminutive of contempt), and 'a foul drunken lubber, swill-belly'. Oatley's combined attack on the alien and professional identities of Lacy/Hans confirms the fusion of the alien with his English trade. There is no separating the alien presence in the English Christian body politic and therefore in those who represent Englishness at different social levels.

To have the alien specifically within the workshop of the shoemakers and to have that alien presence promote the master to a celebration on St Hugh's day further embeds the alien in the confirmation of an Englishness that comprehends itself primarily through demonstrations of class. For all the critical concentration on 'bourgeois' economic issues, money-making is in the end an enabler of issues of national identity. It leads to the final kingly celebration with its layered confirmation of a confident late-medieval 'national identity' in opposition to Frenchness; and it supports the Eyre–Lacy/Hans relationship, read easily as 'hospitality' or 'brotherhood' that asserts a late-sixteenth-century Protestant political-religious power over Catholicism. L. D. Timms notes that Eyre's renaming of Shrove Tuesday as 'St Hugh's Holiday' would have reminded an Elizabethan audience of the coincidence of St Hugh's Day (17 November) with the Accession day of Elizabeth, on which day 'The traditions of the Catholic Saint's Day were absorbed and transformed into a celebration of national achievement and Protestant militancy.'[54] Thus Lacy/Hans' role is as an enabler, embodying the alien confusion that builds Englishness – albeit anachronistically building a modern Protestant individualized figure in happy but not entirely settled subjection to a medieval, communally bound London. Lacy/Hans' role in synthesizing an English inter-class community is not limited to the workshop, of course, but involves his relationship with Rose, which indicates an interclass appreciation and respect at odds with the bitter and underhanded debate between Oatley and Lincoln, or the resentment against the nobility in the Dutch church libel. That Oatley-Lincoln debate, incidentally, is yet another example of Dekker reprising a questionable moral trope of earlier drama and historiography only to pit it against a 'goodness' that overpowers it: the old debate (acted out extensively in Wilson's *The Three Lords*) between the new London as powerful, modern capital city and Lincoln as old, 'foreign', colonized England's Roman capital is refigured in *The Shoemaker's Holiday* as a personal battle between the city mayor Oatley and the foreigner Lincoln (Lacy senior). Diminishing the fracturing of national debate into the bickering of two individuals from the older generation allows the prodigal, Christian, clever, class-joining, alien-enriching Lacy/Hans (and therefore Eyre) to represent the newly upwardly mobile and healthy urban identity of Englishness to succeed in spite of the moral questions that permeate the play.

The name 'Hans' in the plays would have had another major significance, since (as in *Wealth and Health*) it would have reminded the audience of Hanseatic merchants (Merchants of the Intercourse), a coalition of traders from northern German towns formed in the fourteenth century. These stranger merchants operated in several major ports, including London, until the sixteenth century. They were exempted from stranger duties (which were traditionally higher than for English citizens) and drew frequent complaints from English traders for their allegedly questionable dealings. There had apparently been a number of cases such as the one involving one Benedict Spinola, end-enized in 1559: while acting as an agent for an alien trader, he paid only the privileged resident fees to export customs, but took higher strangers' fees from his client, one John Justiniano, and pocketed the difference.[55] We are reminded of Dekker's presentation of a questionable deal in *The Shoemaker's Holiday*, and it would seem likely that the name 'Hans/Hance/Hanse' as a German–Dutch conflation hints at these merchants on the edge between Englishness and alien identity.

Once again, Dekker works into his play a counterbalance to this unwelcome allusion. Because Dekker's character is 'Hans'-eatic, he can be the agent who straddles the English–alien divide and enables the deal between Eyre and the Dutch skipper. Lacy's 'Hans' saves the Dutch skipper additional subsidies as well as providing Eyre with more alien material means to native self-improvement. Subsequently, the inverse becomes true: because he manages to broker the deal, Lacy is 'a Hans'. In the older plays this would unequivocally mean something repellent; Dekker blends the residue of this dramatic heritage with a figure who is more simply a *mensch*, a good, useful fellow. This may be the reason that Eyre continues to refer to Lacy as 'Hans' and 'my Dutchman' after he suspects and then even after he knows Lacy's true identity as an Englishman. In Scene 17, during plans for Lacy and Rose's marriage, Eyre calls Lacy 'Roland Lacy' at line 6 and 'Roland' twenty lines later, but calls him 'Hans' four times, twice before these references and twice after; in Scene 20 Eyre refers to him solely as 'Hans'.[56] To be a 'Hans' (or Hance) in the early interludes was to be 'War' or an economic drain on the country; a 'Hans' by the 1590s could be someone who brings in goods that elevate individual native status. Even this ameliorated process, however, involves a continuation of Wilson's and many other writers' concerns with unnecessary imports, and still encourages currency to 'in ander land lopen' ('walk in another land', *Wealth and Health*, Dv). Moreover, the troubled process in this instant is carried out by an Englishman. Without Dekker's powerful context of forgiveness and his diminution of moral turpitude, it would be tempting to read Lacy/Hans rather as an English-alien vice figure, akin to a figure as devastating as Wilson's Usury, the 'English' representation of a foreign, problematic counterpart. Indeed, we saw in earlier chapters that early modern 'usury' included a number of sharp practices, including brokering.

We may want to pull up short of such an extreme alignment, but Dekker pushes Lacy/Hans close to this position of a tightly confused alien identity through a series of accreting conflations and imbrications involving national identity, human 'nature', and generic overlap or medley. Lacy's journey away from his father and expected social role is reminiscent of Hal's in *Henry IV*; even Lacy's final plea to the king feels like the prince's promises to his father of betterment. Lacy, too, hides himself among Londoners of inferior class. When the mayor finds out that Lacy is hiding in London, disguised, to find Rose, the servant Dodger's words are that he 'Lurks here in London' (9.91). The mayor adapts the phrase with the rhetorical question: 'Lurch in London?' and this skulking, hiding figure they are imagining is talked of in terms of an animal who may be hunted down: 'Well, Master Dodger', says the mayor to his informant, 'you perhaps may start him' (9.95), meaning to flush this prodigal out of his hiding place, like a ferret to a fox. The rhetoric throughout *The Shoemaker's Holiday* demotes estranged characters to the status of animals, suggesting their separation and therefore 'stranger' status from the 'natural' laws or orders of human society as well as from social, cultured English society. Of course, the contiguity and even conflation of the two effects – loss of humanity and loss of Englishness – suggests the drama's promotion of a 'naturalness' of a certain view of Englishness and the inhumanity of all other alien stances. This view of Englishness is a fairly conservative one, for all the play's apparent boisterousness and pushing of behavioural boundaries.

STRANGER JANE

In *The Shoemaker's Holiday*'s other love story, between the journeyman Ralph Damport and his wife, Jane, we see another important adaptation from earlier drama. Symbolic objects such as Christianity's shield in *The Tide Tarrieth* or the stones of Remorse, Care, and Charity in Wilson's *The Three Lords* are moral lessons given in a suggested but not overtly described socio-economic setting.[57] In Dekker, the situation has been inverted, for the object of focus is a commercial product, but it is steeped in a moral narrative that works once again with the connection between alien identity and the confirmation of Englishness. Ralph crafts Jane a pair of unique red shoes by which to remember him before he leaves to fight in the French war. Eventually the shoes will be used to bring the couple together again. In fact, the shoes (and the lovers' love for each other) are the only stable element in this strand of the story, and this bears out the importance of the English product as in turn a producer of Englishness that I mentioned at the beginning of the section on Lacy/Hans.

When Ralph returns from war, he is crippled and almost unrecognizable. He inquires after his wife, and he is told by his former fellow workers that 'Jane is a stranger here' (10.102), for she has fled from troublesome, would-be suitors. The trope of the excursion is doubled (husband and wife) and both parties made 'strange' in preparation for a return to Englishness. Eyre's wife, Margery, greets Ralph with her usual lexical/sexual impropriety: 'Trust me, I am sorry, Ralph, to see thee impotent. Lord, how the wars have made him sunburnt! The left leg is not well; 'twas a fair gift of God the infirmity took not hold a little higher, considering thou camest from France – but let that pass' (10.66–70). The term 'sunburnt' could be used in the early modern period to denote an affliction with venereal disease, and the 'French disease' is of course here referenced, since the 'infirmity' (inability for the 'impotent' to get 'firm') could have gone to the top of Ralph's leg – thus the miracle is that Ralph is still a 'man'. During Jane's separation from Ralph by her 'lying low' and absenting herself from once-familiar company, she is – like Lacy when 'Hans' and like Margery when dressed up out of her familiar social place – animalized: 'We'll ferret her out' (10.105), promises Hodge. The marriage of true love and accord between the French-sunburnt and alien-looking Ralph about whom Margery remarks, 'Perdy, I knew him not' (10.62), and his estranged wife Jane is re-familiarized, re-Englished by means of the recognition of Ralph's own English handiwork on the love-pricked red shoes and by a 'lusty crew of honest shoemakers' (14.60), who will bring them together to their wedding, by force if necessary.

Ralph's experience in France has Dekker again pointing to questions of individual subjects' work and pain before subsuming them into a sphere of communal Englishness. Recent commentary has in particular noticed this communal aspect of the shoe-giving. In spite of Ralph's alteration and injuries, Hodge welcomes him back enthusiastically (Scene 10). 'The shoes commemorate the collaborative work of the guild', write Peter Stallybrass and Ann Rosalind Jones, but they also 'materialise memory' in the personal world of Ralph and Jane.[58] Every time she puts on the shoes, she should remember him; this maintains a material as well as psychological connection between France and England, and it ensures a translation, an Englishing of international relations and the incoming alien. Jonathan Gil Harris similarly notes that 'Ralph ennobles the shoes as the skilful product of collective craftsmanship', and adds that 'In doing so, he invites the audience to view the shoes less as a love-token for Jane than as a homage to the artisans' property of fellowship and association; the placed product in this passage is just as much the relational property of skill, therefore, as the pair of shoes itself.'[59] The status of *being* English is confirmed through communal identity, and the activity of *producing* Englishness requires materials of activity – products of London and properties of the London stage.

David Kastan writes of the reunion with the shoes: 'The reaffirmation of Ralph and Jane's marriage redeems the alienation of working-class lives.'[60] Whether such a concept can be applied with historical accuracy to an Elizabethan shoemaker is debatable, but Marx's problem of the loss of attachment of the worker is helpful for us as readers of culture: 'The worker is related to the product of his labour as to an alien object ... Whatever the product of his labour is, he is not',[61] writes Marx. This problem is nicely defeated in Dekker's play as Ralph and his fellows combine to produce the pair of love-pricked shoes, 'pinked with letters' for Jane's name. This product contains Ralph's wife's and his own identities in a mingled combination not unlike Donne's blood-filled flea. When Firk exclaims 'A shoemaker sell his flesh and blood – O indignity!' (18.96) in response to the intrusive Hammon's offer to 'buy' Jane from Ralph, we cannot help but think again of the shoes she is wearing and that the purchase of the person and the purchase of the shoes are inextricable. The Ralph who put himself into these shoes has been changed by the war, and the shoes are the receptacle of his earlier 'English' self. 'I can know them from a thousand moe' (1.246), Ralph says of the shoes when he gets home, a powerfully somatic moment that recognizes their character(s) – presumably 'J D' for Jane Damport. Ralph 'aliens' the shoes in the legal-economic sense of transferring them as property to another owner, but simultaneously and paradoxically he secures their possession for himself since they are both part of himself, and they are going to that other part of himself, his wife (whom, in another early modern legal sense, he owns). Thus the personal, emotional, metaphorical 'alienation' of the self in Marxist terms can be re-historicized and relocated as a personal, bodily, actual familiarization (repair, completion, consolidation) of the self in early modern dramatic terms. As Bolingbroke and Mowbray found their alternative, eternal dramatic lives through their alien excursions that defeated their talk of death, so Ralph is resurrected. Jane is told by Hammon that Ralph is included in the list of war dead, and on his return Ralph works his way back into himself, from and with the alien to the native. He is a small part of the working-class structure of London; that structure is one of many represented in the Elizabethan drama in the act of incorporating the alien into a re-imagining and ongoing construction of Englishness.

JACK DRUM'S ENTERTAINMENT: THE BEDLAM
SANS MERCY

In *Englishmen for My Money*, Anthony the 'Frenchman' does not end up in Bridewell, in spite of Pisaro's threats, because his plans succeed. In *The Shoemaker's Holiday*, Dekker suppresses the potential moral and personal dangers of 'being the alien' in the figure of Lacy the 'Dutchman'. These emphases are in sharp contrast with the anti-alien imperatives of John Marston's *Jack Drum's Entertainment*. Mamon, the old usurer, is in love with a young woman, Katherine. She already has a young lover, however, called Pasquil, so Mamon attempts to have him killed, and he poisons Katherine when she refuses to return his amorous advances. The comedy of attempted sexual liaisons and misplaced trust runs throughout the play, and indeed the play's 1601 quarto subtitle and running title is *A Pleasant Comedie of Pasquill and Katherine*. But the pleasantry falls away as the play progresses. Public hatred for the usurer is shown in the burning of Mamon's house and all his goods. Finally, he goes mad and is given 'Jack Drum's entertainment' (*OED*: 'a rough reception, turning an unwelcome guest out of doors'), and sent to 'Bedlam' for a whipping.[62] Meanwhile, things get better for the good citizens as Katherine has been cured of Mamon's poison by a wondrous 'Juice of hearbes' (H4).[63]

The torture of whips for Mamon is not designed to make the victim utter comprehensibly, as is the threat against Anthony, but to make him 'sing' only the noises that confirm madness, unlexical sequences of howls that bear no relation to any of the human languages spoken outside the walls of the 'hospital'. This vocality confirms the alien victim's status of self as an unlinguistic madman, to be kept isolated from those with language. Aliens (whose utterances should themselves be illegal, since they clip the king's English) are similarly held to be speakers of something unknown to the proud Englishman, something base, ugly, infectious, likely to breed, non-English, and non-human. Like madmen, suspect aliens in this type of fearful, protective response to the threatening other must be isolated by expulsion (sent out of the gates of London), yet also by enclosure (sent to sing in Bridewell or Bedlam). Behind the obsession with expulsion is the hidden acknowledgement that each member of English society is responsible for articulating the alien element he or she must thereafter account for, control, contain, and build a self's identity around. If Haughton's 'prison' of London is sufficient for containing and teaching a lesson to the aliens, it is not the place for corrupted Englishmen. In this practical age, London is being reclaimed by the

English from Wilson's allegories of rampant alien vice. Until they can be proven good English citizens, the enclosure for deformed or debased English subjects is set up as an independent space, such as Bridewell, or outside the city walls, as is Bedlam.

As both scapegoat for the conscience of the community and figure of real physical danger, Mamon exists in the play solely to be silenced, albeit in order to *say* something about that silencing's effect on Englishness. The play is newly working with the expulsions and escapes of non-Englishness in the early plays; the cries of English representations such as Wilson's Hospitality and Conscience before their demise or abomination are refigured as what is left, or what revives, after the evil part of corrupted Englishness is expelled. Silence follows the cries of protest and pain as one is forced into submission – dragged offstage by Usury, bumped comically by stage-posts or beaten viciously by whips. Marston's Jonsonian lack of sympathy for his character is a reflection of the times and his audience.[64] Mamon is all evil: he is the assassin, the lecher, the old seducer, and the child molester of medieval (anti-Jewish) iconography. That the myths of Jewish child-abuse and diabolism continued right through the Renaissance period, and were ripe for plucking back into the propagandist forefront at any time, is evident from the writings of the traveller William Biddulph. Lucid and acute in his observations elsewhere, he slips into dramatic reportage in his passage on the Turkish Jews:

They observe still all their old Ceremonies and feasts, Sacrifices only excepted, which the *Turkes* will not suffer them to doe: for they were wont amongst them to sacrifice children, but dare not now for feare of the *Turkes*. Yet some of them have confessed, that their Physitians kill some Christian patient or other, whom they have under their hands at that time, in stead of a sacrifice.[65]

As an English usurer with all the vices of the old Jew firmly stuck in his breast, Mamon enacts the infiltration of what Bacon in 'Of Usury' called the 'judaising' vice into English society.[66] It is again a figure of deformation that needs to be overcome while the fruits and inheritance of apparently alien vices are incorporated (usually by a younger generation) to ensure a future of Englishness.

This play seems to push more forcefully than any other since *Wealth and Health* to eradicate the alien in the manner of the simple first alien stage. Mamon's servant, Flawne, has no qualms about playing his part in the downfall of his anti-Christian, usurer master: he revels in the privilege of listing Mamon's bad fortunes, all working to 'laie him up in *Bedlame*, commit him to the mercie of the whip, the entertainment of bread and water, and the sting of a Usurers Conscience for ever' (F3v). And the precious bonds of Mamon as the anti-Christian usurer are shredded. But we have in fact moved on. The effective poisons used by real Jews, such as Abraham in *Selimus*[67] or Barabas against the convent, become in Mamon horrific intent ultimately negated, countered by the Arcadian antidote of 'A skilfull Beldame with the Juice of hearbes' (H4). Indeed, for all *Jack Drum*'s apparent resistance to the second alien stage, the process' irony returns: only through the incorporation of the alien, the recognition of corrupted Englishness, can a response be necessitated that conjures up notions of England as full of natural healing powers, an idyllic utopia of safety and purging. In *Jack Drum*, the context reveals nature's contrapuntal matrix: nature marries cures with diseases, medicines with poisons. The soothing dock leaf grows next to the stinging nettle, and the woman who finds the cure for Katherine is a 'Beldame', the recovery of a name that has been used twice before in the play, contemptuously on both occasions; the epithet also strongly points to someone who, thankfully, will counter the merciless, relentless, and anagrammatical 'Bedlam'.

In an episode reminiscent of Lincoln's cries to the crowd in *Sir Thomas More*, Flawne tells Mamon, 'Your house with all the furniture is burnt, not a ragge left, the people stand warming their hands at the fire, and laugh at your miserie' (F4–F4v).[68] The relation of this act emphasizes the ideological anti-Englishness of Mamon, in so far as the crowd in *Sir Thomas More* was preparing to burn down the houses of the aliens in London. For some members of the audience, at least, this scene would have jogged the memory of a whole trend in the history of the Jews: the final repose of the Jew-like usurer, his house, must be taken, and the Jew must be sent to some house of correction or conversion.[69] In 1215, John Stow tells us, the walls and gates of London that were wrecked by civil war were repaired 'with the stones taken from the Jewes broken houses, namely, *Aeldgate* being then most ruinous'.[70] For centuries, the homes of the Jews had been 'converted' into the very structures that held them in subjection. The homes of the Jews of Elizabethan London were their synagogues, their holy centres, the only domains safe from Christian oppression.[71] One Thomas Wilson (not the writer on usury), a Christian working for a Jewish family, kept a record of the clandestine Jewish services that took place in his employer's household. He mentions that they moved between parishes for ease of worship, 'because they have not been troubled about their Relygyon or use of superstycyous ceremonyes since they came to dwell there as they now do, where before they were constrayned to come and heare servyce at Fanchurche when they dwelt in

Fanchurch streete'.[72] From the real world and the tearing down of the medieval German *Judensynagogs* and their replacement with Christian churches, to the literary imagination, with Barabas' house turned into a Christian convent, house-taking is the final invasion of the Jew's life, the final destruction of his world within the world.[73] So, through Mamon's suffering of house-loss and incarceration, London and rural England purge themselves of the infectious quality they detect in the alien. But there is no denying the vaccinatory benefits of alien confusion; from a reformed, London-based, royalist/conservative point of view, we have seen it make Englishness stronger throughout the plays of the Elizabethan period. The drama encloses, incorporates, and confuses the alien into identities of Englishness – into spaces of urban structure, into acceptable social and moral behaviour, and into the passing of proper justice against malefactors and on behalf of victims.

The justice meted out in *Jack Drum's Entertainment* for folly and evil is the unsatirical story designed to tempt patronage for the recently re-established Paul's Boys of 1600/1, but the hyperbole of the play's romance reveals the underlying viciousness of the intent to do harm, and a very thin line is drawn between English revenge and justice. While the failure of Mamon may be part of Marston's and the Paul's Boys' aim for ethical and political correctness, the way that the play uses stereotype and convention to force realism to its limits is an indicator of the unlikeliness of the play's situation as a whole, including the successful defeat of Mamon in England. As Philip J. Finkelpearl has noticed, Mamon's plots for dastardly deeds are not, in the end, all that different from those of the suspicious lover, Brabant Junior, who is not billed directly as a villain, and who remains at large. Mamon and Pasquil go mad at almost the same time and this may indicate another parallel between the 'good' and 'bad' characters that is hard to ignore.[74] A continuity clearly arises through these plays once more as Englishness and alien identity become confused, from English landlords and foreign immigrants to English and Welsh partners like Hotspur and Glyndwr. In every play discussed in this book, we could say there is a trace, a residue of alien threat in spite of the constant reconfirmation of ideas of Englishness. If Englishness has always relied on the alien to construct and confirm itself, then the alien is always present, threatening to mutate and attack the current notion of Englishness. We have seen, however – whether through deliberate intent or a 'weakness' of national character – that Englishness adapts in response, absorbing and building on aspects of the alien that it would have simply rejected or not have comprehended in a previous decade.

From the equivocality of Wealth in a nation as both good and bad, through Hospitality as a domestic or international phenomenon, to the 'Hans' that enables the confirmation of mayoral authority in London, alien confusion lies behind, before, around, and within Elizabethan English processes of production, exchange, mobility, and authority. The drama represents the alien consistently, but from various angles, as ubiquitous, as something to be feared and resisted, but in the end – whether the plays want to admit it or not – as something confused with Englishness, something to live with, and something that is carried into a new century of outgoing endeavours. The construction of identity that comes out of Elizabethan dramatic and cultural engagement with the alien is a phenomenon to which the later colonial English body and mind must return to take into account its already-altered ideas and ideals of Englishness. Without an appreciation of the ways in which drama revealed the pervasive, invasive, and altering effects of physical and ideological alien confusion, we cannot fully understand English manipulation of otherness in this period or later. If we do not continue to look closely at the alienating processes represented in sixteenth-century moral, comic, and historical drama, we risk misreading and mistaking the rhetorical and physical activities of the colonized and colonizing English both at home and abroad as represented in Jacobean romance, travel, and tragic plays. The postscript builds on this argument for critical awareness of the confused, hybrid, English identity that is brought forward into post-Elizabethan drama.

Postscript: Early modern and post-modern alien excursions

Jeffrey Knapp has argued that England's belatedness and non-involvement in the rich colonizing that was the Iberian experience allowed the English to recast their exclusion from the world of wealthy colonial activity as a valorization of their ethical and religious superiority. This highlighted England's 'abjuration of material or worldly means to power and its extraordinary reliance on God'.[1] This view of the 'sceptered' and 'blessed' 'Isle' pervades the stance of early modern English superiority in the plays of the first alien stage, and it remains as a nostalgic remnant in Shakespeare's histories. But the multinational 'English' force of *Henry V* and the late sixteenth-century popular comedy of foreign contact reminds us that for all the representation of England as an isolated and insular country, it was the deliberate incorporation of British foreignness into 'England' and the influx of a large community of real Continental alien bodies to Elizabethan urban centres that lay behind the ongoing early modern concern to define English selves. The drama, moreover, put physical bodies on stage and in front of English men and women to play out London and England in microcosmic and multivalent reactions to and critiques of the conditions of that English–alien co-habitation.

While this book has attempted to provide a picture of the popular perception of alien confusion in English drama set in England before the permanence of extra-British colonialism, another study might compare these findings with plays set outside England and later in time. The large body of 'colonial' criticism on drama – mostly about Marlowe and Shakespeare, but increasingly about other playwrights, such as James Shirley and Robert Daborne[2] – might begin to make use of the processes of alien confusion in its consideration of English fears, failures, and triumphs abroad. The effect of the incoming alien – foreign persons and influences – forced self-scrutiny, which in turn ignited and continued to fuel a correlating will to expansion. Emily Bartels, for one, has argued that the lack of actual English imperial achievement before the mid-seventeenth century has meant that 'the importance of imperialism to the [Elizabethan] era has, until recently, been greatly underestimated'.[3] Perhaps the term 'imperialist' and the idea of conquest 'across the globe' are concepts for later rhetoric, but we can see evidence of the desire Bartels is thinking of. Hakluyt records Robert Thorne's suggestion to Henry VIII, for example, that the king pursue exploration and exploitation of northern climes, ultimately to attempt a circumnavigation through regions where the Spanish and Portuguese had not yet conquered. The plan is extensive and ambitious, but it is clearly exploratory, preliminary, and aware of England's position as embarrassingly behind in the project of expansion.[4] By 1553, the journey would be attempted by Willoughby and Chancellor. The *concept* of expansion with its accompanying delights and horrors had been alive for some time when Elizabeth settled uneasily into the throne; the desire for and the practical difficulties (tragic and comic) of such exploits are discussed in the creative literature of the period. Such a desire had a need to define a more powerful Englishness through the second half of the sixteenth century, and this involved getting to grips with the alien at home in preparation for tackling the alien abroad. To ignore this burgeoning Tudor awareness of 'imperialism' in studying later periods is to throw out the baby of expansionism and alien confusion along with the (post-)colonial bathwater.

Two useful books by Nabil Matar discuss English 'imperialist' ideals in the context of early modern Anglo-Islamic relations. Matar does tend, however, to simplify literary contributions to English culture. Thus he writes, 'Although there was a momentum for colonization, inspired by the writings of Raleigh, Hakluyt, Purchas, and others, Elizabethan and early Stuart Britons were not yet capable of fulfilling the imperial enterprise',[5] and this observation leads him to downplay the usefulness of popular imaginative literary works to historical understanding, because they do not reveal history, or, as he puts it, 'they sacrifice the truth'.[6] But we can take issue with that 'theologically' definitive notion of 'truth' in literature. Is rewriting or inventing historical relations (literary lying?) a sign of weakness? If the drama is inherently political, is this not at least in part a call for (or will to) change? As English prisoners in the Ottoman Empire converted to Islam (in words, but not heart) in an attempt to gain their freedom and be brought back into the Christian fold, so drama might be involving itself in a fantasy of re-identification of self and 'other' for the purpose of promoting the hope of future restitution and repair of the English national psyche. This seems to be what is happening as the

English draw Britishness into themselves as an essential pre-existing part of the Anglo-centric identity they construct to take abroad and wield throughout the 'British' empire – the empire that *is* Britain itself and the world into which an early modern Britain expands itself. I would argue that the literary material in the present book shows us the pervasiveness of semi-historical fodder for the multi-headed beast that filled the theatre. Moreover, the very spaces in the fuzzy region between political history and the claims of imaginative literature are what worried officials like Edmund Tilney in 'true history'; the incongruities and allusiveness of dramatic representations make a literary study of English trading and (pre-)colonial ideas in the period interesting, just as the spaces between theatres and the cities, courts, and counties they represented/imagined provide gaps in which to play out meaning. The dramatic and popular literature of alien relations in the Elizabethan period seems to me to be much more aware of contemporary political realities and of its own ability to move within and without those political-historical realities than over-bearingly history-bound (rather than appropriately literary-historicized) readings would allow. As I hope I have demonstrated throughout *Aliens and Englishness*, the drama is also more nuanced in its representation of the 'other' than some critics would have us believe.

To comprehend the alien is, to a greater or lesser extent, to become the alien. But, if the evidence of *Sir Thomas More* from Chapter 3 is anything to go by, it seems that such an empathetic position is only possible in the process of incorporating the alien 'other' into a dominant narrative of native identity. In the Elizabethan drama, the English man, woman, or community acknowledges the 'alien within' exclusively for the sake of expanding and confirming Englishness. As critics in the twenty-first century, we have related problems of personal identity to contend with. We profess an inability to put ourselves in the place of an early modern subject, yet we spend our time critically thinking with just such preten-sions, and in doing so we endanger the integrity of the subject of study. Historians and literary scholars enter the sixteenth century as alien archaeologists, likely to disturb (sometimes deliberately, perhaps irrep-arably) what lies there, in the very process of taking samples for analysis. Of course – and with strange, discomforting reverberations of the colonial past – it may be just this danger of destroying what we admire or find marvellous that makes the endeavour such an equivocally exciting and weighty one. Steven Mullaney reminds us of the destructive need for colonial Europe to possess examples or pieces of the alien – a possession ending inevitably in the oblivion of the alien bodies and the absorption of elements of those 'others' (*alia*, aliens). Indeed, the very observation and recording of alien cultural elements is a way literally to inscribe them within the dominant culture.[7] René Girard has argued that by displaying the 'differences' of the alien, a community – even with comic pretensions – creates a tragic and violent scenario in which essential (ethnic) differences are effaced.[8] Any book on the alien, then, must in some ways confess to its kinship with the *Wunderkammer*, even as it tries to organize the alien elements it displays and argue for their appreciation and comprehension. As I write this, I am aware of a further level of fantasy, because this very concern for disturbing or damaging material history suggests a pre-existing, recoverable, holistic past that we could understand if only we lined up our critical ducks in a perfect row. We of course only invent the material past with the rhetorics of the present and in that process create more or less convincing illusions of historical 'truth'.

Aliens and Englishness has been largely concerned with the work that the dramatic text does once it leaves the author's hands. Especially in a historical context where playwrights for the most part sold their plays exclusively without retaining productive control over them, the *creation* of a play's 'real' (in this study, English) identity comes about through a 'pure' authorial text bringing into itself the 'alien' elements of actors, material costume and properties, and playing location. Like the centre of Englishness, the centre of a play's meaning comes into focus as its assumed originary identity fuses with new, semi-predictable elements to create a re-formed world with a new discourse. The text, formally cohesive and coherent, is alienated from itself incrementally and continuously by cultural forces alien to it, but which underlie the context of Englishness. The text, moreover, can be represented as available for duplication (later editions of the *same* play), but the trappings put on the form, the perception of the form by others, and new performance contexts change its identity *as historical event* radically (new frontispieces, revivals of plays alongside sequels, revivals to coincide with major events such as the defeat of the Armada or the execution of Rodrigo Lopez). After all we have seen, it is apparent that such alienated dramatic text – incorporative, changing, reforming – aligns with an Elizabethan, quintessentially English, mode of mutable identity-building and confirmation.

The stage may be England, as we read in the character list of *Grim, The Collier of Croydon*, but in the end all stages are alien. Players are strange: Robert Wilson, Will Kemp, William Shakespeare, and Richard Tarlton convert themselves with apparel, and thereby convert the stage – itself deliberately alienated, in the suburbs or liberties, set apart from London or town authorities. Characters are more strange: figures like Illwill, Newfangle, and Fraud in the moralities, Anthony in *Englishmen*, Roland Lacy and Hal in the comedies and histories alienate themselves from themselves to take on disguises and meta-roles. The deliberate nature of these events lets us know that dramatists and probably playgoers were not so naive as to think that they had no hand in the process of 'Anglicizing' their cities and counties and in the creation of ideas of Englishness. Wherever dramatic imaginative literature fits into the jigsaw of historical 'truth', its premises of action and interaction assure us that we cannot do without its pieces; to '*interact*' in the 'real' world, after all, is to create drama between persons with performance and dialogue. To engage socially upon the stage that is England is to act (and create history) at all times.

The alien is the alien because it is always out of reach; but that makes it akin to evasive notions of native identity. Native and foreign language, as used on the stage and in the streets, are themselves equally alienating forces: languages control entry of 'foreigners' and determine hierarchies within their native ranks. The plays do the same jobs of national gate-keeping and organization. Could staging the alien really alienate the stage, then, as I suggested in Chapter 1? For if the stage was already strange and offensively non-English to English reformers and city authorities, did putting the alien on the stage instead *confirm* its status as a very *English* mechanism for displaying the 'other' and for discovering and delineating the self? We leap across time to look through these dramatic perspectives, ourselves the alien among aliens. We search for selves that we can comprehend in the early modern and post-modern worlds. If we are afraid that in our reading of history through drama we just unravel the threads of a baseless fabric, we also understand that the ideas produced in that destructive critical process are as substantial as any flesh and blood.

Notes

PREFACE

1 I am using the translation of the dedicatory letter provided in Jobst Ammon [i.e. Jost Amman], *The Theatre of Women*, ed. Alfred Aspland (1586; Manchester and London: Holbein Society, 1872). Professors Heather James and Tina Bowman provided me with translations of the Latin text accompanying the image of the married woman of London.

1 INTRODUCTION – ALIENS AND THE ENGLISH IN LONDON

1 Lien Bich Luu, *Immigrants and the Industries of London 1500–1700* (Aldershot: Ashgate, 2005), pp. 3–4. 'Tentative estimates put the immigration to England at 30,000 people in the six years between 1567 and 1573 alone – the period of repression associated with the reign of the Duke of Alva'. Luu estimates the total number of aliens coming to Elizabethan England at about 50,000; they did not all stay, however, and it would seem that the coming-and-going alone of this number of immigrants would give a strong impression among the English of a massive influx of strangers (p. 90).
2 Andrew Pettegree, *Foreign Protestant Communities in Sixteenth-Century London* (Oxford: Clarendon Press, 1986), pp. 24–5, Chap. 2, and *passim*.
3 For a discussion of the arguments between the livery companies, the city, and the Privy Council over alien and denizen rights, see Ian Archer, *The Pursuit of Stability: Social Relations in Elizabethan London* (Cambridge: Cambridge University Press, 1991), pp. 131–40.
4 The figure is from Luu, *Immigrants and the Industries of London*, p. 90; Luu discusses the distribution of aliens in London, pp. 121–6. The phrase 'alien invasion' is taken from the title to Chap. 7 of Richard Vliet Lindabury, *Patriotism in Elizabethan Drama* (Princeton: Princeton University Press, 1931).
5 Luu, *Immigrants and the Industries of London*, pp. 98–9. Alien figures in most recent studies of early modern England use Irene Scouloudi's *Returns of Strangers in the Metropolis 1593, 1627, 1635, 1639: a Study of an Active Minority* (London: Huguenot Society of Great Britain and Ireland, 1985).
6 See Luu, *Immigrants and the Industries of London*, pp. 37–8.
7 Ian Archer, *The Pursuit of Stability*, p. 23.

8 For this notion of citizenship in history and Shakespearean representation, see the Introduction in John Michael Archer, *Citizen Shakespeare: Freemen and Aliens in the Language of the Plays* (New York: Palgrave Macmillan, 2005).

9 Robert Wilson, *An Edition of Robert Wilson's 'The Three Ladies of London' and 'Three Lords and Three Ladies of London'*, ed. H. S. D. Mithal (New York and London: Garland, 1988), p. 48, line 27 (sig. B).

10 John Archer, *Citizen Shakespeare*, p. 17.

11 The distinction between 'denizens', with conflicted rights to escape alien customs duties on imported and traded goods, and 'free denizens' is not entirely clear, and may not have been consistent in the period. Lien Luu makes a strong distinction between the 'free' denizens and those who remained 'alien' in so far as they did not gain freedom of the city and accompanying resident privileges. (See Lien Luu, 'Natural-Born versus Stranger-Born Subjects: Aliens and Their Status in Elizabethan London', in *Immigrants in Tudor and Early Stuart England*, eds. Nigel Goose and Lien Luu (Brighton: Sussex Academic Press, 2005), pp. 57–75, p. 62). Compare Irene Scouloudi's definition of a 'free denizen' as one who 'held the freedom of the City and possibly as well, but not automatically, a Patent of Denization granted by the crown' (Scouloudi, *Returns of Strangers*, p. 9). This note and my understanding of these alien identities has been informed by the work of Jacob Selwood. I am very grateful to Professor Selwood for his helpful correspondence on this issue, including drafts from his forthcoming book on diversity in early modern London (Ashgate, 2009).

12 For discussions of the uncertain status of non-native-born English children and immigrants, and the methods of application for denizenship and citizenship, see Luu, 'Natural-Born versus Stranger-Born Subjects', and Jacob Selwood, '"English-Born Reputed Strangers": Birth and Descent in Seventeenth-Century London', *Journal of British Studies* 44 (2005): 728–53.

13 Luu, *Immigrants and the Industries of London*, pp. 142–6.

14 John Florio, *First Fruits* (London, 1578), N2v.

15 Florio, *First Fruits*, N2.

16 Michael Neill, 'Broken English and Broken Irish: Nation, Language, and the Optic of Power in Shakespeare's Histories', *Shakespeare Quarterly* 45 (1994): 1–32, pp. 3, 14; Andrew Hadfield and Willy Maley, Introduction in *Representing Ireland: Literature and the Origins of Conflict, 1534–1660*, eds. Brendan Bradshaw, Andrew Hadfield, and Willy Maley (Cambridge: Cambridge University Press, 1993), p. 7; Janette Dillon, *Language and Stage in Medieval and Renaissance England* (Cambridge: Cambridge University Press, 1998), pp. 162–3; Eric Griffin, 'From *Ethos* to *Ethnos*: Hispanizing "the Spaniard" in the Old World and the New', *The New Centennial Review* 2.1 (2002): 69–116, p. 71.

17 Richard Helgerson, 'Before National Literary History', *Modern Language Quarterly* 64 (2003): 169–79, p. 171.

18 Helgerson, 'Before National Literary History', p. 173.

19 Jodi Mikalachki, *The Legacy of Boadicea: Gender and Nation in Early Modern England* (London: Routledge, 1998), p. 4.

20 In July 1596, the Privy Council ordered the deportation of all black servants and slaves as payment to the transporter, Casper van Selden, for bringing home English prisoners. (See Great Britain, *Acts of the Privy Council of England, 1452–1628*, 32 vols., ed. John Roche Dasent (London: HMSO, 1890–1907), 26, p. 20). A Proclamation of January(?) 1601 again gave van Selden a warrant for transporting all 'Negroes and blackamoors'; the job had been difficult in the earlier case because the order had required the permission of the masters, which van Selden complained he could not get. See Great Britain, *Tudor Royal Proclamations*, 3 vols., eds. Paul L. Hughes and James F. Larkin (New Haven and London: Yale University Press, (vol. 1) 1964 and (vols. 2 and 3) 1969), 3, pp. 221–2.

21 Thomas Platter, *Thomas Platter's Travels in England*, trans. and intro. Clare Williams (1599; London: Jonathan Cape, 1937), p. 170.

22 Benedict Anderson, *Imagined Communities: Reflections on the Origin and Spread of Nationalism*, rev. edn (London and New York: Verso, 1991), p. 7.

23 Philip Edwards, *Threshold of a Nation: a Study of English and Irish Drama* (Cambridge: Cambridge University Press, 1979), p. 68.

24 See also Cathy Shrank's adjustment of Anderson's assessment of 'national' awareness in *Writing the Nation in Reformation England 1530–1580* (Oxford: Oxford University Press, 2004), pp. 3–7.

25 Emily Bartels uses the term 'self-scrutiny' as a reminder of the need for English inward contemplation, and I have made use of it in the present study. See Emily C. Bartels, *Spectacles of Strangeness: Imperialism, Alienation, and Marlowe* (Philadelphia: University of Pennsylvania Press, 1993). Oseas implores London to look 'with inward eyes' (4.5.70) to learn the lessons of the play (see Thomas Lodge and Robert Greene, *A Looking Glass for London and England*, in *Drama of the English Renaissance 1: the Tudor Period*, eds. Russell A. Fraser and Norman C. Rabkin (New York: Macmillan, 1976)).

26 See Louis Montrose, 'Form and Pressure: Shakespearean Drama and the Elizabethan State', in *Contextualizing the Renaissance Returns to History*, ed. Albert H. Tricomi (Turnhout, Belgium: Brepols, 1999), pp. 171–99.

27 Richard Helgerson, *Forms of Nationhood: the Elizabethan Writing of England* (Chicago: University of Chicago Press, 1992), p. 245.

28 Jean Howard, 'Other Englands: the View from the Non-Shakespearean History Play', in *Other Voices, Other Views: Expanding the Canon in English Renaissance Studies*, eds. Helen Ostovich, Graham Silcox, and Graham Roebuck (London: Associated University Presses, 1999), pp. 135–53; Aaron Landau, '"I Live with Bread like You": Forms of Inclusion in *Richard II*', *Early Modern Literary Studies* 11.1 (2005): 3.1–23. Online, available at: http://purl.oclc.org/emls/11-1/richard.htm (accessed 14 April 2006).

29 Steven Mullaney, *The Place of the Stage: License, Play, and Power in Renaissance England* (Chicago: University of Chicago Press, 1988).

30 This notion of the 'performative' as an imagined 'soul' or centre written on the body for others to read and believe in is drawn from Judith Butler's theory of sexuality in *Gender Trouble: Feminism and Subversion of Identity* (London: Routledge, 1990).

31 Mary Floyd-Wilson, *English Ethnicity and Race in Early Modern Drama* (Cambridge: Cambridge University Press, 2003), pp. 59, 60.
32 Floyd-Wilson's argument returns on occasion to the pattern of an essentialized Englishness defined *in opposition to* the alien. This equation is in danger of perpetuating an ideology of strong, superior Englishness that somehow pre-exists and trumps all other identities. Her discussion of 'nature' versus forgetting 'nature' and the African as the Briton's 'inverse' relies on conflict in contrast to *Aliens and Englishness'* emphasis on the sixteenth-century development of confusion as confluence. See Floyd-Wilson, *English Ethnicity and Race in Early Modern Drama*, p. 7.
33 Floyd-Wilson, *English Ethnicity and Race in Early Modern Drama*, p. 60.
34 John Lyly, *Euphues: the Anatomy of Wit* (1578 and 1580), eds. Morris William Croll and Harry Clemons (New York: Russell and Russell, 1964), p. 421. Cited in Sara Warneke, *Images of the Educational Traveller in Early Modern England* (Leiden: Brill, 1995), p. 88.
35 See J. G. A. Pocock's revised version of 'British History: a Plea for a New Subject', *The Journal of Modern History* 47 (1975): 601–21, p. 610; David Baker, *Between Nations: Shakespeare, Spenser, Marvell, and the Question of Britain* (Stanford: Stanford University Press, 1997), p. 12.
36 Willy Maley, *Nation, State, and Empire in English Renaissance Literature: Shakespeare to Milton* (London: Palgrave Macmillan, 2003), p. 19.

2 DISCOVERING THE ALIEN IN ELIZABETHAN MORAL DRAMA

1 Andrew Pettegree, *Foreign Protestant Communities in Sixteenth-Century London* (Oxford: Clarendon Press, 1986), pp. 113–16. The issue of the cost of denization is arguable, since the process was worked out on a case-by-case and petitioning basis, and fees for residency relative to applicants' incomes do not seem to have been consistent.
2 Robin D. Gwynn, *Huguenot Heritage: the History and Contribution of the Huguenots in Britain* (London: Routledge, 1985), p. 15.
3 Jonathan Gil Harris, *Foreign Bodies and the Body Politic: Discourses of Social Pathology in Early Modern England* (Cambridge: Cambridge University Press, 1998).
4 Laurence Saunders, *A Trewe Mirrour or Glasse Wherin we Maye Beholde the Wofull State of Thys Our Realme of Englande* (London, 1556), A8v.
5 Saunders, *A Trewe Mirrour*, B2.
6 Saunders, *A Trewe Mirrour*, B2v.
7 Anon., *Lamentacion of England* (Germany[?], 1557 and 1558), A3.
8 *Lamentacion of England*, A3v.
9 *Lamentacion of England*, A7. In 1557 Philip had his thirtieth birthday, whereas Mary turned forty-one.
10 *Lamentacion of England*, A6–A6v.
11 *Lamentacion of England*, A8.

12 Eric Griffin, 'From *Ethos* to *Ethnos*: Hispanizing "the Spaniard" in the Old World and the New', *The New Centennial Review* 2.1 (2002): 69–116, p. 76.

13 Griffin, 'From *Ethos* to *Ethnos*', pp. 81–2, 86.

14 Granting monopolies to alien artisans would set up new manufacturing in England, thus decreasing imports of luxury goods. 'In the early years of Elizabeth's reign such projects almost invariably involved foreign projectors', writes Pettegree. William Cecil had a hand in promoting a number of such ventures involving monopolies by aliens in England, including soap manufacture and saltpetre provision (a raw material for dying) (Pettegree, *Foreign Protestant Communities*, pp. 140–1).

15 Great Britain, *Tudor Royal Proclamations*, 3 vols., eds. Paul L. Hughes and James F. Larkin (New Haven and London: Yale University Press, (vol. 1) 1964 and (vols. 2 and 3) 1969), 1, p. 134.

16 Pettegree, *Foreign Protestant Communities*, pp. 273–6.

17 Great Britain, *Tudor Royal Proclamations*, 1, p. 146.

18 Patrick Collinson, 'Europe in Britain: Protestant Strangers and the English Reformation', in *From Strangers to Citizens: the Integration of Immigrant Communities in Britain, Ireland, and Colonial America, 1550–1750*, eds. Randolph Vigne and Charles Littleton (London: Huguenot Society of Great Britain and Ireland, 2001), pp. 57–67, p. 60.

19 Frederick, Duke of Wirtemberg [i.e. Württemberg], *A True and Faithful Narrative*. Quoted in W. B. Rye, ed., *England as Seen by Foreigners* (1865; New York: B. Bloom, 1967).

20 This event is related by Pettegree, *Foreign Protestant Communities*, pp. 273–4.

21 Collinson, 'Europe in Britain', p. 60.

22 See T. W. Craik, 'The Political Interpretation of Two Tudor Interludes: *Temperance and Humility* and *Wealth and Health*', *Review of English Studies* n.s. 4 (1953): 98–108; A. J. Hoenselaars, *Images of Englishmen and Foreigners in the Drama of Shakespeare and His Contemporaries: a Study of Stage Characters and National Identity in English Renaissance Drama, 1558–1642* (London and Toronto: Associated University Presses, 1992), p. 41.

23 M. Beer, *Early British Economics from the XIIIth to the Middle of the XVIIIth Century* (New York: Kelley, 1967), pp. 60–1.

24 Diana Wood, *Medieval Economic Thought* (Cambridge: Cambridge University Press, 2002), pp. 69–70; Beer, *Early British Economics*, p. 63.

25 Thomas Hobbes, *Leviathan* 1651. Renascence Editions. Online, available at: http://darkwing.uoregon.edu/~rbear/hobbes/leviathan2.html (accessed 23 January 2007).

26 See Beer, *Early British Economics*, pp. 94–8.

27 T. W. Craik, 'The Political Interpretation', p. 102; see also Paula Neuss, 'The Sixteenth-Century English "Proverb" Play', *Comparative Drama* 18 (1984): 1–18, p. 14.

28 Anon., *The Bayte and Snare of Fortune*, A2. STC gives 1556 and 1550 as likely publication dates.

29 See Sara Warneke, *Images of the Educational Traveller in Early Modern England* (Leiden: Brill, 1995), Chap. 3.

30 Craik, 'The Political Interpretation', p. 102 n. 3.

31 See for example William Cecil, Lord Burghley, *The Copie of a Letter Sent Out of England to Don Bernadin Mendoza Ambassadour in France for the King of Spaine* (London, 1588); Anon., *A Comparison of the English and Spanish Nation*, trans. from French by Robert Ashley (London, 1589); Anon., *Coppie of the Anti-Spaniard*, trans. from French (a French Gentleman, a Catholic) (London, 1590); Anon., *A Pageant of Spanish Humours*, trans. from Dutch by H. W. (London, 1599).

32 Harris, *Foreign Bodies and the Body Politic*, p. 15.

33 Harris, *Foreign Bodies and the Body Politic*, p. 33.

34 Harris, *Foreign Bodies and the Body Politic*, pp. 40–5.

35 Michel Serres, *The Parasite*, trans. Lawrence Schehr (Baltimore: The Johns Hopkins University Press, 1982).

36 A. J. Hoenselaars, *Images of Englishmen and Foreigners*, p. 41.

37 Laura Hunt Yungblut, 'Strangers and Aliaunts: the "Un-English" among the English in Elizabethan England', in *Crossing Boundaries: Issues of Cultural and Individual Identity in the Middle Ages and the Renaissance*, ed. Sally McKee (Turnhout, Belgium: Brepols, 1999), pp. 263–76, p. 274.

38 Elizabeth Hanson, *Discovering the Subject in Renaissance England* (Cambridge: Cambridge University Press, 1998), p. 26.

39 E. K. Chambers suggests that 'This might be *The Collier* played at Court in 1576', and notes Fleay's assignation of it to the Paul's Boys (*The Elizabethan Stage*, 4 vols. (Oxford: Clarendon Press, 1923), 3, p. 317). In the Introduction to the Malone Society edition of the text, we read, 'the phrase "in the shroudes" (l[ine] 248) may be a hint that *Like Will to Like* was in fact originally designed (and perhaps produced) as a boys' play at St. Paul's'. A note then continues, '(*OED* 'shroud' sb. I.4). It is possible that the playhouse of the Paul's Boys was in the cloister from around 1570' (Ulpian Fulwell, *Like Will to Like Quod the Devil to the Collier*, in *Two Moral Interludes*, ed. Peter Happé (1568; Oxford: Malone Society, 1991), p. 56). The existing texts seem primarily aimed at small, professional troupes, and the stage directions allow for the company's lack of resources: 'Nichol Newfangle must have a Gittorn or some other instrument (if it may be) but if hee have not they must daunce about the place all three, and sing this song that followeth . . .' (A4v).

40 David Bevington, *From Mankind to Marlowe: Growth of Structure in the Popular Drama of Tudor England* (Cambridge, MA: Harvard University Press, 1962), p. 157.

41 Hoenselaars, *Images of Englishmen and Foreigners*, p. 42.

42 Bevington, *From Mankind to Marlowe*, p. 158.

43 See C. L. Kingsford's notes in his edition of John Stow, *A Survey of London*, 2 vols. (1599 and 1603; Oxford: Clarendon Press, 1908), 2, pp. 287, 367–8, and Andrew Pettegree, *Foreign Protestant Communities*, p. 17.

44 Philip Stubbes, *The Anatomie of Abuses* (1595 edn), ed. Margaret Jane Kidnie (Tempe: ACMRS, 2002), pp. 64–5.

45 Hoenselaars, *Images of Englishmen and Foreigners*, p. 43.

46 Charlotte McBride, 'A Natural Drink for an English Man: National Stereotyping in Early Modern Culture', in *A Pleasing Sinne: Drink and Conviviality in Seventeenth-Century England*, ed. Adam Smyth (Woodbridge: D. S. Brewer, 2004), pp. 181–91, pp. 182, 186.

47 David Bevington, *Tudor Drama and Politics* (Cambridge, MA: Harvard University Press, 1968), pp. 134–5.

48 Wapull's play may well be a work from earlier in Elizabeth's reign. While I describe elements of the play as 'echoing' or 'expanding' those that we saw in *Like Will to Like*, then, I mean to continue the notion of a matrix-like relationship between the plays rather than a strict chronological development.

49 Hurtful Help is also given the name 'Hurting Help' at his entrance at A3v.

50 Jean-Christophe Agnew, *Worlds Apart: the Market and the Theater in Anglo-American Thought, 1550–1750* (Cambridge: Cambridge University Press, 1986), Chaps. 1 and 3.

51 Like the usurer and the broker (a professional type discussed below), the covetous landlord had become a stock character for which the morally upright critic could voice disdain, and as a result, the tenant became a common character too; thus Bernard Beckerman can refer to him as a 'generic Tenant'; see Beckerman, 'Playing the Crowd: Structure and Soliloquy in *Tide Tarrieth No Man*', in *Mirror up to Shakespeare*, ed. J. C. Gray (Toronto: University of Toronto Press, 1984), pp. 128–37, p. 134.

52 Neuss, 'The Sixteenth-Century English "Proverb" Play', p. 6. William Wager's *Enough is as Good as a Feast* includes a depressed tenant, the idea taken perhaps from personal experience. As Mark Eccles has discovered, Wager (being a parson) attended the dying Lancelot Fothergill of the Blackfriars and heard his grievances. Apparently Fothergill 'was not able to prefer his poor boy to the lease of his house, he was tied so hard not to alien the lease for twenty-one years that had been made to him by Francis Pitcher', Fothergill's 'leasemonger' (as Satan gleefully calls the corrupted worldly men in *Enough is as Good as a Feast*). (Mark Eccles, 'William Wager and His Plays', *English Language Notes* 18 (1981): 258–62, pp. 259–60.) This reverses Paula Neuss' argument, as the concrete experience produces the dramatic satire. Of course, this does not go against Neuss, but strengthens the likelihood of maturing mimetic moments in the theatre having an increasingly realistic effect on the audiences.

53 For a discussion of brokers as usurers, see the Introduction to *Three Renaissance Usury Plays*, ed. Lloyd Edward Kermode (Revels Plays Companion Library) (Manchester: Manchester University Press, 2008), pp. 1–78.

54 Peter Happé, 'The Devil in the Interludes', *Medieval English Theatre* 11 (1989): 42–55, p. 46.

55 William R. Dynes, '"London, Look On!": the Estates Morality Play and the Moralities of Economy', paper for GEMCS conference, Pittsburgh, 1996. Online, available at: http://english.uindy.edu/dynes/estatesmorality.htm (accessed 23 February 2006).

56 Jonathan Gil Harris, *Sick Economies: Drama, Mercantilism, and Disease in Shakespeare's England* (Philadelphia: University of Pennsylvania Press, 2004), Chap. 4. My thanks are due to Professor Harris for his personal correspondence on this and other related issues.

3 ACCOMMODATING THE ALIEN IN MID-ELIZABETHAN LONDON PLAYS

1 References to *The Three Ladies of London* are from *Three Renaissance Usury Plays*, ed. Lloyd Edward Kermode (Revels Plays Companion Library) (Manchester: Manchester University Press, 2008).

2 Thomas Platter, *Thomas Platter's Travels in England*, trans. and intro. Clare Williams (1599; London: Jonathan Cape, 1937), p. 153.

3 Nigel Goose, 'Immigrants in Tudor and Early Stuart England', in *Immigrants in Tudor and Early Stuart England*, eds. Nigel Goose and Lien Luu (Brighton: Sussex Academic Press, 2005), pp. 1–38, p. 16; see also D. M. Palliser, who calculates that 'By 1547 there were perhaps 5 to 6,000 foreigners in London, amounting to between 5 and 8 per cent of the population; and by 1553 their numbers had risen to perhaps 10,000 or some 10 per cent' (*The Age of Elizabeth: England under the Later Tudors 1547–1603*, 2nd edn (London and New York: Longman, 1992), p. 66); Laura Hunt Yungblut finds that later, 'Despite the increased flow of immigrants into England, particularly in the 1560s and 1570s, the aliens on average rarely represented more than about 4–5 per cent of the total population living in areas in and around the City' (*Strangers Settled Here amongst Us: Policies, Perceptions and the Presence of Aliens in Elizabethan England* (London and New York: Routledge, 1996), p. 29).

4 On Italians in early modern England, see Michael Wyatt, *The Italian Encounter with Tudor England: a Cultural Politics of Translation* (Cambridge: Cambridge University Press, 2005), pp. 138, 144, 148. Wyatt notes that this community 'maintained a sense of their native cultural identity abroad' by closing off a street to create a type of piazza, but 'at no time during the Elizabethan period did the Italian community in London exceed more than several hundred persons, and of them only a very small number were engaged at any given time in professions associated with the promotion of Italian culture'; Alan Haynes provides a detailed summary of positions held by Italians in Elizabethan London – see his 'Italian Immigrants in England, 1550–1603', *History Today* 27.8 (1977): 526–34.

5 See Lien Bich Luu, *Immigrants and the Industries of London 1500–1700* (Aldershot: Ashgate, 2005), p. 90.

6 A. L. Beier, 'Social Problems in Elizabethan London', *Journal of Interdisciplinary History* 9 (1978): 203–21, p. 208.

7 Luu, *Immigrants and the Industries of London*, pp. 150, 156–60.

8 Letter reprinted in *Malone Society Collections* 1.1, ed. W. W. Greg (Oxford: Oxford University Press, 1907/1908), pp. 48–9. The reference to 'unclenly' foreigners is from a separate point in the same letter.

9 Great Britain, *Tudor Royal Proclamations*, 3 vols., eds. Paul L. Hughes and James F. Larkin (New Haven and London: Yale University Press, (vol. 1) 1964 and (vols. 2 and 3) 1969), 2, p. 466. According to the Proclamation, inhabitants of London with fewer than seven years' residency were to leave the city. Palliser questions the efficacy of such an order and, indeed, it could not have been easy removing residents who had established themselves in the capital city several years earlier. Neither was the population increase to be curbed, and Conrad Russell estimates a population approaching half a million by the end of the seventeenth century. See Palliser, *The Age of Elizabeth*, p. 250; Conrad Russell, *The Crisis of Parliaments: English History, 1509–1660* (1971; Oxford and New York: Oxford University Press, 1988), p. 172.

10 35 Eliz. I c. 6. A large proportion of this population came from migration within Britain. Roger Lockyer records the vast influx to the city from the provinces, going as far as to say, 'The increase in the city's population was caused entirely by immigration, for among the residents deaths outnumbered births, and even to maintain a stable level an inflow of 7,000 settlers was needed every year' (*The Early Stuarts: a Political History of England, 1603–1642* (London and New York: Longman, 1989), p. 7).

11 John Stow, *A Survey of London*, 2 vols., ed. C. L. Kingsford (1599 and 1603; Oxford: Clarendon Press, 1908), 1, p. 208.

12 Laura Hunt Yungblut, '"Mayntayninge the indigente and nedie": the Institutionalization of Social Responsibility in the Case of the Resident Alien Communities in Elizabethan Norwich and Colchester', in *From Strangers to Citizens: the Integration of Immigrant Communities in Britain, Ireland, and Colonial America, 1550–1750*, eds. Randolph Vigne and Charles Littleton (London: Huguenot Society of Great Britain and Ireland, 2001), pp. 99–105, 101–3.

13 For the favourable view of English relations with aliens see Steve Rappaport, *Worlds within Worlds: Structures of Life in Sixteenth-Century London* (Cambridge: Cambridge University Press, 1989). Rappaport makes an important, if sanguine, analysis on the insignificance of strangers in causing London's problems in the 1590s: 'In 1593 there were 5450 aliens in London and its environs, mostly French and Dutch, only 2.5 per cent more than in 1573. That area's total population, however, increased more than ten times as much between those years, from about 152,000 to 186,000 people, and thus the alien community actually became relatively smaller by the 1590s when strangers amounted to less than 3 per cent of all people living in London. However persuasive their claims, then, it is likely that the "great hurt of English citizens" which Londoners blamed on aliens was caused instead by economic problems, especially in the city's cloth-related crafts and trade, which began in the early 1560s and for which Dutch, French, and other aliens were not responsible' (p. 58). He continues, 'Indeed the fact that the two communities coexisted within the walls throughout the Tudors' reign must be counted among London's most important accomplishments. The deaths of thousands of Protestants and Catholics, royalists and radicals on the continent

are bloody reminders that in the early modern period brutal repression, expulsion, and even slaughter were at times the means adopted for dealing with religious, political, and other minorities. However grudging their acceptance of foreigners and strangers in their midst, Londoners chose a different course' (p. 60). Rappaport is setting his argument against the 'instability' argument of Peter Clark and Paul Slack in *English Towns in Transition 1500–1700* (Oxford: Oxford University Press, 1976). Rappaport's study itself has been questioned for its optimism by Ian Archer, in *The Pursuit of Stability: Social Relations in Elizabethan London* (Cambridge: Cambridge University Press, 1991).

14 See Joseph P. Ward, 'Fictitious Shoemakers, Agitated Weavers and the Limits of Popular Xenophobia in Elizabethan London', in *From Strangers to Citizens*, eds. Vigne and Littleton, pp. 80–7; Nigel Goose, '"Xenophobia" in Elizabethan and Early Stuart England: an Epithet Too Far?', in *Immigrants in Tudor and Early Stuart England*, eds. Goose and Luu, pp. 110–35.

15 For a discussion of the geohumoral determination of English identity, see Mary Floyd-Wilson, *English Ethnicity and Race in Early Modern Drama* (Cambridge: Cambridge University Press, 2003).

16 Emanuel van Meteren, Antwerp merchant, from his *A True Discourse Historicall, of the Succeeding Governours in the Netherlands* (Dutch, 1599; trans. London, 1602). He travelled in England in 1575, qtd in W. B. Rye, ed., *England as Seen by Foreigners* (1865; New York: B. Bloom, 1967), p. 70.

17 Levinus Lemnius, Dutch physician, 'Notes on England' (1560), in *The Touchstone of Complexions* (London, 1581), qtd in Rye, ed., *England as Seen by Foreigners*, p. 78.

18 Frederick, Duke of Wirtemberg [i.e. Württemberg], *A True and Faithful Narrative*, qtd in Rye, ed., *England as Seen by Foreigners*, p. 7.

19 Luu, *Immigrants and the Industries of London*, p. 41.

20 Daryl Palmer, *Hospitable Performances: Dramatic Genre and Cultural Practices in Early Modern England* (West Lafayette: Purdue University Press, 1992), p. 32.

21 Felicity Heal, *Hospitality in Early Modern England* (Oxford: Oxford University Press, 1990), pp. 322–4.

22 Note the use of 'honest' and 'poor' to describe the destitute English living in the seedy parts of town and following Hospitality at the funeral. It seems that the practice of an honest living cannot be detached from a life of poverty in this vision of corrupted society.

23 See Jonathan Gil Harris, '(Po)X Marks the Spot: How to "Read" "Early Modern" "Syphilis" in *The Three Ladies of London*', in *Sins of the Flesh: Responding to Sexual Disease in Early Modern Europe*, ed. Kevin Siena (Toronto: Center for Reformation and Renaissance Studies, 2005), pp. 111–34, esp. pp. 123–30.

24 Heal, *Hospitality in Early Modern England*, pp. 300–1.

25 In a liminal category is the public feasting of dignitaries, nobles, and royalty by town corporations – public in profile but private in practice, because hosted in large private dwellings or, more often, civic halls with controlled admission.

26 Caleb Dalechamp, *Christian Hospitality* (London, 1632), D2, p. 11.

27 Dalechamp, *Christian Hospitality*, F–Fv, pp. 25–6.

28 This problem is illustrated in the 'Epistle to the Reader' in I. M., *A Health to the Gentlemanly Profession of Servingmen* (London, 1598), qtd in Rye, ed., *England as Seen by Foreigners*, pp. 196–7 n. 27.

29 Yungblut, *Strangers Settled Here amongst Us*, pp. 56–7.

30 Jeffrey Knapp, 'Elizabethan Tobacco', in *New World Encounters*, ed. Stephen Greenblatt (Berkeley and Los Angeles: University of California Press, 1993), pp. 273–312, pp. 273–4.

31 Daniel Vitkus, *Turning Turk: English Theater and the Multicultural Mediterranean, 1570–1630* (New York: Palgrave Macmillan, 2003), esp. Chaps. 1 and 6; for extensive discussions on Anglo-Turkish relations and cultural representations, see Nabil Matar, *Turks, Moors, and Englishmen in the Age of Discovery* (New York: Columbia University Press, 1999), and *Islam in Britain 1558–1685* (Cambridge: Cambridge University Press, 1998); Jonathan Burton, 'Anglo-Ottoman Relations and the Image of the Turk in *Tamburlaine*', *Journal of Medieval and Early Modern Studies* 30 (2000): 125–56, esp. pp. 125–38; on the relation of this history to the play, see Daryl Palmer, 'Merchants and Miscegenation: *The Three Ladies of London*, *The Jew of Malta*, and *The Merchant of Venice*', in *Race, Ethnicity, and Power in the Renaissance*, ed. Joyce Green MacDonald (London: Associated University Presses, 1997), pp. 36–66; Alan Stewart, '"Come from Turkie": Mediterranean Trade in Late Elizabethan London', in *Re-Mapping the Mediterranean in Early Modern English Writings*, ed. Goran V. Stanivukovic (London: Palgrave Macmillan, 2007), pp. 157–77.

32 For an overview of the Anglo-Mediterranean trade in the context of the fraught development of London overseas trade through the early modern period, see Robert Brenner, *Merchants and Revolution: Commercial Change, Political Conflict, and London Overseas Traders, 1550–1653* (Princeton: Princeton University Press, 1993). For a revisionary review of Brenner's thesis, see David Harris Sacks, 'The Metropolis and the Revolution: Commercial, Urban, and Political Culture in Early Modern London', in *The Culture of Capital: Property, Cities, and Knowledge in Early Modern England*, ed. Henry S. Turner (New York and London: Routledge, 2002), pp. 139–62.

33 References to *The Three Lords and Three Ladies of London* are from Robert Wilson, *An Edition of Robert Wilson's 'The Three Ladies of London' and 'Three Lords and Three Ladies of London'*, ed. H. S. D. Mithal (New York and London: Garland, 1988). I give Mithal's line numbers followed by Q sig.

34 These references are taken from Sara Warneke, *Images of the Educational Traveller in Early Modern England* (Leiden: Brill, 1995), pp. 74, 79–82.

35 Philip Stubbes, *The Anatomie of Abuses* (1595 edn), ed. Margaret Jane Kidnie (Tempe: ACMRS, 2002), p. 70. The ongoing importance of these concerns in London seems confirmed by the healthy publishing record of *The Anatomie of Abuses*: two editions in 1583, a third in 1585, and another in 1595.

36 John Deacon, *Tobacco Tortured* (1616; Facsimile. New York: Da Capo Press, 1968). Cited in Sara Warneke, 'A Taste for Newfangledness: the Destructive Potential of Novelty in Early Modern England', *Sixteenth Century Journal* 26 (1995): 881–96, pp. 894–5.

37 Floyd-Wilson, *English Ethnicity and Race*; Warneke, *Images of the Educational Traveller*.

38 Arthur Freeman, 'Marlowe, Kyd, and the Dutch Church Libel', *English Literary Renaissance* 3 (1973): 44–52.

39 John Roche Dasent, ed., *Acts of the Privy Council of England*, n.s. xxiv (1592–3) (London: HMSO, 1901), p. 222.

40 These sources are listed by Alan Dessen, *Shakespeare and the Late Moral Plays* (Lincoln, NE: University of Nebraska Press, 1986), p. 7 and p. 170 n. 11.

41 See Freeman, 'Marlowe, Kyd, and the Dutch Church Libel', p. 50. John Michael Archer relates these lines to *The Merchant of Venice*. See *Citizen Shakespeare: Freemen and Aliens in the Language of the Plays* (New York: Palgrave Macmillan, 2005), pp. 44–5.

42 The Machiavellian merchant of course also recalls Marlowe's Barabas: he is introduced by Machiavel, who asks the audience not to judge Barabas poorly just 'because he favours me'.

43 Louis B. Wright, 'Social Aspects of Some Belated Moralities', *Anglia* 54 (1930): 107–48, p. 129 n. The latter point is made by Teresa Nugent, 'Usury and Counterfeiting in Wilson's *The Three Ladies of London* and *The Three Lords and Three Ladies of London*, and in Shakespeare's *Measure for Measure*', in *Money and the Age of Shakespeare*, ed. Linda Woodbridge (New York: Palgrave Macmillan, 2003), pp. 201–17, pp. 203–4, 207.

44 Nugent, 'Usury and Counterfeiting', pp. 203–4, 207–8, 213.

45 Angela Stock, '"Something done in honour of the city": Ritual, Theatre and Satire in Jacobean Civic Pageantry', in *Plotting Early Modern London: New Essays on Jacobean City Comedy*, eds. Dieter Mehl, Angela Stock, and Anne-Julia Zwierlein (Aldershot: Ashgate, 2004), pp. 125–44, esp. pp. 132–4.

46 Revised by Chettle, Dekker, Heywood, and Shakespeare. See Anthony Munday *et al.*, *Sir Thomas More*, eds. Vittorio Gabrieli and Giorgio Melchiori (Revels) (Manchester and New York: Manchester University Press, 1990), pp. 12–17, 21–7. Line references are from this edition.

47 Complaint from the Lord Mayor and Aldermen to the Privy Council, 13 September 1595. Reprinted in E. K. Chambers, *The Elizabethan Stage*, 4 vols. (Oxford: Clarendon Press, 1923), 4, p. 318.

48 By 28 July 1597, theatres were such health and order problems that the Privy Council ordered 'the Curtayne and the Theatre nere to Shorditch . . . or anie other common playhouse' to be closed for performances and 'plucke[d] downe'. It was added that the 'Justices of Surrey . . . take the like order for the playhouses in the Banckside, in Southwarke or elswhere in the said county within iii miles of London' (see Great Britain, *Acts of the Privy Council of England, 1452–1628*, 32 vols., ed. John Roche Dasent (London: HMSO, 1890–1907) (1597), p. 314). The plucking down order does not seem to have taken

force, although plays were ordered to stop for the summer of 1597. On 15 August 1597, 'very seditious and sclanderous matter' in a play on Bankside (the mysterious *Isle of Dogs*) led to the imprisonment of some of the players and writers. See Great Britain, *Acts of the Privy Council* (1597), p. 338.

49 Great Britain, *Acts of the Privy Council* (1591–2), pp. 506–8.

50 See Scott McMillin, *The Elizabethan Theatre and 'The Book of Sir Thomas More'* (Ithaca, NY: Cornell University Press, 1987), p. 67, and Richard Dutton, *Mastering the Revels: the Regulation and Censorship of English Renaissance Drama* (London: Macmillan, 1991), p. 83.

51 Barbara Freedman also encourages careful reading of Elizabethan uses of the words 'theatre', 'houses', and 'apprentices', all being words – like 'riot' – with multiple referents (see 'Elizabethan Protest, Plague, and Plays: Rereading the "Documents of Control"', *English Literary Renaissance* 26 (1996): 17–45).

52 John Rastell, *An Exposition of Certaine Difficult and Obscure Words, and Termes of the Lawes of This Realme* (London, 1592), Y4.

53 Letter from Sir William Webbe, Lord Mayor, to Lord Burghley, 12 June 1592: 'Beeing informed of a great disorder & tumult lyke to grow yesternight abowt viij of the clock within the Borough of Southwark, I went thither with all speed I could, taking with mee on of the Sherifes, whear I found great multitudes of people assembled togither, & the principall actours to bee certain servants of the ffeltmakers gathered togither out of Barnsey street & the Black fryers, with a great number of lose & maisterles men apt for such pourposes. Whearupon having made proclamation, & dismissed the multitude, I apprehended the chief doers and authors of the disorder, & have committed them to prison to bee farther punished, as they shall bee found to deserve. And having this morning sent for the Deputie & Constable of the Borough with Divers other of best credit, who wear thear present, to examine the cause & manner of the disorder, I found that it began vpon the serving of a warrant from my L. Chamberlain by on of the Knight Mareschalls men vpon a feltmakers servant, who was committed to the Mareschallsea with certein others, that were accused to his L. by the sayed Knight Mareschalls men without cause of offence, as them selves doe affirm. For rescuing of whome the sayed companies assembled themselves by occasion & pretence of their meeting at a play, which bysides the breach of the Sabboth day giveth opportunitie of committing these & such lyke disorders. The principall doers in this rude tumult I mean to punish to the example of others' (reprinted in Chambers, *The Elizabethan Stage*, 4, p. 310).

54 My reading of the relatively low level of 'riot' could, however, be influenced by deliberate Elizabethan government policy. Harsh punishment for misdemeanour offences seems to have been part of a strategy in the period for preventing escalation of minor disorders. A Proclamation of 1598, for instance, asserted that 'divers routs' have escalated to 'robberies and murders' and ordered a round-up of idle persons. A week after the Essex rebellion of 1601, another Proclamation imposes martial law over those who have not necessarily offended in any significant way but that sort 'being of likelihood

ready to lay hold of any occasion to enter into any tumult and disorder, thereby to seek rapine and pillage' (Great Britain, *Tudor Royal Proclamations*, 3, pp. 196–7, 232). The former document also mentions that the petty disorderlies became violent when confronted with officers of the law; assertions of power and rebellious responses can spiral upward, requiring more officers who in turn provoke louder calls by the citizens against oppression. Freedman also notes a good reason to side with McMillin's and Dutton's reading of the level of violence: 'One good reason to minimize social disorder in official reports was economic. When disorder was reported adequately, the Privy Council automatically appointed provost-marshals, with the result that communities such as Southwark were highly taxed for disciplinary services. Another good reason to minimize disorder was to avoid court interference in city affairs. Elizabeth's preference for martial law and exemplary punishment was well known. So, too, were its incendiary effects' (Freedman, 'Elizabethan Protest', p. 24).

55 McMillin, *The Elizabethan Theatre*, p. 72.
56 On 16 April the Privy Council sent a letter to the Lord Mayor of London: 'Whereas there was a lewde and vyle ticket or placarde set up upon some post in London purportinge some determynacion and intencion the apprentyces should have to attempt some vyolence on the strangers, and your Lordship as we understande hath by your carefull endevour apprehended one that is to be suspected and thought likelie to have written the same. Because oftentymes it doth fall out of soche lewde beginninges that further mischeife doth ensue yf in tyme it be not wyselie prevented ... wee thincke it convenient that he shalbe punyshed by torture used in like cases and so compelled to reveale the same. Wee truste you are so carefull in the government of the citty as yf some lewde persons had soche wicked purpose to attempt any thinge againste strangers that by your carefull foresighte the same shalbe prevented' (Great Britain, *Acts of the Privy Council* (1592–3), p. 187). This final sentence might imply the existence of a break between the attitude of the central Council and the officers for the parishes and wards. Some of the local officials may have been turning blind eyes to acts with which they could sympathize, even if not publicly approve.
57 Great Britain, *Acts of the Privy Council* (1592–3), pp. 200–1.
58 Thomas Platter wrote in the final year of the century that the Dutch and French immigrants 'have been very kindly received' (*Thomas Platter's Travels in England*, p. 156). We can question whether he was thinking of the behaviour of the aliens' peers or the protection afforded them by the government against native hostility.
59 Great Britain, *Acts of the Privy Council* (1592–3), p. 187.
60 Great Britain, *Acts of the Privy Council* (1592–3), p. 222.
61 Reprinted in Chambers, *The Elizabethan Stage*, 4, p. 293.
62 In his reprint edition of the play for the Malone Society, W. W. Greg keeps the Clown's speech in an appendix (Anthony Munday *et al.*, *The Book of Sir Thomas More*, ed. W. W. Greg (Malone Society) (Oxford: Oxford University

Press, 1911), Addition 11 (B, C) (Fol. 7a, b)); see Greg's explanation of the revision on p. 69. Gabrieli and Melchiori favour the text of the addition as intended to replace the original scene. However, this addition was probably made in 1603, and not during the 1592–3 attempts to get the play through the Master of the Revels, Edmund Tilney. (See Munday *et al.*, *Sir Thomas More*, p. 19, and pp. 37–40, detailing correspondences between Gabrieli's and Greg's edition with the Harley MS 7368; also McMillin, *The Elizabethan Theatre*, p. 153ff.)

63 Jean E. Howard and Phyllis Rackin, *Engendering a Nation: a Feminist Account of Shakespeare's English Histories* (New York: Routledge, 1997), pp. 198–200.

64 Dutton, *Mastering the Revels*, pp. 82–3.

65 The relevant crime would be 'rout', the stage before 'riot'. John Rastell writes, 'Rout, is when people do assemble them selves together & after do proceed or ride, or go forth, or do move by the instigation of one or more . . . that is a rout & against the law although they have not done or put in execution their mischevous entent. See the statute 1. Mar. c. 12' (Rastell, *An Exposition of Certaine Difficult and Obscure Words*, Y4–Y4v).

66 For a fuller discussion of the sensibilities of Tilney, see Dutton, *Mastering the Revels*, Chap. 3.

67 Munday *et al.*, *Sir Thomas More*, p. 30; Tracey Hill, '"The Cittie is in an uproare": Staging London in *The Booke of Sir Thomas More*', *Early Modern Literary Studies* 11.1 (2005): 2.1–19. Online, available at: http://purl.oclc.org/emls/11–1/more.htm (accessed 7 April 2006), Para. 5.

68 Hill, '"The Cittie is in an uproare"', para. 10.

69 Ian Munro, *The Figure of the Crowd in Early Modern London: the City and Its Double* (New York: Palgrave Macmillan, 2005), pp. 20–4.

70 Hill, '"The Cittie is in an uproare"', para. 16 (Hill's argument for the change in character of the rebel leaders runs through paras. 12–19). Hill refers to the Second Addition as it is set off in W. W. Greg's Malone Society edition of the play; in the Gabrieli and Melchiori edition, this addition is in the main body of the text of Act 2 (see n. 62 above for further details).

71 Joan Fitzpatrick, 'Food and Foreignness in *Sir Thomas More*', *Early Theatre* 7 (2004): 33–47, esp. pp. 33–40. I examine a couple of the same passages as Fitzpatrick, and the reader is encouraged to read her essay for comparison.

72 See Fitzpatrick, 'Food and Foreignness' for further discussion of the relationship between food, sex, and masculinity.

73 Munday *et al.*, *Sir Thomas More*, p. 85.

4 INCORPORATING THE ALIEN IN SHAKESPEARE'S SECOND TETRALOGY

1 Anon., *A Comparison of the English and Spanish Nation*, trans. from French by Robert Ashley (London, 1589), B3, p. 5.

2 Jane Kingsley-Smith, *Shakespeare's Drama of Exile* (London: Palgrave Macmillan, 2003), p. 29.

3 See William Shakespeare, *The Second Part of King Henry IV* (Updated edn), ed. Giorgio Melchiori (Cambridge: Cambridge University Press, 2007), pp. 55–61.

4 I am alluding to the argument by Scott McMillin and Sally-Beth MacLean that the Queen's Men were largely put together as a provincial mouthpiece for the Elizabethan regime (*The Queen's Men and Their Plays, 1583–1603* (Cambridge: Cambridge University Press, 1998)), and to Paula Blank's concern with the various competing English dialects and 'British' languages in the early modern period (*Broken English: Dialects and the Politics of Language in Renaissance Writings* (London and New York: Routledge, 1996)).

5 John Morrill, 'The British Problem, *c.* 1534–1707', in *The British Problem, c. 1534–1707: State Formation in the Atlantic Archipelago*, eds. Brendan Bradshaw and John Morrill (New York: St Martin's Press, 1996), pp. 1–38, p. 17.

6 David Read, 'Losing the Map: Topographical Understanding in the "Henriad"', *Modern Philology* 94 (1997): 475–95, p. 488.

7 Aaron Landau, '"I Live with Bread Like You": Forms of Inclusion in *Richard II*', *Early Modern Literary Studies* 11.1 (2005): 3.1–23. Online, available at: http://purl.oclc.org/emls/11-1/richard.htm (accessed 14 April 2006), Paras. 4–6.

8 Lisa Hopkins, *Shakespeare on the Edge: Border-Crossing in the Tragedies and the Henriad* (Aldershot: Ashgate, 2005), p. 18.

9 Bernhard Klein, *Maps and the Writing of Space in Early Modern England and Ireland* (New York: Palgrave Macmillan, 2001), p. 3.

10 John Michael Archer, *Citizen Shakespeare: Freemen and Aliens in the Language of the Plays* (New York: Palgrave Macmillan, 2005), p. 97; Kingsley-Smith, *Shakespeare's Drama of Exile*, p. 62.

11 Kingsley-Smith, *Shakespeare's Drama of Exile*, p. 62.

12 The Chorus uses 'imaginary' twice in his first speech; 'imagined' and six other orders to 'see' things in the 'mind' in his third; in his fourth speech, he has two calls to 'mind' things as they are meant rather than as they are; and the fifth asks the audience once to 'imagine' and three times to use their 'thought(s)'.

13 I was prompted to think along these lines by Peter Womack's 'Imagining Communities: Theatres and the English Nation in the Sixteenth Century', in *Culture and History 1350–1600: Essays on English Communities, Identities, and Writing*, ed. David Aers (Detroit: Wayne State University Press, 1992), pp. 91–145, pp. 92–3.

14 I am defending my argument here from a possible objection that could arise from Jonathan Gil Harris and Natasha Korda's Introduction to *Staged Properties in Early Modern English Drama* (Cambridge: Cambridge University Press, 2002), in which they correct the long-standing critical bias for a 'bare stage' over property-filled production. On p. 9, they highlight the Chorus' 'wooden O' speech as the archetypal nexus for such non-material fetishism.

15 Kingsley-Smith, *Shakespeare's Drama of Exile*, p. 59.

16 Kingsley-Smith notes that Foxe represents Protestant exile in this way (*Shakespeare's Drama of Exile*, p. 17).

17 Kingsley-Smith, *Shakespeare's Drama of Exile*, p. 15.

18 Christopher Highley, *Shakespeare, Spenser, and the Crisis in Ireland* (Cambridge: Cambridge University Press, 1997), p. 86–7.

19 Highley, *Shakespeare, Spenser, and the Crisis in Ireland*, p. 87.

20 Christopher Highley, 'Wales, Ireland, and *1 Henry IV*', *Renaissance Drama* n.s. 21 (1990): 91–114, pp. 95, 96–7.

21 Highley, *Shakespeare, Spenser, and the Crisis in Ireland*, pp. 6–7, 9, 67, 70, 76, 87.

22 Highley, *Shakespeare, Spenser, and the Crisis in Ireland*, pp. 93–4, 95, 97.

23 Philip Jenkins, 'The Plight of Pygmy Nations: Wales in Early Modern Europe', *North American Journal of Welsh Studies* 2 (2002): 1–11, p. 1.

24 Terence Hawkes, 'Bryn Glas', in *Post-Colonial Shakespeares*, eds. Ania Loomba and Martin Orkin (London and New York: Routledge, 1998), pp. 117–40, pp. 136–7.

25 Mark Netzloff, *England's Internal Colonies: Class, Capital, and the Literature of Early Modern English Colonialism* (New York: Palgrave Macmillan, 2003), p. 7; see also Michael Hechter, *Internal Colonialism: the Celtic Fringe in British National Development, 1536–1966* (1975; New Brunswick, NJ: Transaction Publishers, 1999).

26 Michael Neill, 'Broken English and Broken Irish: Nation, Language, and the Optic of Power in Shakespeare's Histories', *Shakespeare Quarterly* 45 (1994): 1–32, p. 16.

27 Neill, 'Broken English and Broken Irish', pp. 4–5.

28 Willy Maley, *Nation, State, and Empire in English Renaissance Literature: Shakespeare to Milton* (London: Palgrave Macmillan, 2003) p. 26.

29 Philip Schwyzer, *Literature, Nationalism, and Memory in Early Modern England and Wales* (Cambridge: Cambridge University Press, 2004), p. 6.

30 William Shakespeare, *The First Quarto of King Henry V*, ed. Andrew Gurr (Cambridge: Cambridge University Press, 2000), pp. 10, 22.

31 Maley, *Nation, State, and Empire*, p. 21.

32 The use of the trope 'mother earth' is contemporary, Sebastian Münster's *Cosmographia* (1574) employing it (see Klein, *Maps and the Writing of Space*, p. 38).

33 Old spelling text cited in Atsuhiko Hirota, 'The Romanticization of a British Past: Early Modern English Nationalism and the Literary Representations of Wales' (Ph.D. Diss., Claremont Graduate University, 2001), p. 166. (Lines 2817–20, my modernization.)

34 See Blank, *Broken English*, Chap. 5: 'Language, Laws, and Blood: the King's English and His Empire'.

35 Jacqueline Vanhoutte, *Strange Communion: Motherland and Masculinity in Tudor Plays, Pamphlets, and Politics* (Newark: University of Delaware Press, 2003), p. 165.

36 See John Gillies, *Shakespeare and the Geography of Difference* (Cambridge: Cambridge University Press, 1994), pp. 70–98; John Gillies and Virginia

Mason Vaughan, eds., *Playing the Globe: Genre and Geography in English Renaissance Drama* (Madison: Farleigh Dickinson University Press, 1998).

37 For *Tamburlaine*'s place in the recognition of a shift in the concepts and uses of map-making, see Klein, *Maps and the Writing of Space*, pp. 15–20.

38 David Armitage, *The Ideological Origins of the British Empire* (Cambridge: Cambridge University Press, 2000), pp. 7–8.

39 Matthew Greenfield, '*1 Henry IV*: Metatheatrical Britain', in *British Identities and English Renaissance Literature*, eds. David J. Baker and Willy Maley (Cambridge: Cambridge University Press, 2002), pp. 71–80, p. 72.

40 Andrew Hadfield and Willy Maley, Introduction in *Representing Ireland: Literature and the Origins of Conflict, 1534–1660*, eds. Brendan Bradshaw, Andrew Hadfield, and Willy Maley (Cambridge: Cambridge University Press, 1993), p. 11 (citing the Introduction in S. G. Ellis, *Tudor Ireland: Crown, Community and the Conflict of Cultures, 1470–1603* (London: Longman, 1985)).

41 Janette Dillon, *Language and Stage in Medieval and Renaissance England* (Cambridge: Cambridge University Press, 1998), p. 178.

42 Claire McEachern, *The Poetics of English Nationhood 1590–1612* (Cambridge: Cambridge University Press, 1996), p. 108.

43 Schwyzer, *Literature, Nationalism, and Memory*, p. 37.

44 Greenfield, '*1 Henry IV*', p. 75.

45 Highley, *Shakespeare, Spenser, and the Crisis in Ireland*, p. 96

46 Bruce Avery, 'Gelded Continents and Plenteous Rivers: Cartography as Rhetoric in Shakespeare', in *Playing the Globe*, eds. Gillies and Vaughan, pp. 46–62, p. 57.

47 Glanmor Williams, 'Religion and Welsh Literature in the Age of the Reformation', *Proceedings of the British Academy* 69 (1983): 371–408, p. 403; see also Williams, 'Prophecy, Poetry, and Politics in Medieval and Tudor Wales', in *British Government and Administration*, eds. H. Hearder and H. R. Loyn (Cardiff: University of Wales Press, 1974), pp. 104–16.

48 Hawkes, 'Bryn Glas', p. 119. In his essay, named after the place of battle and mutilation of the English in Holinshed, Terence Hawkes uses the idea of interactive juxtaposed texts in Derrida's 'Glas' as the epitome of the cross-border relationship of 'Great Britain' (pp. 117–18). Read from one side to the other, the 'texts' of Wales and England vary, interdepend, cast backward and forward, and re-signify.

49 Hawkes, 'Bryn Glas', p. 135.

50 Patricia Parker, 'Uncertain Unions: Welsh Leeks in *Henry V*', in *British Identities and English Renaissance Literature*, eds. Baker and Maley, pp. 81–100; Lisa Hopkins, 'Fluellen's Name', *Shakespeare Studies* 24 (1996): 148–55.

51 After all, Henry Tudor had come with French forces from his exile, and in the mid 1590s, there were strong rumours about the imminent arrival of Spanish support for the Irish resistance. For more on Milford Haven as a 'stand in for all of Wales', see Garrett A. Sullivan, *The Drama of Landscape: Land, Property, and Social Relations on the Early Modern Stage* (Stanford: Stanford University

Press, 1998), p. 139; see his Chap. 4, 'Civilizing Wales', p. 136 and *passim* for the balancing of Milford Haven as port of celebration and fear.

52 Hopkins, *Shakespeare on the Edge*, pp. 13–33.

53 Hopkins, *Shakespeare on the Edge*, p. 26.

54 Hopkins points out a similar ever-present but very suppressed threat in the second tetralogy: the relentless danger of women's roles through their equivocal lineage and language, sexuality and violence ('Fluellen's Name', pp. 150–4).

55 This point about the map in *1 Henry IV* is made by Avery, 'Gelded Continents and Plenteous Rivers', p. 58. For further discussion of the completeness and 'semiotic residue' of maps in *Henry IV* and *King Lear*, see also John Gillies, 'The Scene of Cartography in *King Lear*', in *Literature, Mapping, and the Politics of Space in Early Modern Britain*, eds. Andrew Gordon and Bernhard Klein (Cambridge: Cambridge University Press, 2001), pp. 109–37.

56 Ronald Boling briefly reads this term backward through the lens of *Cymbeline*, where Cloten is an 'irregulous devil' (4.2.317), reminding us of the related fear of the 'irregular' 'damned' 'devil' Glyndwr (1.3.82 & 2.5.337); see 'Anglo-Welsh Relations in *Cymbeline*', *Shakespeare Quarterly* 51 (2000): 33–66, p. 50.

57 See Howard's footnote to *1 Henry IV* 1.1.40 in *The Norton Shakespeare*, eds. Stephen Greenblatt *et al.* (New York and London: W. W. Norton, 1997), p. 1158.

58 See Paul Brown, 'This Thing of Darkness I Acknowledge Mine: *The Tempest* and the Discourse of Colonialism', in *Political Shakespeare: Essays in Cultural Materialism*, eds. Jonathan Dollimore and Alan Sinfield (Ithaca, NY: Cornell University Press, 1985), p. 54 for a discussion and contextualization of the 'wild' man performed for Elizabeth in 1575. See G. M. Pinciss, 'The Savage Man in Spenser, Shakespeare, and Renaissance Drama', *The Elizabethan Theatre* 8 (1982): 69–89, for an extended examination of wild man plays. For the Irish and American wild 'savage' connection, see Ronald Takaki, '*The Tempest* in the Wilderness: the Racialization of Savagery', *Journal of American History* 79 (1992): 892–912. For a reassessment of the English view via non-dramatic literature of the savagery and uses of Ireland and the Irish, see Andrew Hadfield, *Edmund Spenser's Irish Experience: Wilde Fruit and Salvage Soyl* (Oxford: Clarendon Press, 1997), and Willy Maley, *Salvaging Spenser: Colonialism, Culture and Identity* (New York: St Martin's Press, 1997).

59 Morrill, 'The British Problem', p. 7.

60 Archer, *Citizen Shakespeare*, p. 108.

61 Williams, 'Religion and Welsh Literature', p. 401. Blank cites George Owen's characterization of Pembrokeshire in 1603 as 'a kind of cultural oasis, another English island encircled by a (Welsh) "sea"' (Blank, *Broken English*, p. 131).

62 The quotation is from Blank, *Broken English*, p. 128.

63 Megan Lloyd, *'Speak it in Welsh': Wales and the Welsh Language in Shakespeare* (Lanham, MD: Rowman and Littlefield, 2007), p. 1.

64 Steven Mullaney, 'Strange Things, Gross Terms, Curious Customs: the Rehearsal of Cultures in the Late Renaissance', in *Representing the Renaissance*, ed. Stephen Greenblatt (Berkeley and Los Angeles: University of California Press, 1988), pp. 65–92, p. 81.

65 Hawkes, 'Bryn Glas', p. 127; David Steinsaltz, 'The Politics of French Language in Shakespeare's History Plays', *Studies in English Literature 1500–1900* 42 (2002): 317–34, p. 331.

66 Peter Roberts, 'Tudor Legislation and the Political Status of "the British Tongue"', in *The Welsh Language before the Industrial Revolution*, ed. Geraint H. Jenkins (Cardiff: University of Wales Press, 1997), p. 136; see also Blank, *Broken English*, p. 133.

67 William P. Griffith notes the influence of English language and values in Wales 'long before the Acts of Union'. There are men of standing in both north and south Wales in the fifteenth and sixteenth centuries who had courtly and English upbringings and educations, although the matter should not be exaggerated ('Humanist Learning, Education and the Welsh Language', in *The Welsh Language before the Industrial Revolution*, ed. Jenkins, pp. 289–315, pp. 289–90).

68 Roberts, 'Tudor Legislation', p. 123; Williams, 'Religion and Welsh Literature', pp. 392–3. 'Official permission to produce the Scriptures in the vernacular was extended to the native Irish as well in the 1560s, following what appears to have been a general decision of policy to encourage the spread of Protestantism', and significant money was spent on casting new type for the project before a drop-off in financial support (Roberts, 'Tudor Legislation', p. 146); see also Peter Roberts, 'Tudor Wales, National Identity and the British Inheritance', in *British Consciousness and Identity: the Making of Britain, 1533–1707*, eds. Brendan Bradshaw and Peter Roberts (Cambridge: Cambridge University Press, 1998), pp. 8–42.

69 Roberts, 'Tudor Legislation', p. 148.

70 Williams, 'Religion and Welsh Literature', pp. 383–4.

71 Williams, 'Religion and Welsh Literature', p. 400.

72 There is the intriguing hypothesis that Falstaff originally survived through an earlier draft of *Henry V* and that after he is killed off, his potential role was taken over and shared by the other semi-Welsh characters, Captain Gower and Williams (Joan Rees, 'Shakespeare's Welshmen', in *Literature and Nationalism*, eds. Vincent Newey and Ann Thompson (Liverpool: Liverpool University Press, 1991), pp. 22–40, pp. 31–2). The folio stage direction that begins 3.6 reads: 'Enter Captains, English and Welsh, Gower and Fluellen' (*First Folio* 434). *The Norton Shakespeare* deletes the phrase 'English and Welsh', but the point is being made that Gower, in spite of his Welsh-sounding name, is English. This is not done, however, for the soldier Williams. That Falstaff is Captain of a ragged band (*1 HIV* 4.2) and that one Captain without accent and one English soldier should be given such Welsh names seems to lend some support to the substitution hypothesis.

73 Hirota, 'The Romanticization of a British Past', p. 167.

74 See David Baker's similar reading of this passage in *Between Nations: Shakespeare, Spenser, Marvell, and the Question of Britain* (Stanford: Stanford University Press, 1997), pp. 57–8.

75 Baker observes that the name MacMorris is taken from an Old English family (*Between Nations*, p. 36). A foundational reading of this scene is Graham Holderness, '"What Ish My Nation?": Shakespeare and National Identities', *Textual Practice* 5 (1991): 74–93.

76 Archer, *Citizen Shakespeare*, p. 117.

77 McEachern, *The Poetics of English Nationhood*, pp. 109–10.

78 Read, 'Losing the Map', p. 485.

79 Schwyzer, *Literature, Nationalism, and Memory*, p. 126.

80 Willy Maley, 'Postcolonial Shakespeare: British Identity Formation and *Cymbeline*', in *Shakespeare's Late Plays: New Readings*, eds. J. Richards and J. Knowles (Edinburgh: Edinburgh University Press, 1999), pp. 145–57, p. 146.

81 Maley, 'Postcolonial Shakespeare', p. 149.

82 Maley, 'Postcolonial Shakespeare', p. 150.

83 Avraham Oz, 'Extending Within: Placing Self and Nation in the Epic of *Cymbeline*', *Journal of Theatre and Drama* 4 (1998): 81–97, p. 83.

84 Claire McEachern, *The Poetics of English Nationhood 1590–1612* (Cambridge: Cambridge University Press, 1996), p. 30.

85 Jodi Mikalachki, *The Legacy of Boadicea: Gender and Nation in Early Modern England* (London: Routledge, 1998), pp. 110–11.

86 See the Introduction to Stephen Greenblatt, *Renaissance Self-Fashioning: from More to Shakespeare* (Chicago: Chicago University Press, 1980), pp. 1–9.

87 Moreover, with Jodi Mikalachki's reading in mind, we have to remain aware that this play, with its combination of charm and harsh nationalism, articulates its rejections and incorporations of identity around a strongly masculinized sense of Roman and British heritage. See Mikalachki, *The Legacy of Boadicea*, pp. 96–114.

88 Sullivan cites Humfrey Lluyd's *The Breviary of Britaine* (1573). See Sullivan, *The Drama of Landscape*, p. 146.

89 Huw Griffiths, 'The Geographies of Shakespeare's *Cymbeline*', *English Literary Renaissance* 34 (2004): 339–58, pp. 352–3.

5 BEING THE ALIEN IN LATE-ELIZABETHAN LONDON PLAYS

1 Jean Howard, 'Women, Foreigners, and the Regulation of Urban Space in *Westward Ho*', in *Material London, ca. 1600*, ed. Lena Cowen Orlin (Philadelphia: University of Pennsylvania Press, 2000), pp. 150–67, pp. 152–3.

2 Laura Caroline Stevenson, *Praise and Paradox: Merchants and Craftsmen in Elizabethan Popular Literature* (Cambridge: Cambridge University Press, 1984), p. 30.

3 Peter McCluskey, '"Shall I betray my brother?": Anti-Alien Satire and Its Subversion in *The Shoemaker's Holiday*', *Tennessee Philological Bulletin* 37 (2000): 43–54, pp. 44–5.

4 Andrew Fleck, 'Marking Difference and National Identity in Dekker's *The Shoemaker's Holiday*', *Studies in English Literature 1500–1900* 46 (2006): 349–70, pp. 358–9.

5 Quoted in Louis B. Wright, *Middle-Class Culture in Elizabethan England* (Chapel Hill: University of North Carolina Press, 1955), p. 36. Wright quotes from Thomas Johnson's *Cornucopiae, or Divers Secrets* (1596), F2–F2v.

6 For a discussion of Anglo-Jewish contact and relations in this decade, see Theodore K. Rabb, 'The Stirrings of the 1590s and the Return of the Jews to England', *Transactions of the Jewish Historical Society of England* 26 (1974–8): 26–33.

7 We have records of sixteenth-century Jewish activity in Seething Lane (Sydon Lane), Crutched Friars, Hart Street, Fenchurch, and Duke's Place. For the return of Jews to England in the late-fifteenth to mid-sixteenth centuries see Lucien Wolf's ground-breaking 'Jews in Elizabethan England', *Transactions of the Jewish Historical Society of England* 11 (1924–7), 1–91; C. J. Sisson, 'A Colony of Jews in Shakespeare's London', *Essays and Studies* 23 (1938): 38–52; Albert M. Hyamson, *The Sephardim of England: History of the Spanish and Portuguese Jewish Community, 1492–1951* (New York: AMS Press, 1951); Cecil Roth, *A History of the Jews in England*, 3rd edn (Oxford: Clarendon Press, 1964); Roger Prior, 'A Second Jewish Community in Tudor London', *Transactions of the Jewish Historical Society of England* 31 (1989–90): 137–52; James Shapiro, *Shakespeare and the Jews* (New York: Columbia University Press, 1996), pp. 68–76 and *passim*; David S. Katz, *The Jews in the History of England, 1485–1850* (Oxford: Clarendon Press, 1995).

8 Samuel Purchas, *Hakluytus Posthumus, or Purchas His Pilgrimes*, 20 vols. (1625; Glasgow: James MacLehose & Sons, 1905), 10, p. 427. At Coryate's time of writing (1613) Amis was sixty years old, and he left London when he was thirty; so he was in London from 1553 to 1583.

9 All references to *Englishmen for My Money* are from *Three Renaissance Usury Plays*, ed. Lloyd Edward Kermode (Revels Plays Companion Library) (Manchester: Manchester University Press, 2008).

10 For a very useful study of the features of the stage usurer, see Celeste Turner Wright, 'Some Conventions regarding the Usurer in Elizabethan Literature', *Studies in Philology* 31 (1934): 176–97. This work highlights the contemporary confusions in identifying a figure of the 'other' in racial and religious terms, while pointing to prejudicial behavioural and physical features. For social issues and the appearance of Jews in Europe see Alfred Rubens, *A History of Jewish Costume* (1967; London: Weidenfeld and Nicolson, 1973), and Rubens, *A Jewish Iconography* (London: The Jewish Museum, 1954).

11 Pisaro's oath may suggest conversion to Catholicism, which would do him little good in Elizabethan England; Marina's rejection of nunhood pushes in the other direction. These seem like dramatic commonplaces, however, like Aaron calling Lucius 'popish' in *Titus Andronicus* (5.1.76).

12 For an extended overview of this non-dramatic context, see the Introduction to *Three Renaissance Usury Plays*, ed. Kermode, pp. 1–78, pp. 1–28.

The better-known extant usury tracts include Thomas Wilson, *A Discourse upon Usury*, ed. R. H. Tawney (London, 1572); Phillip Caesar, *A General Discourse against the Damnable Sect of Usurers* (London, 1578); Henry Smith, *An Examination of Usurie* (London, 1591); the anonymous *The Death of Usury, or the Disgrace of Usurers* (Cambridge, 1594); and Miles Mosse, *The Arraignment and Conviction of Usury* (London, 1595). It is not unreasonable to assume a sizeable readership for the books printed in London. Mosse makes the point that printing in London (rather than at one of the universities) makes the work available to the general – and usurious – public.

13 For the play entry, see Philip Henslowe, *Henslowe's Diary*, eds. R. A. Foakes and R. T. Rickert (Cambridge: Cambridge University Press, 1961), p. 89.

14 The quotation is from Theodore B. Leinwand, *The City Staged: Jacobean Comedy, 1603–1613* (Madison: University of Wisconsin Press, 1986), p. 53. Stevenson, drawing on Lawrence Stone's *The Crisis of the Aristocracy, 1558–1641* (1965; Oxford: Clarendon Press, 1979), reminds us of this climate of credit (Stevenson, *Praise and Paradox*, p. 94).

15 Shapiro, *Shakespeare and the Jews*, p. 186.

16 For one assessment of the problems of the decade, see M. J. Power, 'London and the Control of the "Crisis" of the 1590s', *History* 70 (1985): 371–85.

17 A. J. Hoenselaars, *Images of Englishmen and Foreigners in the Drama of Shakespeare and His Contemporaries: a Study of Stage Characters and National Identity in English Renaissance Drama, 1558–1642* (London and Toronto: Associated University Presses, 1992), p. 57.

18 Henslowe, *Henslowe's Diary*, pp. 87, 89.

19 For a good study of the place of language in (anti-)alien drama, see Chap. 7 of Janette Dillon's *Language and Stage in Medieval and Renaissance England* (Cambridge: Cambridge University Press, 1998). Dillon frames the chapter with a reading of *The Spanish Tragedy*, and includes a significant section on *Henry V*. She also makes some interesting observations about *Three Ladies* and *Englishmen for My Money*. Her balanced historical overview is also useful. However, her use of 'racist' to describe English prejudice against European languages and their import (e.g. pp. 164, 167, 176) allows her to elide English–European conflict and the English colonial experience of distant others (e.g. p. 176) a little too easily.

20 Hoenselaars, *Images of Englishmen*, p. 58.

21 Dillon notes the strategic use of English characters' 'failure' to speak foreign languages as part of an oppressive, co-opting (or colonizing) system that controls the alien. See Dillon, *Language and Stage*, pp. 169, 182.

22 See Teresa Nugent, 'Usury and Counterfeiting in Wilson's *The Three Ladies of London* and *The Three Lords and Three Ladies of London*, and in Shakespeare's *Measure for Measure*', in *Money and the Age of Shakespeare*, ed. Linda Woodbridge (New York: Palgrave Macmillan, 2003), pp. 201–17, pp. 203–4, 207–8, 213.

23 Firk's line to the injured Ralph, 'Thou lie with a woman, to build nothing but Cripplegates!' (14.67) could be compared. In this case, the vaguer alien

reference seems to be to the return of soldiers from wars, forced to beg and burden society.

24 Emma Smith sees such assertive power as an inherited and gendered national trait: 'In his play, Haughton has killed off the mother but not her tongue: Pisaro's wife had given her language, and with it her national status, to her daughters' ('"So much English by the Mother": Gender, Foreigners, and the Mother Tongue in William Haughton's *Englishmen for My Money*, *Medieval and Renaissance Drama in England* 13 (2001): 165–81, p. 176).

25 Edmund Valentine Campos, 'Jews, Spaniards, and Portingales: Ambiguous Identities of Portuguese *Marranos* in Elizabethan England', *ELH* 69 (2002): 599–616, p. 613.

26 Diane Cady, 'Linguistic Dis-ease: Foreign Language as Sexual Disease in Early Modern England', in *Sins of the Flesh: Responding to Sexual Disease in Early Modern Europe*, ed. Kevin Siena (Toronto: Center for Reformation and Renaissance Studies, 2005), pp. 159–86, pp. 179, 161.

27 Leinwand, *The City Staged*; Jean Howard, *Theater of a City: the Places of London Comedy, 1598–1642* (Philadelphia: University of Pennsylvania Press, 2007).

28 I do not agree with Angela Stock, who argues that elements of London description are brought into the play as a satirical response to the (just about to be) published *Survey of London* by John Stow. See 'Stow's *Survey* and the London Playwrights', in *John Stow and the Making of the English Past*, eds. Ian Gadd and Alexandra Gillespie (London: British Library, 2004), pp. 89–98.

29 Thomas Nashe, *The Works of Thomas Nashe*, 5 vols., ed. Ronald B. McKerrow (Oxford: Basil Blackwell, 1966), 2, p. 312. The middle of the seventeenth century sees the publication of Thomas Browne's *Pseudodoxia Epidemica*. In Chap. 10, Browne dismisses the theory of a 'Jewish smell', since the Jews are not a racially distinct group, but intermingled with others; since they eat more carefully than other people; and since the smell is not evident in the synagogues. The theory arose, Browne supposes, from the literalizing of the metaphorical assertion that the Jews' antipathy to Christians 'made them abominable and stinck in the nostrils of all men', and Jacob's comment that his sons' abomination had made him 'stinke in the land' (Gen. 24) (*Sir Thomas Browne's Pseudodoxia Epidemica*, ed. Robin Robbins, 2 vols. (1646; Oxford: Clarendon Press, 1981), 1, pp. 324–9).

30 Andrew Gurr, 'The Bare Island', *Shakespeare Survey* 47 (1994): 29–43, p. 36.

31 In his edition of the play, A. C. Baugh identified the conduit at the junction of Leadenhall and Cornhill streets as the one referred to in this instant (William Haughton, *Englishmen for My Money*, ed. Albert Croll Baugh (Ph.D. Diss., University of Pennsylvania, 1917), p. 226). John Stow writes that a forcier conveyed Thames water through the main pipe, which 'with foure spoutes did at every tyde runne (according to covenant) four wayes, plentifully serving to the commoditie of the inhabitants neare adjoyning in their houses, and also cleansed the Chanels of the streete towarde Bishopsgate, Aldgate, the bridge, and the Stocks Market' (*A Survey of London*, 2 vols., ed.

C. L. Kingsford (1599 and 1603; Oxford: Clarendon Press, 1908), 1, p. 188). Stow also notes that the highly beneficial conduit was built by one Peter Morris, a German, in 1582.

32 John Orrell, 'The Architecture of the Fortune Playhouse', *Shakespeare Survey* 47 (1994): 15–27, pp. 23–6. A combination of the Greek derivative 'Herm', from the god of passing-over, Hermes, and the Roman 'Term', from *terminus*, or boundary, gives us a richly suggestive etymological and semiotic context in which to think about the trope of foreigners being kept within limits by hitting their heads on the posts, while being directed to cross over the boundary of the city in the fiction of the play, while in reality heading for the groundling audience at the limit of the stage. Orrell points out the continuation of the iconography of Terms in frontispiece engravings (illus., p. 25).

33 Christopher Marlowe, *Edward II*, eds. Martin Wiggins and Robert Lindsey (New Mermaids) (London: A & C Black, 1997), 5.4.31; Nashe, *The Works*, 2, p. 298.

34 The term 'Bridewell-bird' was current in the 1580s and 1590s (*OED* 'Bridewell'). Shapiro notes that, in response to the Dutch church libel, the Privy Council 'not only ordered a search and apprehension of those suspected of writing the poem, but sanctioned the use of torture at Bridewell prison', presumably to make the inmates 'sing' (*Shakespeare and the Jews*, p. 184).

35 Fleck, 'Marking Difference', pp. 352–3.

36 Janette Dillon points out that *Henry V* does a similar job of censuring hierarchical contravention when it has Williams complain that he only talked to the king as brashly as he did because the king was not in his proper place; had the king in fact been a commoner, Williams would have committed no offence (see *Language and Stage*, p. 181).

37 Ronda A. Arab, 'Work, Bodies, and Gender in *The Shoemaker's Holiday*', *Medieval and Renaissance Drama in England* 13 (2001): 182–212, pp. 184–8.

38 Jonathan Gil Harris and Natasha Korda discuss this shift in the medieval and early modern senses of 'property' in their Introduction to *Staged Properties in Early Modern English Drama.*, eds. Jonathan Gil Harris and Natasha Korda (Cambridge: Cambridge University Press, 2002).

39 Line references are to Anthony Parr's New Mermaids edition of the play, 2nd edn (London: A & C Black, 1990).

40 Alexander Leggatt for one notices the play's 'deliberate suppression of material' found in Deloney's source text *The Gentle Craft* on this issue; see *Citizen Comedy in the Age of Shakespeare* (Toronto: University of Toronto Press, 1973), p. 18.

41 Silk weaving was a very prominent resident alien occupation in late-sixteenth-century London. The Ellesmere MS version of the 1593 return of strangers records 219 alien silk weavers in the Metropolis plus 136 in other silk-production jobs (355 total), out of 704 alien workers in all clothing and cloth jobs. By comparison, there were only 66 shoemakers, 20 cobblers, 6 bakers, 85 brewers, and 158 merchants in the return. After our period, in the 1635 return, only 12 aliens were listed as silk weavers among 609 weavers in general (Irene Scouloudi, *Returns of Strangers in the Metropolis 1593, 1627, 1635, 1639: a Study of an*

Active Minority (London: Huguenot Society of Great Britain and Ireland, 1985), pp. 131, 133. See also Lien Luu's chapter on the silk industry in *Immigrants and the Industries of London 1500–1700* (Aldershot: Ashgate, 2005), pp. 175–217.

42 Jean MacIntyre thinks that Eyre displays 'an egalitarian indifference to garments that display a man's rank. This contrasts him with his wife, Margery, for whom a French hood, a periwig, and a farthingale are the purpose of promotion to office' ('Shore's Wife and *The Shoemaker's Holiday*', *Cahiers Elisabethains* 12 (1991): 17–28, p. 22). In fact, as the quotation in the main text makes clear, it is Eyre who gives Margery the French hood with some pride. Eyre loves the 'idea' of his new apparel and understands its social importance.

43 Robert Tittler, *Architecture and Power: the Town Hall and the English Urban Community* (Oxford: Clarendon Press, 1991), esp. Chap. 5, 'Oligarchy, Deference, and the Built Environment'; see also Tittler, 'The End of the Middle Ages in the English Country Town', *Sixteenth Century Journal* 4 (1987): 471–87.

44 In addition to Ann Rosalind Jones and Peter Stallybrass, *Renaissance Clothing and the Materials of Memory* (Cambridge: Cambridge University Press, 2000), earlier work addresses other aspects of stage apparel: see Peter Hyland, 'Disguise and Renaissance Tragedy', *University of Toronto Quarterly* 55 (1985–6): 161–71; Muriel Bradbrook, 'Shakespeare and the Use of Disguise in Elizabethan Drama', *Essays in Criticism* 2 (1952): 159–68; and Victor O. Freeburg's traditional *Disguise Plots in Elizabethan Drama: a Study in Stage Tradition* (1915; New York: Benjamin Blom, 1965). Roze Hentschell's essay 'Treasonous Textiles: Foreign Cloth and the Construction of English-ness', *Journal of Medieval and Early Modern Studies* 32 (2002): 543–70, usefully discusses the role of clothing as a marker of nationality.

45 Jonathan Gil Harris, 'Properties of Skill: Product Placement in Early English Artisanal Drama', in *Staged Properties in Early Modern English Drama*, eds. Harris and Korda, pp. 35–66, p. 54.

46 Julia Gasper, *The Dragon and the Dove: the Plays of Thomas Dekker* (Oxford: Clarendon Press, 1990), p. 19.

47 Gasper, *The Dragon and the Dove*, p. 20.

48 Gasper, *The Dragon and the Dove*, p. 19.

49 Joseph P. Ward, 'Fictitious Shoemakers, Agitated Weavers and the Limits of Popular Xenophobia in Elizabethan London', in *From Strangers to Citizens: the Integration of Immigrant Communities in Britain, Ireland, and Colonial America, 1550–1750*, eds. Randolph Vigne and Charles Littleton (London: Huguenot Society of Great Britain and Ireland, 2001), pp. 80–7, p. 85.

50 See Thomas Dekker, *The Shoemaker's Holiday*, in *Drama of the English Renaissance 1: the Tudor Period*, eds. Russell A. Fraser and Norman Rabkin (New York: Macmillan, 1976), 1.iv.52 n., p. 489.

51 These points are made by McCluskey, ' "Shall I betray my brother?" ', pp. 44 and 49, and Andrew Fleck, 'Marking Difference', p. 363.

52 McCluskey, '"Shall I betray my brother?"', p. 49.

53 Gerald Porter, 'Cobblers All: Occupation as Identity and Cultural Message', *Folk Music Journal* 7 (1995): 43–61, p. 46.

54 L. D. Timms, 'Dekker's *The Shoemaker's Holiday* and Elizabeth's Accession Day', *Notes and Queries* 230 (1985): 58.

55 Scouloudi, *Returns of Strangers*, p. 24.

56 Between these two uses of 'Roland', Eyre turns to his wife and scolds her suggestion that he get rid of 'Hans': 'Why, my sweet Lady Madgy, think you Simon Eyre can forget his fine Dutch journeyman? No, vah! Fie, I scorn it! It shall never be cast in my teeth that I was unthankful. Lady Madgy, thou hadst never covered thy Saracen's head with this French flap, nor loaden thy bum with this farthingale – 'tis trash, trumpery, vanity! – Simon Eyre had never walked in a red petticoat, nor wore a chain of gold, but for my fine journeyman's portagues; and shall I leave him? No. Prince am I none, yet bear a princely mind' (17.12–20). It is interesting that Eyre's everyday discourse takes on 'Dutchisms'. In one of his tirades against the workers and women who frustrate him, we hear, 'Avaunt, kitchen-stuff! Rip, you brown-bread *tannikin*, out of my sight!' (7.63–4, my emphasis).

57 See Robert Wilson, *An Edition of Robert Wilson's 'The Three Ladies of London' and 'Three Lords and Three Ladies of London'*, ed. H. S. D. Mithal (New York and London: Garland, 1988), lines 2105–69; sig. I–Iv.

58 Jones and Stallybrass, *Renaissance Clothing and the Materials of Memory*, pp. 204–5.

59 Harris, 'Properties of Skill', pp. 51–2.

60 David Scott Kastan, 'Workshop and/as Playhouse: Comedy and Commerce in *The Shoemaker's Holiday*', *Studies in Philology* 84 (1987): 324–37, p. 330.

61 Karl Marx and Friedrich Engels, *Economic and Philosophic Manuscripts of 1844*, in *The Marx–Engels Reader*, 2nd edn, ed. Robert C. Tucker (New York: W. W. Norton, 1978), p. 72.

62 *OED* 'drum', entry 3b (the play is not cited by the *OED*). For use of the full term see Robert Wilson, *The Three Ladies of London*, in *Three Renaissance Usury Plays*, ed. Kermode, 8.127; Nashe, *The Works*, 2, p. 218; and Shakespeare, *All's Well that Ends Well*, 3.6.34. A book from 1581 warned travellers to Rome that they could expect to find in that city, 'no hoste to intertaine you, unlesse perhappes, some prettie noppes to make a ridying stocke: would graunt you a breakefaste, and after she had laughed her fill, give you Jacke Drommes, entertainment, and thrust the contemner of Beautie, the dispraiser of Love, the despiser of women, and the disparager of their honours, out of the doores' (Barnabe Rich, *The Straunge and Wonderfull Adventures of Don Simonides, a Gentilman Spaniarde* (London, 1581), S3).

63 Signature citations are from Q1 1601.

64 Marston's satirical characterization in *Jack Drum* and his involvement in the war of the theatres more generally have been dealt with by a number of authorities including E. K. Chambers, *The Elizabethan Stage*, 4 vols. (Oxford: Clarendon Press, 1923), 3, p. 428, citing the representation of Jonson in the play in the character of Brabant Senior; see also Anthony

Caputi, *John Marston, Satirist* (Ithaca, NY: Cornell University Press, 1961); Philip J. Finkelpearl, *John Marston of the Middle Temple* (Cambridge, MA: Harvard University Press, 1969); R. W. Ingram, *John Marston* (Boston: G. K. Hall, 1978), Chaps. 4–5; Michael Scott, *John Marston's Plays: Theme, Structure, and Performance* (London: Macmillan, 1978); Morse S. Allen, *The Satire of John Marston* (New York: Haskell House, 1965).

65 William Biddulph, *The Travels of Certaine Englishmen into Africa, Asia, Troy, Bythinia, Thracia, and into the Black Sea* (1609; Facsimile. New York: Da Capo Press, 1968), M4v (p. 74).

66 Francis Bacon, 'Of Usury', in *The Essays or Counsells, Civill and Morall*, ed. Michael Kiernan (Cambridge, MA: Harvard University Press, 1985), pp. 124–5.

67 Robert Greene, *Selimus* (London, 1594), G4v.

68 See Anthony Munday *et al.*, *Sir Thomas More*, eds. Vittorio Gabrieli and Giorgio Melchiori (Revels) (Manchester: Manchester University Press, 1990), 2.1.21–2.

69 For this practice in Italy, see Poul Borchsenius, *Behind the Wall: the Story of the Ghetto*, trans. Reginald Spink (London: George Allen and Unwin, 1964), p. 94. For England, see Michael Adler, *Jews of Medieval England* (London: The Jewish Historical Society, 1939), Chap. 6.

70 Stow, *Survey*, I, p. 30.

71 C. J. Sisson concludes that 'the whole colony of Portuguese Jews . . . did in fact practise their true religion in secret, throughout the Tudor period' ('A Colony of Jews in Shakespeare's London', *Essays and Studies* 23 (1938): 38–52, p. 49).

72 Sisson, 'A Colony of Jews', pp. 45–6.

73 For broadsheets of evicted Jews see David Kunzle, *The Early Comic Strip: Narrative Strips and Picture Stories in the European Broadsheet from* c. *1450 to 1825* (Berkeley: University of California Press, 1972).

74 Finkelpearl, *John Marston of the Middle Temple*, p. 135.

POSTSCRIPT: EARLY MODERN AND POST-MODERN
ALIEN EXCURSIONS

1 Jeffrey Knapp, *An Empire Nowhere: England, America, and Literature from* Utopia *to* The Tempest (Berkeley and Los Angeles: University of California Press, 1992), p. 4.

2 See, for example, Barbara Fuchs' essay, 'Faithless Empires: Pirates, Renegadoes, and the English Nation', *ELH* 67 (2000): 45–69; also Daniel Vitkus' edition of *Three Turk Plays from Early Modern England:* Selimus, A Christian Turned Turk, *and* The Renegado (New York: Columbia University Press, 2000).

3 Emily C. Bartels, *Spectacles of Strangeness: Imperialism, Alienation, and Marlowe* (Philadelphia: University of Pennsylvania Press, 1993), p. xiv. Jonathan Burton counters that 'Bartels' notion of the Elizabethan period as marking "a critical beginning in the drive toward domination" seems to me a backward projection of the later British Empire' ('Anglo-Ottoman Relations and the

Image of the Turk in *Tamburlaine*', *Journal of Medieval and Early Modern Studies* 30 (2000): 125–56, p. 129). But Bartels has already defended her position: 'Yet it was precisely because there was no established empire that the promotion of the imperialist cause was so crucial. For how was the state to impose its dominance across the globe until the ideological backing was vitally and visibly in place at home?' (*Spectacles of Strangeness*, p. xiv).

4 R. H. Tawney and E. Power, eds., *Tudor Economic Documents*, 3 vols. (London: Longmans, Green, and Co., 1924), 2, p. 19.

5 Nabil Matar, *Turks, Moors, and Englishmen in the Age of Discovery* (New York: Columbia University Press, 1999), p. 11.

6 Nabil Matar, *Islam in Britain 1558–1685* (Cambridge: Cambridge University Press, 1998), p. 52.

7 Steven Mullaney, 'Strange Things, Gross Terms, Curious Customs: the Rehearsal of Cultures in the Late Renaissance', in *Representing the Renaissance*, ed. Stephen Greenblatt (Berkeley and Los Angeles: University of California Press, 1988), pp. 65–92, p. 73. (Originally published in *Representations* 3 [1983]: 40–67. Revised as Chap. 3 in Mullaney, *The Place of the Stage: License, Play and Power in Renaissance England* (Chicago and London: University of Chicago Press, 1988), p. 69.)

8 René Girard, *Violence and the Sacred*, trans. Patrick Gregory (Paris, 1972; Baltimore and London: The Johns Hopkins University Press, 1979), p. 47.

Bibliography

PLAYS

(Spelling and capitalization of titles have been modernized.)

Anon. *Wealth and Health* (London, n.d.).

Dekker, Thomas. *The Shoemaker's Holiday*, in *Drama of the English Renaissance 1: the Tudor Period*, eds. Russell A. Fraser and Norman C. Rabkin (New York: Macmillan, 1976).

    The Shoemaker's Holiday, 2nd edn, ed. Anthony Parr (New Mermaids) (London: A & C Black, 1990).

Fulwell, Ulpian. *Like Will to Like Quod the Devil to the Collier* (London, 1568).

    Like Will to Like Quod the Devil to the Collier, in *Two Moral Interludes*, ed. Peter Happé (1568; Oxford: Malone Society, 1991).

Greene, Robert. *Selimus* (London, 1594).

Haughton, William. *Englishmen for My Money*, ed. Albert Croll Baugh (Ph.D. Diss., University of Pennsylvania, 1917).

    Englishmen for My Money, in *Three Renaissance Usury Plays*, ed. Lloyd Edward Kermode (Revels Plays Companion Library) (Manchester: Manchester University Press, 2008).

Heywood, Thomas. *2 If You Know Not Me, You Know Nobody* (London, 1605).

Lodge, Thomas, and Robert Greene. *A Looking Glass for London and England*, in *Drama of the English Renaissance 1: the Tudor Period*, eds. Russell A. Fraser and Norman C. Rabkin (New York: Macmillan, 1976).

Marlowe, Christopher. *Edward II*, eds. Martin Wiggins and Robert Lindsey (New Mermaids) (London: A & C Black, 1997).

Marston, John. *Jack Drum's Entertainment* (London, 1601).

Munday, Anthony, *et al.* *Sir Thomas More*, eds. Vittorio Gabrieli and Giorgio Melchiori (Revels) (Manchester: Manchester University Press, 1990).

    The Book of Sir Thomas More, ed. W. W. Greg (Malone Society) (Oxford: Oxford University Press, 1911).

Shakespeare, William. *The First Quarto of King Henry V*, ed. Andrew Gurr (Cambridge: Cambridge University Press, 2000).

    The Second Part of King Henry IV (Updated edn), ed. Giorgio Melchiori (Cambridge: Cambridge University Press, 2007).

The Norton Shakespeare, 2nd edn, eds. Stephen Greenblatt, Walter Cohen, Jean E. Howard, and Katharine Eisaman Maus (New York and London: W. W. Norton, 2008).

Wapull, George. *The Tide Tarrieth No Man* (London, 1576).

Wilson, Robert. *The Three Ladies of London*, in *Three Renaissance Usury Plays*, ed. Lloyd Edward Kermode (Revels Plays Companion Library) (Manchester: Manchester University Press, 2008).

An Edition of Robert Wilson's 'The Three Ladies of London' and 'Three Lords and Three Ladies of London', ed. H. S. D. Mithal (New York and London: Garland, 1988).

PRIMARY EARLY MODERN WORKS AND REFERENCE

(Capitalization of early printed titles is modernized.)

Amman, Jost. *The Theatre of Women*, ed. Alfred Aspland (1586; Manchester and London: Holbein Society, 1872).

Anon. *The Bayte and Snare of Fortune* (?1556, ?1550).

A Comparison of the English and Spanish Nation, trans. from French by Robert Ashley (1589).

Coppie of the Anti-Spaniard, trans. from French (a French Gentleman, a Catholic) (1590).

The Death of Usury, or the Disgrace of Usurers (Cambridge, 1594).

Lamentacion of England (Germany[?], 1557 and 1558).

A Pageant of Spanish Humours, trans. from Dutch by H. W. (1599).

Bacon, Francis. 'Of Usury', in *The Essays or Counsells, Civill and Morall*, ed. Michael Kiernan (Cambridge, MA: Harvard University Press, 1985), pp. 124–5.

Biddulph, William. *The Travels of Certaine Englishmen into Africa, Asia, Troy, Bythinia, Thracia, and into the Black Sea* (1609; Facsimile. New York: Da Capo Press, 1968).

Browne, Thomas. *Sir Thomas Browne's Pseudodoxia Epidemica*, 2 vols., ed. Robin Robbins (1646; Oxford: Clarendon Press, 1981).

Burghley, William Cecil, Lord. *The Copie of a Letter Sent Out of England to Don Bernadin Mendoza Ambassadour in France for the King of Spaine* (London, 1588).

Caesar, Phillip. *A General Discourse against the Damnable Sect of Usurers* (London, 1578).

Dalechamp, Caleb. *Christian Hospitality* (London, 1632).

Deacon, John. *Tobacco Tortured* (1616; Facsimile. New York: Da Capo Press, 1968).

Florio, John. *First Fruits* (London, 1578).

Great Britain. *Acts of the Privy Council of England, 1452–1628*, 32 vols., ed. John Roche Dasent (London: HMSO, 1890–1907).

The Statutes of the Realm, 11 vols., eds. Alexander Luders *et al.* (London: HMSO, 1810–28).

Tudor Royal Proclamations, 3 vols., eds. Paul L. Hughes and James F. Larkin (New Haven and London: Yale University Press, (vol. 1) 1964 and (vols. 2 and 3) 1969).

Greg, W. W., ed. 'Letter from Mayor Woodrofe to Lord Burghley' (1580), in *Malone Society Collections* 1.1 (Oxford: Oxford University Press, 1907/ 1908).

Henslowe, Philip. *Henslowe's Diary*, eds. R. A. Foakes and R. T. Rickert (Cambridge: Cambridge University Press, 1961).

Hobbes, Thomas. *Leviathan 1651*. Renascence Editions. Online, available at: http:// darkwing.uoregon.edu/~rbear/hobbes/leviathan2.html (accessed 23 January 2007).

Johnson, Thomas. *Cornucopiae, or Divers Secrets* (London, 1596).

Lemnius, Levinus. 'Notes on England' (1560), from *The Touchstone of Complexions* (London, 1581), in *England as Seen by Foreigners*, ed. Rye, pp. 75–80.

Lyly, John. *Euphues: the Anatomy of Wit* (1578 and 1580), eds. Morris William Croll and Harry Clemons (New York: Russell and Russell, 1964).

M., I. *A Health to the Gentlemanly Profession of Servingmen* (London, 1598), in *England as Seen by Foreigners*, ed. Rye, pp. 196–7.

Meteren, Emanuel van. *A True Discourse Historicall, of the Succeeding Governours in the Netherlands* (Dutch, 1599; trans. London, 1602), in *England as Seen by Foreigners*, ed. Rye, pp. 67–73.

Mosse, Miles. *The Arraignment and Conviction of Usury* (London, 1595).

Münster, Sebastian. *Cosmographia* (London, 1574).

Nashe, Thomas. *The Works of Thomas Nashe*, 5 vols., ed. Ronald B. McKerrow (Oxford: Basil Blackwell, 1966).

Platter, Thomas. *Thomas Platter's Travels in England*, trans. and intro. Clare Williams (1599; London: Jonathan Cape, 1937).

Purchas, Samuel. *Hakluytus Posthumus, or Purchas His Pilgrimes*, 20 vols. (1625; Glasgow: James MacLehose & Sons, 1905).

Rastell, John. *An Exposition of Certaine Difficult and Obscure Words, and Termes of the Lawes of This Realme* (London, 1592).

Rich, Barnabe. *The Straunge and Wonderfull Adventures of Don Simonides, a Gentilman Spaniarde* (London, 1581).

Rye, W. B., ed. *England as Seen by Foreigners* (1865; New York: B. Bloom, 1967).

Saunders, Laurence. *A Trewe Mirrour or Glasse Wherin We Maye Beholde the Wofull State of Thys Our Realme of Englande* (London, 1556).

Scouloudi, Irene. *Returns of Strangers in the Metropolis 1593, 1627, 1635, 1639: a Study of an Active Minority* (London: Huguenot Society of Great Britain and Ireland, 1985).

Smith, Henry. *An Examination of Usurie* (London, 1591).

Stow, John. *A Survey of London*, 2 vols., ed. C. L. Kingsford (1599 and 1603; Oxford: Clarendon Press, 1908).

Stubbes, Philip. *The Anatomie of Abuses*, ed. Margaret Jane Kidnie (1595; Tempe: Arizona Center for Medieval and Renaissance Studies, 2002).

Tawney, R. H., and E. Power, eds. *Tudor Economic Documents*, 3 vols. (London: Longmans, Green and Co., 1924).

Wilson, Thomas. *A Discourse upon Usury*, ed. R. H. Tawney (1572; London: G. Bell, 1925).

Wirtemberg [i.e. Württemberg], Frederick, Duke of. *A True and Faithful Narrative of the Bathing Excursion . . . to the Far-Famed Kingdom of England* (Tübingen, 1602), in *England as Seen by Foreigners*, ed. Rye, pp. 5–53.

SECONDARY MODERN WORKS

Adler, Michael. *Jews of Medieval England* (London: The Jewish Historical Society, 1939).

Agnew, Jean-Christophe. *Worlds Apart: the Market and the Theater in Anglo-American Thought, 1550–1750* (Cambridge: Cambridge University Press, 1986).

Allen, Morse S. *The Satire of John Marston* (New York: Haskell House, 1965).

Anderson, Benedict. *Imagined Communities: Reflections on the Origin and Spread of Nationalism*, rev. edn (London and New York: Verso, 1991).

Arab, Ronda A. 'Work, Bodies, and Gender in *The Shoemaker's Holiday*', *Medieval and Renaissance Drama in England* 13 (2001): 182–212.

Archer, Ian. *The Pursuit of Stability: Social Relations in Elizabethan London* (Cambridge: Cambridge University Press, 1991).

Archer, John Michael. *Citizen Shakespeare: Freemen and Aliens in the Language of the Plays* (New York: Palgrave Macmillan, 2005).

Armitage, David. *The Ideological Origins of the British Empire* (Cambridge: Cambridge University Press, 2000).

Avery, Bruce. 'Gelded Continents and Plenteous Rivers: Cartography as Rhetoric in Shakespeare', in *Playing the Globe*, eds. Gillies and Vaughan, pp. 46–62.

Baker, David. *Between Nations: Shakespeare, Spenser, Marvell, and the Question of Britain* (Stanford: Stanford University Press, 1997).

Baker, David J., and Willy Maley. *British Identities and English Renaissance Literature* (Cambridge: Cambridge University Press, 2002).

Bartels, Emily C. *Spectacles of Strangeness: Imperialism, Alienation, and Marlowe* (Philadelphia: University of Pennsylvania Press, 1993).

Beckerman, Bernard. 'Playing the Crowd: Structure and Soliloquy in *Tide Tarrieth No Man*', in *Mirror up to Shakespeare*, ed. J. C. Gray (Toronto: University of Toronto Press, 1984), pp. 128–37.

Beer, M. *Early British Economics from the XIIIth to the Middle of the XVIIIth Century* (New York: Kelley, 1967).

Beier, A. L. 'Social Problems in Elizabethan London', *Journal of Interdisciplinary History* 9 (1978): 203–21.

Bevington, David. *From* Mankind *to* Marlowe: *Growth of Structure in the Popular Drama of Tudor England* (Cambridge, MA: Harvard University Press, 1962).

Tudor Drama and Politics (Cambridge, MA: Harvard University Press, 1968).

Blank, Paula. *Broken English: Dialects and the Politics of Language in Renaissance Writings* (London and New York: Routledge, 1996).

Boling, Ronald J. 'Anglo-Welsh Relations in *Cymbeline*', *Shakespeare Quarterly* 51 (2000): 33–66.

Borchsenius, Poul. *Behind the Wall: the Story of the Ghetto*, trans. Reginald Spink (London: George Allen and Unwin, 1964).

Bradbrook, Muriel. 'Shakespeare and the Use of Disguise in Elizabethan Drama', *Essays in Criticism* 2 (1952): 159–68.

Bradshaw, Brendan, Andrew Hadfield, and Willy Maley, eds. *Representing Ireland: Literature and the Origins of Conflict, 1534–1660* (Cambridge: Cambridge University Press, 1993).

Bradshaw, Brendan, and Peter Roberts, eds. *British Consciousness and Identity: the Making of Britain, 1533–1707* (Cambridge: Cambridge University Press, 1998).

Brenner, Robert. *Merchants and Revolution: Commercial Change, Political Conflict, and London Overseas Traders, 1550–1653* (Princeton: Princeton University Press, 1993).

Brown, Paul. 'This Thing of Darkness I Acknowledge Mine: *The Tempest* and the Discourse of Colonialism', in *Political Shakespeare: Essays in Cultural Materialism*, eds. Jonathan Dollimore and Alan Sinfield (Ithaca, NY: Cornell University Press, 1985), pp. 48–71.

Burton, Jonathan. 'Anglo–Ottoman Relations and the Image of the Turk in *Tamburlaine*', *Journal of Medieval and Early Modern Studies* 30 (2000): 125–56.

Butler, Judith. *Gender Trouble: Feminism and Subversion of Identity* (London: Routledge, 1990).

Cady, Diane. 'Linguistic Dis-ease: Foreign Language as Sexual Disease in Early Modern England', in *Sins of the Flesh*, ed. Siena, pp. 159–86.

Campos, Edmund Valentine. 'Jews, Spaniards, and Portingales: Ambiguous Identities of Portuguese *Marranos* in Elizabethan England', *ELH* 69 (2002): 599–616.

Caputi, Anthony. *John Marston, Satirist* (Ithaca, NY: Cornell University Press, 1961).

Chambers, E. K. *The Elizabethan Stage*, 4 vols. (Oxford: Clarendon Press, 1923).

Clark, Peter, and Paul Slack. *English Towns in Transition 1500–1700* (Oxford: Oxford University Press, 1976).

Collinson, Patrick. 'Europe in Britain: Protestant Strangers and the English Reformation', in *From Strangers to Citizens*, eds. Vigne and Littleton, pp. 57–67.

Craik, T. W. 'The Political Interpretation of Two Tudor Interludes: *Temperance and Humility* and *Wealth and Health*', *Review of English Studies* n.s. 4 (1953): 98–108.

Dessen, Alan. *Shakespeare and the Late Moral Plays* (Lincoln, NE: University of Nebraska Press, 1986).

Dillon, Janette. *Language and Stage in Medieval and Renaissance England* (Cambridge: Cambridge University Press, 1998).

Dutton, Richard. *Mastering the Revels: the Regulation and Censorship of English Renaissance Drama* (London: Macmillan, 1991).

Dynes, William R. "'London, Look On!": the Estates Morality Play and the Moralities of Economy', paper for GEMCS conference, Pittsburgh, 1996. Online, available at: http://english.uindy.edu/dynes/estatesmorality.htm (accessed 23 February 2006).

Eccles, Mark. 'William Wager and His Plays', *English Language Notes* 18 (1981): 258–62.

Edwards, Philip. *Threshold of a Nation: a Study of English and Irish Drama* (Cambridge: Cambridge University Press, 1979).

Ellis, S. G. *Tudor Ireland: Crown, Community and the Conflict of Cultures, 1470–1603* (London: Longman, 1985).

Finkelpearl, Philip J. *John Marston of the Middle Temple* (Cambridge, MA: Harvard University Press, 1969).

Fitzpatrick, Joan. 'Food and Foreignness in *Sir Thomas More*', *Early Theatre* 7 (2004): 33–47.

Fleck, Andrew. 'Marking Difference and National Identity in Dekker's *The Shoemaker's Holiday*', *Studies in English Literature 1500–1900* 46 (2006): 349–70.

Floyd-Wilson, Mary. *English Ethnicity and Race in Early Modern Drama* (Cambridge: Cambridge University Press, 2003).

Freeburg, Victor O. *Disguise Plots in Elizabethan Drama: a Study in Stage Tradition* (1915; New York: Benjamin Blom, 1965).

Freedman, Barbara. 'Elizabethan Protest, Plague, and Plays: Rereading the "Documents of Control"', *English Literary Renaissance* 26 (1996): 17–45.

Freeman, Arthur. 'Marlowe, Kyd, and the Dutch Church Libel', *English Literary Renaissance* 3 (1973): 44–52.

Fuchs, Barbara. 'Faithless Empires: Pirates, Renegadoes, and the English Nation', *ELH* 67 (2000): 45–69.

Gasper, Julia. *The Dragon and the Dove: the Plays of Thomas Dekker* (Oxford: Clarendon Press, 1990).

Gillies, John. 'The Scene of Cartography in *King Lear*', in *Literature, Mapping, and the Politics of Space in Early Modern Britain*, eds. Andrew Gordon and Bernhard Klein (Cambridge: Cambridge University Press, 2001), pp. 109–37.

  Shakespeare and the Geography of Difference (Cambridge: Cambridge University Press, 1994).

Gillies, John, and Virginia Mason Vaughan, eds. *Playing the Globe: Genre and Geography in English Renaissance Drama* (Madison: Farleigh Dickinson University Press, 1998).

Girard, René. *Violence and the Sacred*, trans. Patrick Gregory (Paris, 1972; Baltimore and London: The Johns Hopkins University Press, 1979).

Goose, Nigel. 'Immigrants in Tudor and Early Stuart England', in *Immigrants in Tudor and Early Stuart England*, eds. Goose and Luu, pp. 1–38.

'"Xenophobia" in Elizabethan and Early Stuart England: an Epithet Too Far?', in *Immigrants in Tudor and Early Stuart England*, eds. Goose and Luu, pp. 110–35.

Goose, Nigel, and Lien Luu, eds. *Immigrants in Tudor and Early Stuart England* (Brighton: Sussex Academic Press, 2005).

Greenblatt, Stephen. *Renaissance Self-Fashioning: From More to Shakespeare* (Chicago: Chicago University Press, 1980).

Greenfield, Matthew. '*1 Henry IV*: Metatheatrical Britain', in *British Identities and English Renaissance Literature*, eds. Baker and Maley, pp. 71–80.

Griffin, Eric. 'From *Ethos* to *Ethnos*: Hispanizing "the Spaniard" in the Old World and the New', *The New Centennial Review* 2.1 (2002): 69–116.

Griffith, William P. 'Humanist Learning, Education and the Welsh Language', in *The Welsh Language before the Industrial Revolution*, ed. Geraint H. Jenkins (Cardiff: University of Wales Press, 1997), pp. 289–315.

Griffiths, Huw. 'The Geographies of Shakespeare's *Cymbeline*', *English Literary Renaissance* 34 (2004): 339–58.

Gurr, Andrew. 'The Bare Island', *Shakespeare Survey* 47 (1994): 29–43.

Gwynn, Robin D. *Huguenot Heritage: the History and Contribution of the Huguenots in Britain* (London: Routledge, 1985).

Hadfield, Andrew. *Edmund Spenser's Irish Experience: Wilde Fruit and Salvage Soyl* (Oxford: Clarendon Press, 1997).

Hadfield, Andrew, and Willy Maley. 'Introduction', in *Representing Ireland*, eds. Bradshaw, Hadfield, and Maley, pp. 1–23.

Hanson, Elizabeth. *Discovering the Subject in Renaissance England* (Cambridge: Cambridge University Press, 1998).

Happé, Peter. 'The Devil in the Interludes', *Medieval English Theatre* 11 (1989): 42–55.

Harris, Jonathan Gil. *Foreign Bodies and the Body Politic: Discourses of Social Pathology in Early Modern England* (Cambridge: Cambridge University Press, 1998).

'(Po)X Marks the Spot: How to "Read" "Early Modern" "Syphilis" in *The Three Ladies of London*', in *Sins of the Flesh*, ed. Siena, pp. 111–34.

'Properties of Skill: Product Placement in Early English Artisanal Drama', in *Staged Properties in Early Modern English Drama*, eds. Harris and Korda, pp. 35–66.

Sick Economies: Drama, Mercantilism, and Disease in Shakespeare's England (Philadelphia: University of Pennsylvania Press, 2004).

Harris, Jonathan Gil, and Natasha Korda, eds. *Staged Properties in Early Modern English Drama* (Cambridge: Cambridge University Press, 2002).

Hawkes, Terence. 'Bryn Glas', in *Post-Colonial Shakespeares*, eds. Ania Loomba and Martin Orkin (London and New York: Routledge, 1998), pp. 117–40.

Haynes, Alan. 'Italian Immigrants in England, 1550–1603', *History Today* 27.8 (1977): 526–34.

Heal, Felicity. *Hospitality in Early Modern England* (Oxford and New York: Oxford University Press, 1990).

Hechter, Michael. *Internal Colonialism: the Celtic Fringe in British National Development, 1536–1966* (1975; New Brunswick, NJ: Transaction Publishers, 1999).

Helgerson, Richard. 'Before National Literary History', *Modern Language Quarterly* 64 (2003): 169–79.

Forms of Nationhood: the Elizabethan Writing of England (Chicago and London: University of Chicago Press, 1992).

Hentschell, Roze. 'Treasonous Textiles: Foreign Cloth and the Construction of Englishness', *Journal of Medieval and Early Modern Studies* 32 (2002): 543–70.

Highley, Christopher. *Shakespeare, Spenser, and the Crisis in Ireland* (Cambridge: Cambridge University Press, 1997).

'Wales, Ireland, and *1 Henry IV*', *Renaissance Drama* n.s. 21 (1990): 91–114.

Hill, Tracey. '"The Cittie is in an uproare": Staging London in *The Booke of Sir Thomas More*', *Early Modern Literary Studies* 11 (2005) 2.1–19. Online, available at: http://purl.oclc.org/emls/11–1/more.htm (accessed 7 April 2006).

Hirota, Atsuhiko. 'The Romanticization of a British Past: Early Modern English Nationalism and the Literary Representations of Wales' (Ph.D. Diss., Claremont Graduate University, 2001).

Hoenselaars, A. J. *Images of Englishmen and Foreigners in the Drama of Shakespeare and his Contemporaries: a Study of Stage Characters and National Identity in English Renaissance Drama, 1558–1642* (London and Toronto: Associated University Presses, 1992).

Holderness, Graham. '"What Ish My Nation?": Shakespeare and National Identities', *Textual Practice* 5 (1991): 74–93.

Hopkins, Lisa. 'Fluellen's Name', *Shakespeare Studies* 24 (1996): 148–55.

Shakespeare on the Edge: Border-Crossing in the Tragedies and the Henriad (Aldershot: Ashgate, 2005).

Howard, Jean. 'Other Englands: the View from the Non-Shakespearean History Play', in *Other Voices, Other Views*, ed. Ostovich, Silcox, and Roebuck, pp. 135–53.

Theater of a City: the Places of London Comedy, 1598–1642 (Philadelphia: University of Pennsylvania Press, 2007).

'Women, Foreigners, and the Regulation of Urban Space in *Westward Ho*', in *Material London, ca. 1600*, ed. Lena Cowen Orlin (Philadelphia: University of Pennsylvania Press, 2000), pp. 150–67.

Howard, Jean E., and Phyllis Rackin. *Engendering a Nation: a Feminist Account of Shakespeare's English Histories* (New York: Routledge, 1997).

Hyamson, Albert M. *The Sephardim of England: History of the Spanish and Portuguese Jewish Community, 1492–1951* (New York: AMS Press, 1951).

Hyland, Peter. 'Disguise and Renaissance Tragedy', *University of Toronto Quarterly* 55 (1985–6): 161–71.

Ingram, R. W. *John Marston* (Boston: G. K. Hall, 1978).

Jenkins, Geraint H., ed. *The Welsh Language before the Industrial Revolution* (Cardiff: University of Wales Press, 1997).

Jenkins, Philip. 'The Plight of Pygmy Nations: Wales in Early Modern Europe', *North American Journal of Welsh Studies* 2 (2002): 1–11.

Jones, Ann Rosalind, and Peter Stallybrass. *Renaissance Clothing and the Materials of Memory* (Cambridge: Cambridge University Press, 2000).

Kastan, David Scott. 'Workshop and/as Playhouse: Comedy and Commerce in *The Shoemaker's Holiday*', *Studies in Philology* 84 (1987): 324–37.

Katz, David S. *The Jews in the History of England, 1485–1850* (Oxford: Clarendon Press, 1995).

Kermode, Lloyd Edward. 'After Shylock: the "Judaiser" in England', *Renaissance and Reformation* 20 (1996): 5–25.

'Introduction' in *Three Renaissance Usury Plays*, ed. Lloyd Edward Kermode (Revels Plays Companions Library) (Manchester: Manchester University Press, 2008), pp. 1–78.

'The Playwright's Prophecy: Robert Wilson's *The Three Ladies of London* and the "Alienation" of the English', *Medieval and Renaissance Drama in England* 11 (1999): 60–87.

Kingsley-Smith, Jane. *Shakespeare's Drama of Exile* (London: Palgrave Macmillan, 2003).

Klein, Bernhard. *Maps and the Writing of Space in Early Modern England and Ireland* (New York: Palgrave Macmillan, 2001).

Knapp, Jeffrey. 'Elizabethan Tobacco', in *New World Encounters*, ed. Stephen Greenblatt (Berkeley and Los Angeles: University of California Press, 1993), pp. 273–312.

An Empire Nowhere: England, America, and Literature from Utopia *to* The Tempest (Berkeley and Los Angeles: University of California Press, 1992).

Kunzle, David. *The Early Comic Strip: Narrative Strips and Picture Stories in the European Broadsheet from* c. *1450 to 1825* (Berkeley and Los Angeles: University of California Press, 1972).

Landau, Aaron. '"I Live with Bread like You": Forms of Inclusion in *Richard II*', *Early Modern Literary Studies* 11 (2005): 3.1–23. Online, available at: http://purl.oclc.org/emls/11-1/richard.htm (accessed 14 April 2006).

Leggatt, Alexander. *Citizen Comedy in the Age of Shakespeare* (Toronto and Buffalo: University of Toronto Press, 1973).

Leinwand, Theodore B. *The City Staged: Jacobean Comedy, 1603–1613* (Madison: University of Wisconsin Press, 1986).

Lindabury, Richard Vliet. *Patriotism in Elizabethan Drama* (Princeton: Princeton University Press, 1931).

Lloyd, Megan. *'Speak it in Welsh': Wales and the Welsh Language in Shakespeare* (Lanham, MD: Rowman and Littlefield, 2007).

Lockyer, Roger. *The Early Stuarts: a Political History of England, 1603–1642* (London and New York: Longman, 1989).

Luu, Lien Bich. *Immigrants and the Industries of London 1500–1700* (Aldershot: Ashgate, 2005).

'Natural-Born versus Stranger-Born Subjects: Aliens and Their Status in Elizabethan London', in *Immigrants in Tudor and Early Stuart England*, eds. Goose and Luu, pp. 57–75.

MacIntyre, Jean. 'Shore's Wife and *The Shoemaker's Holiday*', *Cahiers Elisabethains* 12 (1991): 17–28.

Maley, Willy. *Nation, State, and Empire in English Renaissance Literature: Shakespeare to Milton* (London: Palgrave Macmillan, 2003).

'Postcolonial Shakespeare: British Identity Formation and *Cymbeline*', in *Shakespeare's Late Plays: New Readings*, eds. J. Richards and J. Knowles (Edinburgh: Edinburgh University Press, 1999), pp. 145–57.

Salvaging Spenser: Colonialism, Culture and Identity (New York: St Martin's Press, 1997).

Marx, Karl, and Friedrich Engels. *Economic and Philosophic Manuscripts of 1844*, in *The Marx–Engels Reader*, 2nd edn, ed. Robert C. Tucker (New York: W. W. Norton, 1978).

Matar, Nabil. *Islam in Britain 1558–1685* (Cambridge: Cambridge University Press, 1998).

Turks, Moors, and Englishmen in the Age of Discovery (New York: Columbia University Press, 1999).

McBride, Charlotte. 'A Natural Drink for an English Man: National Stereotyping in Early Modern Culture', in *A Pleasing Sinne: Drink and Conviviality in Seventeenth-Century England*, ed. Adam Smyth (Woodbridge: D. S. Brewer, 2004), pp. 181–91.

McCluskey, Peter M. '"Shall I betray my brother?": Anti-Alien Satire and Its Subversion in *The Shoemaker's Holiday*', *Tennessee Philological Bulletin* 37 (2000): 43–54.

McEachern, Claire. *The Poetics of English Nationhood 1590–1612* (Cambridge: Cambridge University Press, 1996).

McMillin, Scott. *The Elizabethan Theatre and 'The Book of Sir Thomas More'* (Ithaca, NY: Cornell University Press, 1987).

McMillin, Scott, and Sally-Beth MacLean. *The Queen's Men and Their Plays, 1583–1603* (Cambridge: Cambridge University Press, 1998).

Mikalachki, Jodi. *The Legacy of Boadicea: Gender and Nation in Early Modern England* (London: Routledge, 1998).

Montrose, Louis. 'Form and Pressure: Shakespearean Drama and the Elizabethan State', in *Contextualizing the Renaissance Returns to History*, ed. Albert H. Tricomi (Turnhout, Belgium: Brepols, 1999), pp. 171–99.

Morrill, John. 'The British Problem, *c.* 1534–1707', in *The British Problem, c. 1534–1707: State Formation in the Atlantic Archipelago*, eds. Brendan Bradshaw and John Morrill (New York: St Martin's Press, 1996), pp. 1–38.

Mullaney, Steven. *The Place of the Stage: License, Play, and Power in Renaissance England* (Chicago and London: University of Chicago Press, 1988).

'Strange Things, Gross Terms, Curious Customs: the Rehearsal of Cultures in the Late Renaissance', in *Representing the Renaissance*, ed. Stephen Greenblatt (Berkeley and Los Angeles: University of California Press, 1988), pp. 65–92. (Originally published in *Representations* 3 [1983]: 40–67. Revised as Chapter 3 in Mullaney, *The Place of the Stage*.)

Munro, Ian. *The Figure of the Crowd in Early Modern London: the City and Its Double* (New York: Palgrave Macmillan, 2005).

Neill, Michael. 'Broken English and Broken Irish: Nation, Language, and the Optic of Power in Shakespeare's Histories', *Shakespeare Quarterly* 45 (1994): 1–32.

Netzloff, Mark. *England's Internal Colonies: Class, Capital, and the Literature of Early Modern English Colonialism* (New York: Palgrave Macmillan, 2003).

Neuss, Paula. 'The Sixteenth-Century English "Proverb" Play', *Comparative Drama* 18 (1984): 1–18.

Nugent, Teresa. 'Usury and Counterfeiting in Wilson's *The Three Ladies of London* and *The Three Lords and Three Ladies of London*, and in Shakespeare's *Measure for Measure*', in *Money and the Age of Shakespeare*, ed. Linda Woodbridge (New York: Palgrave Macmillan, 2003), pp. 201–17.

Orrell, John. 'The Architecture of the Fortune Playhouse', *Shakespeare Survey* 47 (1994): 15–27.

Ostovich, Helen, Graham Silcox, and Graham Roebuck, eds. *Other Voices, Other Views: Expanding the Canon in English Renaissance Studies* (London: Associated University Presses, 1999).

Oz, Avraham. 'Extending Within: Placing Self and Nation in the Epic of *Cymbeline*', *Journal of Theatre and Drama* 4 (1998): 81–97.

Palliser, D. M. *The Age of Elizabeth: England under the Later Tudors 1547–1603*, 2nd edn (London and New York: Longman, 1992).

Palmer, Daryl. *Hospitable Performances: Dramatic Genre and Cultural Practices in Early Modern England* (West Lafayette: Purdue University Press, 1992).

'Merchants and Miscegenation: *The Three Ladies of London*, *The Jew of Malta*, and *The Merchant of Venice*', in *Race, Ethnicity, and Power in the Renaissance*, ed. Joyce Green MacDonald (London: Associated University Presses, 1997), pp. 36–66.

Parker, Patricia. 'Uncertain Unions: Welsh Leeks in *Henry V*', in *British Identities and English Renaissance Literature*, eds. Baker and Maley, pp. 81–100.

Pettegree, Andrew. *Foreign Protestant Communities in Sixteenth-Century London* (Oxford: Clarendon Press, 1986).

Pinciss, G. M. 'The Savage Man in Spenser, Shakespeare, and Renaissance Drama', *The Elizabethan Theatre* 8 (1982): 69–89.

Pocock, J. G. A. 'British History: a Plea for a New Subject', *The Journal of Modern History* 47 (1975): 601–21.

Porter, Gerald. 'Cobblers All: Occupation as Identity and Cultural Message', *Folk Music Journal* 7 (1995): 43–61.

Power, M. J. 'London and the Control of the "Crisis" of the 1590s', *History* 70 (1985): 371–85.

Prior, Roger. 'A Second Jewish Community in Tudor London', *Transactions of the Jewish Historical Society of England* 31 (1989–90): 137–52.

Rabb, Theodore K. 'The Stirrings of the 1590s and the Return of the Jews to England', *Transactions of the Jewish Historical Society of England* 26 (1974–8): 26–33.

Rackin, Phyllis. *Stages of History: Shakespeare's English Chronicles* (London: Routledge, 1990).

Rappaport, Steve. *Worlds within Worlds: Structures of Life in Sixteenth-Century London* (Cambridge: Cambridge University Press, 1989).

Read, David. 'Losing the Map: Topographical Understanding in the "Henriad"', *Modern Philology* 94 (1997): 475–95.

Rees, Joan. 'Shakespeare's Welshmen', in *Literature and Nationalism*, eds. Vincent Newey and Ann Thompson (Liverpool: Liverpool University Press, 1991), pp. 22–40.

Roberts, Peter. 'Tudor Legislation and the Political Status of "the British Tongue"', in *The Welsh Language before the Industrial Revolution*, ed. Jenkins, pp. 123–52.

    'Tudor Wales, National Identity and the British Inheritance', in *British Consciousness and Identity*, eds. Bradshaw and Roberts, pp. 8–42.

Roth, Cecil. *A History of the Jews in England*, 3rd edn (Oxford: Clarendon Press, 1964).

Rubens, Alfred. *A History of Jewish Costume* (1967; London: Weidenfeld and Nicolson, 1973).

    A Jewish Iconography (London: The Jewish Museum, 1954).

Russell, Conrad. *The Crisis of Parliaments: English History, 1509–1660* (1971; Oxford and New York: Oxford University Press, 1988).

Sacks, David Harris. 'The Metropolis and the Revolution: Commercial, Urban, and Political Culture in Early Modern London', in *The Culture of Capital*, ed. Turner, pp. 139–62.

Schwyzer, Philip. *Literature, Nationalism, and Memory in Early Modern England and Wales* (Cambridge: Cambridge University Press, 2004).

Scott, Michael. *John Marston's Plays: Theme, Structure, and Performance* (London: Macmillan, 1978).

Selwood, Jacob. '"English-Born Reputed Strangers": Birth and Descent in Seventeenth-Century London', *Journal of British Studies* 44 (2005): 728–53.

Serres, Michel. *The Parasite*, trans. Lawrence Schehr (Baltimore: The Johns Hopkins University Press, 1982).

Shapiro, James. *Shakespeare and the Jews* (New York: Columbia University Press, 1996).

Shrank, Cathy. *Writing the Nation in Reformation England 1530–1580* (Oxford: Oxford University Press, 2004).

Siena, Kevin, ed. *Sins of the Flesh: Responding to Sexual Disease in Early Modern Europe* (Toronto: Center for Reformation and Renaissance Studies, 2005).

Sisson, C. J. 'A Colony of Jews in Shakespeare's London', *Essays and Studies* 23 (1938): 38–52.

Smith, Emma. "'So much English by the Mother": Gender, Foreigners, and the Mother Tongue in William Haughton's *Englishmen for My Money*', *Medieval and Renaissance Drama in England* 13 (2001): 165–81.

Steinsaltz, David. 'The Politics of French Language in Shakespeare's History Plays', *Studies in English Literature 1500–1900* 42 (2002): 317–34.

Stevenson, Laura Caroline. *Praise and Paradox: Merchants and Craftsmen in Elizabethan Popular Literature* (Cambridge: Cambridge University Press, 1984).

Stewart, Alan. "'Come from Turkie": Mediterranean Trade in Late Elizabethan London', in *Re-Mapping the Mediterranean in Early Modern English Writings*, ed. Goran V. Stanivukovic (London: Palgrave Macmillan, 2007), pp. 157–77.

Stock, Angela. "'Something done in honour of the city": Ritual, Theatre and Satire in Jacobean Civic Pageantry', in *Plotting Early Modern London: New Essays on Jacobean City Comedy*, eds. Dieter Mehl, Angela Stock, and Anne-Julia Zwierlein (Aldershot: Ashgate, 2004), pp. 125–44.

'Stow's *Survey* and the London Playwrights', in *John Stow and the Making of the English Past*, eds. Ian Gadd and Alexandra Gillespie (London: British Library, 2004), pp. 89–98.

Stone, Lawrence. *The Crisis of the Aristocracy, 1558–1641* (1965; Oxford: Clarendon Press, 1979).

Sullivan, Garrett A. *The Drama of Landscape: Land, Property, and Social Relations on the Early Modern Stage* (Stanford: Stanford University Press, 1998).

Takaki, Ronald. '*The Tempest* in the Wilderness: the Racialization of Savagery', *Journal of American History* 79 (1992): 892–912.

Timms, L. D. 'Dekker's *The Shoemaker's Holiday* and Elizabeth's Accession Day', *Notes and Queries* 230 (1985): 58.

Tittler, Robert. *Architecture and Power: the Town Hall and the English Urban Community* (Oxford: Clarendon Press, 1991).

'The End of the Middle Ages in the English Country Town', *Sixteenth Century Journal* 4 (1987): 471–87.

Turner, Henry S., ed. *The Culture of Capital: Property, Cities, and Knowledge in Early Modern England* (New York and London: Routledge, 2002).

Vanhoutte, Jacqueline. *Strange Communion: Motherland and Masculinity in Tudor Plays, Pamphlets, and Politics* (Newark: University of Delaware Press, 2003).

Vigne, Randolph, and Charles Littleton, eds. *From Strangers to Citizens: the Integration of Immigrant Communities in Britain, Ireland, and Colonial America, 1550–1750* (London: Huguenot Society of Great Britain and Ireland, 2001).

Vitkus, Daniel, ed. *Three Turk Plays from Early Modern England:* Selimus, A Christian Turned Turk, *and* The Renegado (New York: Columbia University Press, 2000).

Turning Turk: English Theater and the Multicultural Mediterranean, 1570–1630 (New York: Palgrave Macmillan, 2003).

Ward, Joseph P. 'Fictitious Shoemakers, Agitated Weavers and the Limits of Popular Xenophobia in Elizabethan London', in *From Strangers to Citizens*, eds. Vigne and Littleton, pp. 80–7.

Metropolitan Communities: Trade Guilds, Identity, and Change in Early Modern London (Stanford: Stanford University Press, 1997).

Warneke, Sara. *Images of the Educational Traveller in Early Modern England* (Leiden: Brill, 1995).

'A Taste for Newfangledness: the Destructive Potential of Novelty in Early Modern England', *Sixteenth Century Journal* 26 (1995): 881–96.

Williams, Glanmor. 'Prophecy, Poetry, and Politics in Medieval and Tudor Wales', in *British Government and Administration*, eds. H. Hearder and H. R. Loyn (Cardiff: University of Wales Press, 1974), pp. 104–16.

'Religion and Welsh Literature in the Age of the Reformation', *Proceedings of the British Academy* 69 (1983): 371–408.

Wolf, Lucien. 'Jews in Elizabethan England', *Transactions of the Jewish Historical Society of England* 11 (1924–7): 1–91.

Womack, Peter. 'Imagining Communities: Theatres and the English Nation in the Sixteenth Century', in *Culture and History 1350–1600: Essays on English Communities, Identities, and Writing*, ed. David Aers (Detroit: Wayne State University Press, 1992), pp. 91–145.

Wood, Diana. *Medieval Economic Thought* (Cambridge: Cambridge University Press, 2002).

Wright, Celeste Turner. 'Some Conventions regarding the Usurer in Elizabethan Literature', *Studies in Philology* 31 (1934): 176–97.

Wright, Louis B. *Middle-Class Culture in Elizabethan England* (Chapel Hill: University of North Carolina Press, 1955).

'Social Aspects of Some Belated Moralities', *Anglia* 54 (1930): 107–48.

Wyatt, Michael. *The Italian Encounter with Tudor England: a Cultural Politics of Translation* (Cambridge: Cambridge University Press, 2005).

Yungblut, Laura Hunt. '"Mayntayninge the indigente and nedie": the Institutionalization of Social Responsibility in the Case of the Resident Alien Communities in Elizabethan Norwich and Colchester', in *From Strangers to Citizens*, eds. Vigne and Littleton, pp. 99–105.

'Strangers and Aliaunts: the "Un-English" among the English in Elizabethan England', in *Crossing Boundaries: Issues of Cultural and Individual Identity in the Middle Ages and the Renaissance*, ed. Sally McKee (Turnhout, Belgium: Brepols, 1999), pp. 263–76.

Strangers Settled Here amongst Us: Policies, Perceptions and the Presence of Aliens in Elizabethan England (London and New York: Routledge, 1996).

Index